Business Tax

(Finance Act 2015)

Tutorial

for assessments from January 2016

Aubrey Penning
Bob Thomas

Published by Osborne Books Limited
Unit 1B Everoak Estate
Bromyard Road, Worcester WR2 5HP
Tel 01905 748071
Email books@osbornebooks.co.uk
Website www.osbornebooks.co.uk

Design by Laura Ingham

Printed by CPI Group (UK) Limited, Croydon, CRO 4YY, on environmentally friendly, acid-free paper from managed forests.

British Library Cataloguing in Publication Data
A catalogue record for this book is available from the British Library

ISBN 978 1909173 613

Contents

Please note that the eight chapters and subsequent sections of the book each have a self-contained numbering system, rather than the traditional form of pagination which runs through the book.

Acknowledgements

The publisher wishes to thank the following for their help with the reading and production of the book: Jon Moore, Cathy Oliver and Bee Pugh. Thanks are also due Laura Ingham for her designs for this series.

The publisher is indebted to the Association of Accounting Technicians for its help and advice to our authors and editors during the preparation of this text.

The publisher would also like to thank HM Revenue & Customs for its help, advice and kind permission to reproduce tax forms obtained from www.gov.uk.

Author and Technical Editor

Aubrey Penning has many years experience of teaching accountancy on a variety of courses in Worcester and Gwent. He is a Certified Accountant, and before his move into full-time teaching he worked for the health service, a housing association and a chemical supplier. For many years he was the AAT course coordinator at Worcester College of Technology, specialising in the areas of management accounting and taxation.

Bob Thomas, the Technical Editor of this book and the Osborne Books' *Personal Tax*, has been involved with the Education and Training activities of the AAT since 1986, including the development and piloting of the skills-based scheme. He is an external verifier, a simulation writer, a moderator and a contributor at workshops, training days, conferences and master classes. Until recently he was a member of the Learning and Development Board and Chairman of the Assessment Panel.

Introduction

what this book covers

This book has been written specifically to cover the 'Business Tax' Unit which is an option in the AAT Level 4 Diploma in Accounting.

The book contains a clear text with worked examples and case studies, chapter summaries and key terms to help with revision. Each chapter has a wide range of activities, many in the style of the computer-based assessments used by AAT. Note that the pagination of each chapter is self-contained, eg Chapter 1 contains pages 1.2 to 1.23.

Exams, Finance Acts and Tax Years

This book has been designed to include guidance and exercises based on Tax Year 2015/16 (Finance Act (No 1) 2015). We understand that the AAT plan to assess this legislation from 1 January 2016 to 31 December 2016. Tutors and students are advised to check this with the AAT and ensure that they sit the correct Computer Based Assessment.

Osborne Workbooks

Osborne Workbooks contain practice material which helps students achieve success in their assessments. *Business Tax (Finance Act 2015) Workbook* contains a number of paper-based 'fill in' practice exams in the style of the computer-based assessment. Please visit www.osbornebooks.co.uk for further details and access to our online shop.

Tax data

NATIONAL INSURANCE

Tax Year 2015/16

Self-employed National Insurance contributions (sole traders and partners)

Class 2 contributions are payable at a flat rate of £2.80 per week (unless below the 'small profits threshold), and in addition,

Class 4 contributions are payable on the profits as follows:

9% of profits for the year between £8,060 and £42,385, plus

2% of profits above £42,385

CORPORATION TAX

'Augmented Profits'	Financial Year 2014 (i.e. 1/4/2014 – 31/3/2015)	Financial Year 2015 (i.e. 1/4/2015 – 31/3/2016)
£0 – £300,000	Small Profits Rate (20%)	Main Rate (20%)
£300,001 – £1,500,000	Main Rate (21%) less marginal relief	
£1,500,001 and over	Main Rate (21%)	

Marginal relief (applicable to FY2014)

Marginal relief formula:

Standard Fraction x (Upper Limit of Band – Augmented Profits) x Normal TTP / Augmented Profits

or: *Fraction x (U – A) x (N/ A)*

where   U   =   Upper Limit of Band
          A   =   'Augmented Profits'
          N   =   Normal Taxable Total Profits

The fraction is:
*   1/400 for the financial year 2014

INCOME TAX

Personal Allowance for tax year 2015/16: £10,600

Tax bands 2015/16
(General Income)

	£
Basic rate 20%	0 – 31,785
Higher rate 40%	31,786 to 150,000
Additional rate 45%	over 150,000

CAPITAL GAINS TAX – FOR INDIVIDUALS

2015/16

Annual Exempt Amount   £11,100

Rates

Gains   18% and/or 28% (for higher/additional rate income tax payers)
                 (10% where entrepreneurs' relief is claimed)

RETAIL PRICE INDEX (for indexation allowance for companies only)

	Jan	Feb	Mar	Apr	May	Jun	Jul	Aug	Sept	Oct	Nov	Dec
2015	255.4	256.7	257.1	258.0								
2014	252.6	254.2	254.8	255.7	255.9	256.3	256.0	257.0	257.6	257.7	257.1	257.5
2013	245.8	247.6	248.7	249.5	250.0	249.7	249.7	251.0	251.9	251.9	252.1	253.4
2012	238.0	239.9	240.8	242.5	242.4	241.8	242.1	243.0	244.2	245.6	245.6	246.8
2011	229.0	231.3	232.5	234.4	235.2	235.2	234.7	236.1	237.9	238.0	238.5	239.4
2010	218.0	219.2	220.7	222.8	223.6	224.1	223.6	224.5	225.3	225.8	226.8	228.4
2009	210.1	211.4	211.3	211.5	212.8	213.4	213.4	214.4	215.3	216.0	216.6	218.0
2008	209.8	211.4	212.2	214.0	215.1	216.8	216.5	217.2	218.4	217.7	216.0	212.9
2007	201.6	203.1	204.4	205.4	206.2	207.3	206.1	207.3	208.0	208.9	209.7	210.9
2006	193.4	194.2	195.0	196.5	197.7	198.5	198.5	199.2	200.1	200.4	201.8	202.7
2005	188.9	189.6	190.5	191.6	192.0	192.0	192.2	192.6	193.1	193.3	193.6	194.1
2004	183.1	183.8	184.6	185.7	186.5	186.8	186.8	187.4	188.1	188.6	189.0	189.9
2003	178.4	179.3	179.9	181.2	181.5	181.3	181.3	181.6	182.5	182.6	182.7	183.5
2002	173.3	173.8	174.5	175.7	176.2	176.2	175.9	176.4	177.6	177.9	178.2	178.5
2001	171.1	172.0	172.2	173.1	174.2	174.4	173.3	174.0	174.6	174.3	173.6	173.4
2000	166.6	167.5	168.4	170.1	170.7	171.1	170.5	170.5	171.7	171.6	172.1	172.2
1999	163.4	163.7	164.1	165.2	165.6	165.6	165.1	165.5	166.2	166.5	166.7	167.3
1998	159.5	160.3	160.8	162.6	163.5	163.4	163.0	163.7	164.4	164.5	164.4	164.4
1997	154.4	155.0	155.4	156.3	156.9	157.5	157.5	158.5	159.3	159.5	159.6	160.0
1996	150.2	150.9	151.5	152.6	152.9	153.0	152.4	153.1	153.8	153.8	153.9	154.4
1995	146.0	146.9	147.5	149.0	149.6	149.8	149.1	149.9	150.6	149.8	149.8	150.7
1994	141.3	142.1	142.5	144.2	144.7	144.7	144.0	144.7	145.0	145.2	145.3	146.0
1993	137.9	138.8	139.3	140.6	141.1	141.0	140.7	141.3	141.9	141.8	141.6	141.9
1992	135.6	136.3	136.7	138.8	139.3	139.3	138.8	138.9	139.4	139.9	139.7	139.2
1991	130.2	130.9	131.4	133.1	133.5	134.1	133.8	134.1	134.6	135.1	135.6	135.7
1990	119.50	120.20	121.40	125.10	126.20	126.70	126.80	128.10	129.30	130.30	130.00	129.90
1989	111.00	111.80	112.30	114.30	115.00	115.40	115.50	115.80	116.60	117.50	118.50	118.80

	Jan	Feb	Mar	Apr	May	Jun	Jul	Aug	Sept	Oct	Nov	Dec
1988	103.30	103.70	104.10	105.80	106.20	106.60	106.70	107.90	108.40	109.50	110.00	110.30
1987	100.00	100.40	100.60	101.80	101.90	101.90	101.80	102.10	102.40	102.90	103.40	103.30
1986	96.25	96.60	96.73	97.67	97.85	97.79	97.52	97.82	98.30	98.45	99.29	99.62
1985	91.20	91.94	92.80	94.78	95.21	95.41	95.23	95.49	95.44	95.59	95.92	96.05
1984	86.84	87.20	87.48	88.64	88.97	89.20	89.10	89.94	90.11	90.67	90.95	90.87
1983	82.61	82.97	83.12	84.28	84.64	84.84	85.30	85.68	86.06	86.36	86.67	86.89
1982	-	-	79.44	81.04	81.62	81.85	81.88	81.90	81.85	82.26	82.66	82.51

1 Introduction to business taxation

this chapter covers...

In this chapter we provide a brief review of the various types of UK tax that apply to businesses and are studied in this book. Corporation Tax is payable by limited companies, while sole traders and partnerships are subject to Income Tax. We will also look at the role of HM Revenue and Customs, and see how sources of law relate to tax.

We will briefly look at how tax computations for both Corporation Tax and Income Tax work, before examining how income is divided up into categories for these taxes.

We need to understand how income and profits are taxed under these two taxes, and we will examine the impact of financial years and tax years on the calculation and reporting of tax. This includes a study of the way that tax returns work and when they need to be submitted by and the payment dates of tax.

Next we will learn how National Insurance is calculated for the self-employed and those in partnership.

Finally we will examine the responsibilities of the tax practitioner, including those relating to confidentiality and record keeping.

WHAT IS 'BUSINESS TAX'?

The 'business tax' that we are going to study in this book is not a single tax, but instead is a number of UK taxes that have an impact on businesses.

The specific taxes that affect any business in the UK will depend primarily on the legal structure of the business. You will probably be aware from your accounting studies of the three main ways (listed below) that businesses can be formed. We are going to examine the tax situation for

- limited companies
- sole traders, and
- partnerships

Limited companies (whether public or private) are incorporated bodies and therefore have their own legal existence that is quite separate from that of the owners. The profits that limited companies generate are subject to **Corporation Tax**.

Sole traders and **partnerships** are both unincorporated businesses, which means that there is no legal separation between the owner(s) of the business and the business itself. For this reason the profits from these businesses are dealt with under **Income Tax**, where they are assessed directly in relation to the business owners – the sole trader or partners. This is the same Income Tax that most of us pay on our income from employment or savings. If you have studied the learning area 'personal tax', you will have seen how Income Tax works in some detail. To succeed in the 'business tax' Unit you only have to understand the impact of Income Tax on business profits.

In the first part of this book we will be examining how Corporation Tax works, and how we can calculate how much Corporation Tax limited companies should pay. To do this we will need to work out the amount of trading profits that are subject to Corporation Tax. We will also need to work out the chargeable gains that result from the disposal of certain assets, and incorporate this along with other company profits in the Corporation Tax computation. The tax return for a limited company will also be studied so that we can complete it.

In the second part of the book we will be looking at how the profits of sole traders and partnerships are assessed under Income Tax. We will also see how Capital Gains Tax can affect these business owners if they dispose of certain business assets. We will also learn how to complete the parts of the Income Tax return that deal with self-employment, and partnerships.

We will also look at the impact of National Insurance on the self-employed and those in partnerships, and learn how to calculate the amounts that need to be paid.

The table on the opposite page shows the topics we will study in this Unit. The content of the Unit 'Personal Tax' is also shown for comparison. There are other taxes, such as Value Added Tax and Inheritance Tax, which affect businesses, but they are beyond the requirements of your studies here and so are not covered in this book.

THE TAX SYSTEM

We will first look at the background to the way that the tax system works. We will then outline the way in which numerical tax calculations are carried out.

HM Revenue & Customs

HM Revenue & Customs was formed in 2005 by an amalgamation of the Inland Revenue and HM Customs & Excise. Income tax, Corporation Tax and Capital Gains Tax are all administered by HM Revenue & Customs, which also collects National Insurance Contributions and VAT. This is a government organisation that has an administrative structure containing the following three parts:

- taxpayer service offices are the main offices that individual taxpayers deal with, and handle much of the basic Income Tax assessment and collection functions
- taxpayer district offices deal with Corporation Tax and more complex Income Tax issues
- tax enquiry centres deal with enquiries and provide forms and leaflets to taxpayers

These three functions are located in offices throughout the UK. In smaller centres some functions may be combined into one office, while in larger towns and cities they may be located separately.

the law governing tax – statute law

The authority to levy taxes comes from two sources. The first is legislation passed by Parliament, known as **statute law**. You may have heard of the Finance Acts. These are generally published each year and give details of any changes to taxes. These changes will have been proposed by the Chancellor of the Exchequer (usually in the budget) and passed by Parliament. In this book we will be using information from the Finance Act (No 1) 2015, which relates to the financial year 2015 for companies and the tax year 2015/16 for individuals.

We will see exactly what is meant by financial years and tax years later in this chapter. There are also other relevant statute laws that were designed to create frameworks for the way that certain taxes work.

If a second 2015 Finance Act introduces any changes to tax for this year it will be ignored in this book and in your assessment.

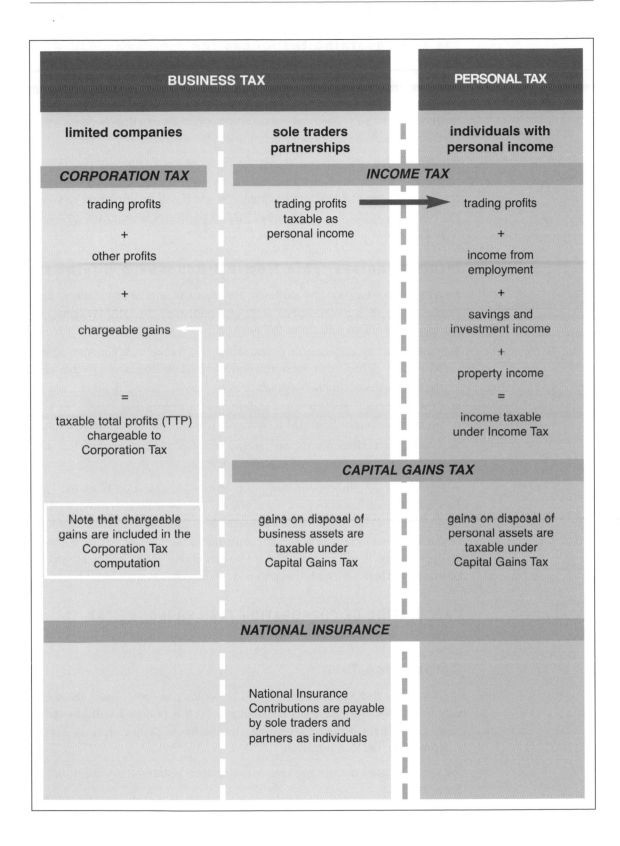

BUSINESS TAX		PERSONAL TAX
limited companies	**sole traders partnerships**	**individuals with personal income**
CORPORATION TAX	*INCOME TAX*	
trading profits	trading profits taxable as personal income →	trading profits
+		+
other profits		income from employment
+		+
chargeable gains		savings and investment income
		+
		property income
=		=
taxable total profits (TTP) chargeable to Corporation Tax		income taxable under Income Tax
	CAPITAL GAINS TAX	
Note that chargeable gains are included in the Corporation Tax computation	gains on disposal of business assets are taxable under Capital Gains Tax	gains on disposal of personal assets are taxable under Capital Gains Tax
	NATIONAL INSURANCE	
	National Insurance Contributions are payable by sole traders and partners as individuals	

the law governing tax – case law

The second source of tax law is called **'case law'**, and draws its authority from decisions taken in court cases. Taxation can be very complicated, and sometimes disagreements between HM Revenue & Customs and taxpayers result in court cases. The final outcome of such cases can then become 'case law' and influences future interpretation of statute law.

Although there is a substantial amount of statute law and case law that is relevant to the taxation of businesses in the UK, this book will try to keep references to specific law to a minimum. While it will be important to know the rules that apply to certain situations, you will not be required to quote from the legislation or cases in your examination.

information available from HM Revenue & Customs

In addition to the tax law outlined above, there are interpretations and explanations of various issues that are published by HM Revenue & Customs. The main ones are as follows:

- extra-statutory concessions issued when HM Revenue & Customs agree to impose a less strict interpretation of the law than would otherwise apply in particular circumstances
- HM Revenue & Customs statements of practice are public announcements of how HM Revenue & Customs interpret specific rules
- Guides and Help Sheets are issued to help taxpayers complete the necessary return forms and calculate their tax

A large array of publications and forms can be downloaded from the HM Revenue & Customs website at www.gov.uk. This website also provides data on Corporation Tax and Income Tax rates for a range of tax years. You will find it useful to have a look at what is available on this site when you have an opportunity. It will also mean that you can obtain copies of tax returns to practice on when you reach that part of your business tax studies.

CALCULATION OF CORPORATION TAX AND INCOME TAX

Corporation Tax

In Chapters 2 to 5 in this book we will be looking in some detail about the way in which Corporation Tax is calculated. At this point we will just show how the system works in outline, by using a simple format for a **Corporation Tax computation**.

We will then use a numerical example that reflects a straightforward situation for a company.

an outline Corporation Tax computation		
		£
	Trading Profits	X
+	Income from Investments	X
+	Chargeable Gains	X
=	Taxable Total Profits (TTP)	X
	Corporation Tax on TTP	X

A simple Corporation Tax computation would look like this if we assume the following figures:

Corporation Tax Computation for AB Company Limited
for year ended 31/3/2016

	£
Trading Profits	1,300,000
Income from Investments	400,000
Chargeable Gains	300,000
Taxable Total Profits (TTP)	2,000,000
Corporation Tax on TTP (£2,000,000 x 20%*)	400,000

*We will see later the other Corporation Tax rates that apply to the financial year 2014.

Income Tax

In the later chapters in this book we will be looking at how trading profits are assessed under Income Tax. Although we will not need to use a full Income Tax computation in this learning area, we will now just briefly see how it will appear. This is so that you can envisage how the trading profit figures would be used to work out Income Tax.

an outline Income Tax computation

		£
	Income – earnings and other income	X
	Less personal allowance	(X)
=	Taxable income	X
	Tax payable on taxable income	X

A simple Income Tax computation for a sole trader might appear as follows:

Income Tax Computation

	£
Trading Profits	15,000
Other General Income	1,000
	16,000
Less Personal Allowance	10,600
Taxable income	5,400
Tax payable at 20%*	1,080

*Other rates of Income Tax can also apply.

HOW INCOME IS CATEGORISED FOR TAX PURPOSES

The income that a company or an individual receives is divided into categories, depending on what sort of income it is and where it comes from. These categories apply to both Corporation Tax and Income Tax, and are based on descriptions of income. This is done so that:

■ the correct rules on how to work out the income are used (since these vary with the categories), and

■ the correct rates of tax are used (since they can also depend on the type of income when applying income tax)

When studying this learning area we will only need to know the outline detail of most of these categories, because we will be mainly concentrating on trading income. The list and descriptions shown below have been simplified to include only the categories that you need to know about in this learning area. It does not include, for example, the categories that relate to overseas income.

'Property Income' – Rental income from land and property

'Trading Income' – Profits of trades and professions

'Savings & Investment Income' – UK Interest

FINANCIAL YEARS AND TAX YEARS

Corporation Tax – financial years

The rates of Corporation Tax are changed from time-to-time (normally in the Chancellor's budget) and relate to specific **financial years.** These years run from 1 April in one calendar year to 31 March in the following year. The year that runs from 1 April 2015 to 31 March 2016 is known as the financial year 2015 – in other words, the financial year is named after the calendar year that most of it falls into. We will see in the next chapters exactly how companies use the tax rates that apply to each financial year to calculate the correct amount of Corporation Tax.

Income Tax – tax years

For Income Tax purposes time is divided into **tax years** (sometimes called **fiscal years**). Individuals' income and Income Tax is worked out separately for each tax year. The tax year runs from 6 April in one calendar year to 5 April in the next calendar year. The tax year running from 6 April 2015 to 5 April 2016 would be described as the 2015/16 tax year.

HOW TAX RETURNS WORK

A **Tax Return** is a document issued by HM Revenue & Customs and used to collect information about a company's or an individual's income and gains. The Company Tax Return (the CT600 form) is used to collect information for Corporation Tax purposes, whereas the tax return for individuals provides data relating to Income Tax and Capital Gains Tax. Both companies and individuals are subject to the **self-assessment** system of tax. This means that they declare their profits and other taxable income on the tax return, and can then pay their own tax without HM Revenue & Customs sending them a bill. Individuals who submit a paper-based return within a certain deadline can ask HM Revenue & Customs to work the tax out for them, but otherwise the taxpayer (company or individual) or their agent must calculate the tax. Where the income tax return is submitted online, the tax is calculated automatically.

The tax forms relevant to your studies for this learning area are reproduced in the Appendix to this book. The forms are also available for download from the HM Revenue & Customs website: www.gov.uk or the Resources Sections of www.osbornebooks.co.uk As we progress through this book we will examine how the various relevant parts of the returns should be completed.

tax returns for limited companies

A company must submit a CT600 form (see opposite for page 1 of the short version) for every **chargeable accounting period** (CAP). Provided the accounts are produced for a period of twelve months or less, the company's normal accounting period will be the same as the CAP. Longer accounting periods are divided into two CAPs, one based on the first twelve months of the accounting period, and the other based on the remainder of the period. We will look at the practicalities of dividing up the figures for a long accounting period later in the book.

Note that the company tax return relates to the company's chargeable accounting period, not a particular financial year. The form sets out the information that is needed by HM Revenue & Customs, and provides a standard format for calculations. It must be submitted within twelve months after the end of the company's accounting period from which the CAP was derived. All companies must file returns online. The short CT600 version shown in the Appendix to this book is the one that you will need to be able to complete. You will not be asked to complete any supplementary pages for the company tax return that you may see referred to within the form, or the 'full' version of the form.

tax returns for individuals

Individuals with complex tax affairs (including all those in business as sole traders or partners) need to complete a separate tax return for each tax year. Note that individuals' tax returns relate to tax years, not accounting periods. The normal way that accounting periods are linked to tax years under Income Tax is that the assessable profits for a particular tax year are derived from the accounting period that ends in that tax year. This is known as a basis period for the tax year. For example a sole trader who makes accounts up to 31 December each year would use the accounts for the year ended 31/12/2015 as the basis period for the tax year 2015/16.

Later on in this book we will look at the rules that link accounting periods to tax years in various special situations.

HM Revenue & Customs

Page 1

Company - Short Tax Return form
CT600 (Short) (2008) Version 2
for accounting periods ending on or after 1 July 1999

Your company tax return

If we send the company a *Notice* to deliver a company tax return (form *CT603*) it has to comply by the filing date, or we charge a penalty, even if there is no tax to pay. A return includes a company tax return form, any Supplementary Pages, accounts, computations and any relevant information.

Is this the right form for the company? Read the advice on pages 3 to 6 of the Company tax return guide (the *Guide*) before you start.

The forms in the CT600 series set out the information we need and provide a standard format for calculations. Use the *Guide* to help you complete the return form. It contains general information you may need and box by box advice.

Company information

Company name

Company registration number

Tax Reference as shown on the CT603

Type of company

Registered office address

Postcode

About this return

This is the above company's return for the period

from (dd/mm/yyyy)   to (dd/mm/yyyy)

Put an 'X' in the appropriate box(es) below

A repayment is due for this return period

A repayment is due for an earlier period

Making more than one return for this company now

This return contains estimated figures

Company part of a group that is not small

Disclosure of tax avoidance schemes

Notice of disclosable avoidance schemes

Transfer pricing

Compensating adjustment claimed

Company qualifies for SME exemption

Accounts
I attach accounts and computations

• for the period to which this return relates

• for a different period

If you are not attaching accounts and computations, say why not

Supplementary Pages
If you are enclosing any Supplementary Pages put an 'X' in the appropriate box(es)

Loans to participators by close companies, form *CT600A*

Charities and Community Amateur Sports Clubs (CASCs), form *CT600E*

Disclosure of tax avoidance schemes, form *CT600J*

HMRC 09/08

CT600 (Short) (2008) Version 2

structure of the income tax return

Because different individuals have different circumstances, the tax return is divided into two parts.

The first part is used by every person that needs to complete a tax return, and is therefore common to all returns. It requests general information, as well as details of certain personal income.

The second part of the tax return consists of a series of supplementary pages that are only used by relevant taxpayers. In this text we will only be looking at these business-related supplementary pages, since some other parts of the return are dealt with in Osborne Books' *Personal Tax* text, which covers the 'personal tax' Unit.

There are supplementary pages for income from **self-employment** (ie for sole traders) and income from **partnerships**. For those in partnership, the supplementary page is completed for the individual's share of partnership profits. The partnership as a whole will also need to submit a form that summarises the total profits of the partnership.

scheduling of the income tax return

Individuals and partnerships can submit their tax returns either in the traditional paper format, or online. HMRC are encouraging the use of online submissions, and have introduced the following different deadlines for each method of tax return submission:

■ submission of paper-based tax returns must be made by the 31 October following the end of the tax year. This means that the 2015/16 return would need to be submitted by 31 October 2016. If required, HMRC will calculate the tax relating to a properly completed return if it meets this deadline

■ submission of an online return can be made at any time up to 31 January following the end of the tax year. The amount of tax is automatically calculated by the computer program once the online form has been completed, and the taxpayer can print out a copy for their records. An online return for the tax year 2015/16 would therefore need to be submitted by 31 January 2017

WHEN TO PAY TAX

The payment dates for companies and individuals differ, so we will examine them separately.

companies – Corporation Tax

We saw in the last section that company tax returns are completed for each chargeable accounting period (CAP). Unless instalment payments are necessary, the Corporation Tax that has been calculated is normally payable nine months and one day after the end of the chargeable accounting period that it relates to. For example, the Corporation Tax relating to the chargeable accounting period 1/1/2015 to 31/12/2015 will normally be payable on 1/10/2016. If the period falls into more than one financial year this will be taken account of in the tax calculation, but it does not affect the payment date. The payment date relates only to the period, not to the financial year.

If a company is 'large', then it will pay most of its Corporation Tax earlier in instalments, with only the final amount falling due on the date referred to above. We will look at this situation in more detail after we have seen how Corporation Tax is calculated.

Notice that for companies the payment of tax is due before the final filing date for the tax return. This means that the tax calculation will have to have been carried out by the payment date (so that the payment amount is known), even though the actual form need not be submitted until nearly three months later! The return can always be submitted early if desired.

individuals – Income Tax

For income from trading profits there is no system set up to automatically deduct Income Tax as there is for employees. The outstanding balance of Income Tax that relates to business profits and other income from which tax has not been deducted will need to be paid to HM Revenue & Customs according to the following rules.

The *final* date for payment of the Income Tax that relates to a tax year is the 31 January *following the end of that tax year*.

For some taxpayers there may also be payments on account that must be made before the final date. These are due as follows:

- first payment on account is due on 31 January within the tax year
- second payment on account is due on 31 July following the end of the tax year

For the tax year 2015/16 the payment dates would be:

> 31 January 2016 for the first payment on account,
>
> 31 July 2016 for the second payment on account, and
>
> 31 January 2017 for the final payment

Notice that when payments on account are required, two payments will be due on each 31 January. For example, on 31 January 2016 there would be due both:

> the final payment for the tax year 2014/15, and
>
> the first payment on account for the tax year 2015/16

Later in the book we will see how the payments on account are calculated, and which taxpayers need to make these early payments.

We saw earlier that 31 January following the tax year was also the final date for submitting an online tax return, so for Income Tax these two dates coincide.

The table below illustrates the main points relating to tax returns and payment dates.

Companies	Individuals (Sole Traders and Partnerships)
Corporation Tax	**Income Tax**
Company Tax Return (CT600) includes calculation of Corporation Tax for chargeable accounting period (CAP).	Tax return includes supplementary pages for sole traders and partners, and relates to tax year.
Return submitted online by 12 months after end of period that accounts are based on.	Paper return submitted by 31 Oct following tax year, or online return submitted by 31 Jan following tax year.
Final payment by 9 months and 1 day after end of CAP.	Final payment by 31 Jan following tax year.
Large companies also make earlier instalment payments.	Many taxpayers also make two payments on account.

DIVERSE ACCOUNTING PRACTICE: TAX RETURNS

It is August 2015. You are a trainee employed by the Diverse Accounting Practice, working in their tax department. The practice uses online submission for all tax returns. You are currently scheduling work related to two clients as follows:

The Mammoth Company Limited produces annual accounts to the 31 January. The accounts for the year ended 31/1/2015 have been completed and are awaiting the necessary tax work.

Jo Small is a sole trader who has been trading for many years. The practice has produced accounts for her for the year ended 30/6/2015.

required

State the type of tax return that will need to be completed for each of the clients. Explain how each return is related to the client's accounting period, and the latest submission dates for the returns. State the final date for the payment of outstanding tax after any instalments or payments on account have been made.

solution

The Mammoth Company Limited will require a company tax return (form CT600). This will relate to the chargeable accounting period (CAP) 1/2/2014 to 31/1/2015. The form must be submitted online by 12 months after the end of the accounting period – 31/1/2016. The final Corporation Tax payment must be made by 1/11/2015 (nine months and one day after the end of the CAP).

Jo Small will need a tax return for the tax year 2015/16. The accounting period of 1/7/2014 to 30/6/2015 will form the basis period for this tax year. The main part of the form will need to be completed, along with the supplementary pages relating to self-employment. The online tax return must be submitted by 31/1/2017. The final Income Tax payment relating to 2015/16 will also have to be made by 31/1/2017.

NATIONAL INSURANCE

If you are an employee, you are probably familiar with employee National Insurance Contributions (NIC), which are deducted through Pay-As-You-Earn, along with Income Tax. In our study of business tax we will be looking at National Insurance Contributions, payable by self-employed individuals (sole traders and partners) in respect of their own profits.

self-employed National Insurance contributions

There are two classes of NIC that apply to both sole traders and partners.

■ **Class 2 contributions** are payable at a flat rate of £2.80 per week (unless the profits are below the 'small profits threshold' [see below]), and, in addition,

■ **Class 4 contributions** are payable on profits above £8,060 per year

The profits for self-employed NIC purposes are the same ones that are used for Income Tax purposes – the assessable trading profits. Where profits are less than £5,965 (2015/16) then the small profits threshold means that Class 2 contributions need not be paid.

Neither Class 2 nor Class 4 NIC is payable by those either under 16 years of age or over pensionable age at the start of the tax year.

The rates for Class 4 contributions for 2015/16 are:

■ 9% of profits for the year between £8,060 and £42,385, plus

■ 2% of profits above £42,385

If profits are below £8,060 then there are no Class 4 contributions.

example – NI for the self-employed

Sonita is a sole trader with trading profits of £50,000 in 2015/16.

Her NIC liability for the year would be:

		£	£
Class 2 contributions:	£2.80 x 52 =		145.60
Class 4 contributions:	(£42,385 – £8,060) x 9% =	3,089.25	
	plus		
	(£50,000 – £42,385) x 2% =	152.30	
			3,241.55
			3,387.15

Both Class 2 and Class 4 contributions are calculated at the same time as Income Tax under the self-assessment system, and entered on the tax return and paid along with the Income Tax for the year.

THE DUTIES AND RESPONSIBILITIES OF A TAX PRACTITIONER

A person who acts as a professional by helping clients (either companies or individuals) with their tax affairs has responsibilities:

- to the client, and
- to HM Revenue & Customs

The AAT has published a revised **Code of Professional Ethics** that deals with these and other issues. This applies to both AAT students and members and the document can be downloaded from the website www.aat.org.uk

confidentiality

Keeping a client's or customer's dealings confidential is an essential element of professional ethics. As far as confidentiality for a tax practitioner is concerned, the Code referred to above states that confidentiality should always be observed, unless either

- authority has been given to disclose the information (by the client), or
- there is a legal or professional right or duty to disclose

The Code also says that:

'Information about a past, present, or prospective client's or employer's affairs, or the affairs of clients of employers, acquired in a work context is likely to be confidential if it is not a matter of public knowledge.'

The rules of confidentiality apply in a social environment as well as a business one, and care should be taken to not inadvertently disclose confidential information. The need to comply also extends after a business relationship has ended – for example if there was a change of employment.

One important **exception to the normal rules of confidentiality** is where **'money laundering'** is known or suspected. 'Money laundering' includes any process of concealing or disguising the proceeds of any criminal offence, including tax evasion.

Where a practitioner has knowledge or suspicion that his client is money laundering, then he has a duty to inform the relevant person or authority. For those in a group practice this would be the Money Laundering Reporting Officer (MLRO), and for sole practitioner the National Crime Agency (NCA).

It is an offence to warn the client that a report of this type is going to be made about him. Money laundering therefore is not a situation where authority would be sought from the client to disclose information!

taxation services

The Code states the following regarding taxation services:

'A member providing professional tax services has a duty to put forward the best position in favour of a client or an employee. However the service must be carried out with professional competence, must not in any way impair integrity or objectivity, and must be consistent with the law.'

The Code also states that:

'A member shall only undertake taxation work on the basis of full disclosure by the client or employer. The member, in dealing with the tax authorities, must act in good faith and exercise care in relation to facts and information presented on behalf of the client or employer. It will normally be assumed that facts and information on which business tax computations are based were provided by the client or employer as the taxpayer, and the latter bears ultimate resopnsibility for the accuracy of the facts, information and tax computations. The member shall avoid assuming responsibility for the accuracy of facts, etc. outside his or her knowledge.

'When a member learns of a material error or omission in a tax return of a prior year, or of a failure to file a required tax return, the member has a responsibility to advise promptly the client or employer of the error or omission and recommend that disclosure be made to HMRC. If the client or employer, after having had a reasonable time to reflect, does not correct the error, the member shall inform the client or employer in writing that it is not possible for the member to act for them in connection with that return or other related information submitted to the authorities.'

dealing with professional ethics problems

Dealing with professional ethics can be a difficult and complex area, and we have only outlined some main points. If you find yourself in a position where you are uncertain how you should proceed because of an ethical problem then you should first approach your supervisor or manager. If you are still unable to resolve the problem then further professional or legal advice may need to be obtained.

tax records

It is also important to know what records will need to be kept regarding the client's income and tax affairs, and to ensure that such records are kept secure. The records must be sufficient to substantiate the information provided to HM Revenue & Customs. This would include documentation such as invoices, receipts, and working papers.

These records must be kept as follows:

- **companies** must keep records relating to the information in their tax returns until at least 6 years after the end of the accounting period. For example, records relating to the chargeable accounting period (CAP) from 1/4/2015 until 31/3/2016 must be kept until 31/3/2022

- **individuals** in business (sole traders and partners) must keep records for approximately 5 years plus 10 months from the end of the tax year to which they relate. For example documents relating to 2015/16 must be retained until 31 January 2022

For both types of organisation this date for record keeping is 5 years after the latest filing date for the return (assuming the income tax return is submitted online). If there is a formal HM Revenue & Customs enquiry into a taxpayer's affairs then the records need to be kept at least until the end of the enquiry.

There can be a penalty for not keeping the required records of up to £3,000 for each tax year (for individuals) or £3,000 per accounting period (for companies).

compliance checks

HMRC can carry out 'compliance checks' relating to a range of taxes including Corporation Tax, Income Tax and Capital Gains Tax to ensure that the correct amount of tax is paid and that proper records are kept. HMRC have powers to:

- visit businesses to inspect premises, assets and records
- ask taxpayers and third parties (for example tax practitioners) for more information and documents

In most situations at least seven days prior notice would be given of a visit. HMRC are required by law to 'act reasonably' with regard to compliance checks.

Chapter Summary

- The taxes that UK businesses are subject to will depend on the type of organisation.

- The profits and gains of limited companies are subject to Corporation Tax, while sole traders and partners' trading profits are subject to Income Tax, along with any other personal income. The self-employed are also subject to Capital Gains Tax on the disposal of certain business assets. National Insurance contributions are applied to the self-employed and partners on their profits.

- Income Tax and Corporation Tax are administered by HM Revenue & Customs, which collects tax and National Insurance Contributions. It is also responsible for publishing documents and forms to gather information about how much tax is owed and is governed by statute law and case law.

- Under both Corporation Tax and Income Tax, the assessable amount is divided into categories so that appropriate rules can be applied to calculate the amount of each different form of income.

- Corporation Tax rates relate to financial years that run from 1 April. The tax is calculated separately for each Chargeable Accounting Period (CAP) that is linked to the period for which the accounts are produced.

- The Company Tax Return (CT600) is based on the CAP. Corporation tax is payable within nine months and one day after the end of the CAP. Large companies must also make instalment payments.

- Income tax, which applies to individuals (sole traders and partners), is calculated separately for each tax year (6 April to the following 5 April). An Income Tax computation is used to calculate the tax by totalling the income from various sources, and subtracting the personal allowance. Each tax year has a separate tax return, which is used to collect information about the income and tax of individuals. It consists of a common section plus supplementary pages relating to self-employment. Income tax must be paid to HM Revenue & Customs by the 31 January following the end of the tax year. For some taxpayers there is also a requirement to make payments on account before this date.

■ National Insurance is applied to the self-employed and partners in respect of their profits. They must pay a flat rate (Class 2), plus an amount calculated as percentages of their profits (Class 4).

■ Tax practitioners have responsibilities to their clients (including confidentiality) and to HM Revenue & Customs. They must also ensure that all necessary records are kept for the required period of time.

Key Terms		
Limited Company	a limited company is a separate legal entity from its owners (the shareholders). Its profits are subject to Corporation Tax
Sole Trader	an individual who is self-employed on his or her own. There is no legal distinction between the business entity and the individual, and the sole trader is subject to Income Tax on the profits of the business
Partnership	an organisation made up of several individuals who share the responsibilities and profits of the partnership. Since there is no legal separation between the partnership and the individuals who are partners, they are individually subject to Income Tax on their share of the profits. Effectively, a partnership is a collection of sole traders
Corporation Tax	a tax that applies to the trading and other profits of limited companies, including any chargeable gains
Income Tax	the tax that individuals (including sole traders and partners) pay on their income, including business profits
Capital Gains Tax	the tax that applies to certain disposals that individuals make on business and private assets
National Insurance	effectively a tax that is applied to the self-employed and partners
Statute Law	legislation that is passed by Parliament, for example the annual Finance Act
Case Law	the result of decisions taken in court cases that have an impact on the interpretation of law
Financial Year (Corporation Tax)	each financial year runs from 1 April to 31 March Corporation Tax rates are based on financial years

Tax Year (Income Tax)	each tax year runs from 6 April to the following 5 April. Tax years are also known as fiscal years
Company Tax Return	this document (the CT600) is filed online for each Chargeable Accounting Period, normally the period for which the company prepares accounts
Tax Return (individuals)	the self-assessment tax return is issued for each tax year to certain taxpayers and relates to Income Tax and Capital Gains Tax. It is divided into a common section, plus supplementary pages including pages relating to sole traders and partners. It can be submitted in paper form, or online

Activities

1.1 The following statements are made by a trainee in the tax department of Jenner & Co.

Indicate whether each statement is true or false.

(a)	One of the reasons that income is divided into categories is so that the correct rules can be applied to each type of income.	
(b)	The only law that is relevant to tax matters is the current Finance Act.	
(c)	Companies must complete a separate CT600 tax return for every financial year in which they operate.	
(d)	A Corporation Tax Computation is the name given to the calculation of Corporation Tax, based on the taxable total profits chargeable to Corporation Tax for the chargeable accounting period.	
(e)	A sole trader with profits assessable in 2015/16 of £20,000, and no other taxable income, would pay Income Tax of £1,880.	
(f)	It is the job of a tax practitioner to ensure that his client pays the least amount of tax. This may involve bending the rules, or omitting certain items from a tax computation.	
(g)	Most self-employed people pay tax under PAYE and so don't have to worry about completing tax returns.	

1.2 DonCom plc has the following assessable income agreed for the chargeable accounting period from 1/4/2015 to 31/3/2016:

Trading Profits	£1,300,000
Chargeable Gains	£500,000
Profits from renting property	£100,000

Required:

(a) Assuming a Corporation Tax rate of 20%, use a Corporation Tax computation to calculate the tax liability for DonCom plc.

(b) State the filing date of the CT600 form, and the date by which the final Corporation Tax payment must be made.

1.3 Parmajit is trading in partnership. Her share of the partnership profits for the accounting period 1/6/2014 to 31/5/2015 was £16,000. In addition she had other general taxable income in the tax year 2015/16 of £2,000. She uses paper-based tax returns.

Required:

(a) Assuming that Parmajit is entitled to a personal allowance of £10,600 for 2015/16, and pays Income Tax at 20% for that year, calculate her Income Tax liability.

(b) State the date that her tax return must be submitted if HM Revenue & Customs were to calculate her tax, and the date by which the balance of Income Tax must be paid for the tax year.

1.4 John is self-employed, and has assessable trading profits for the tax year 2015/16 of £25,000.

Required:

Calculate the National Insurance Contribution liability under each class for John.

State how payment would be made.

1.5   You are a trainee employed by Osborne Accounting Practice, working in their tax department. The practice uses online return submission for Income Tax. You are currently scheduling work related to two clients as follows:

The Walvern Water Company Limited produces annual accounts to 31 July. The accounts for the year ended 31/7/2015 have been completed and are awaiting the necessary tax work.

Wally Weaver is a sole trader who has been trading for many years. The practice has produced accounts for him for the year ended 31/7/2015.

Required:

- State the type of tax return that will need to be completed for each of the clients

- Explain how each tax return is related to the client's accounting period, and state the latest submission dates for the returns.

- State in each case the final date for the payment of outstanding tax after any instalments or payments on account have been made.

1.6   **(1)**   Which of the following statements is correct?

(a)	Every self employed taxpayer must pay Class 2 NIC, irrespective of the level of profits	
(b)	Self employed taxpayers pay either Class 2 or Class 4, but not both	
(c)	Class 4 NIC is based on the amount of money taken out of the business by the taxpayer	
(d)	An individual failing to keep appropriate records for the correct length of time is subject to a penalty of up to £3,000 for each tax year	

(2)   A taxpayer has self employed income of £70,000 for 2015/16.

The amount chargeable to NIC at 2% would be   £

(3)   A taxpayer has self employed income of £35,000 for 2015/16.

The amount of total Class 4 NIC payable would be   £

2 Corporation tax – trading profits

this chapter covers...

In this chapter we provide a brief review of the Corporation Tax computation, and examine the step by step procedures for compiling the computation, before concentrating on the calculation of adjusted trading profits.

We examine in detail how to adjust the data provided in an income statement so that it is valid for tax purposes. This involves adjusting income and expenditure. We will note the main types of expenditure that cannot be set against trading income, as well as specific examples of expenditure that is allowable.

There will be opportunities to practice adjusting accounts that have been prepared for internal purposes, as well as using published accounts.

We will then see how to deal with the situation when accounts have been prepared for a long period and need to be split into two Chargeable Accounting Periods.

Finally, we will learn the rather complex rules about the options that are available to companies to offset any trade losses that they incur.

THE CORPORATION TAX COMPUTATION

We saw in the last chapter that the Corporation Tax computation comprises a summary of profits from various sources that are chargeable to Corporation Tax. The computation then goes on to calculate the amount of Corporation Tax that is payable. A simple version of this computation is repeated here:

	Trading Income	X
+	Profits from Investments	X
+	Chargeable Gains	X
=	Taxable Total Profits (TTP)	X
	Corporation Tax on taxable total profits	X

Note that 'taxable total profits' were previously known as 'profits chargeable to Corporation Tax' (PCTCT).

You will notice that 'Trading Income' is listed as the first item in the computation, and is often the most important one. We will be looking in detail in this chapter at why and how the trading profits from the financial accounts are adjusted for tax purposes.

Before we do that, we will examine briefly the main steps that need to be undertaken to complete the full Corporation Tax computation. We can then refer to this procedure as we look at the components in detail over the next chapters. The following diagram shows in summary how it all fits together.

In this chapter we are going to learn how to adjust the trading profit (the top left-hand box in the diagram). We will also see how trade losses can be set against profits to reduce total taxable profits.

In Chapter Three we will see how to calculate capital allowances so that we can incorporate the result into the trading income assessment.

In Chapter Four we will examine chargeable gains and then we will see how it all fits together.

In Chapter Five we will explain how to calculate the Corporation Tax liability.

ADJUSTMENT OF PROFITS

The starting point for the calculation of trading profits is the statement of profit or loss (income statement) that has been prepared by the company. Whether you are asked to work from a set of accounts prepared for internal use, or in published format, the process is the same.

The 'basis of assessment' for trading profits is the **tax-adjusted trading profits** of the **chargeable accounting period**, prepared on an accruals basis. In this section of the book we will start by using accounts that have been prepared for the chargeable accounting period (ie no more than 12 months). We will see later how we deal with accounts that have been prepared for a longer period. Since the financial accounts that will be our starting point will always have been prepared on an accruals basis, that aspect should not cause us any problems.

The reason that accounts need to be adjusted for tax purposes is not because they are wrong, but because Corporation Tax does not use exactly the same rules as financial accounting. We need to arrive at a profit figure that is based on the tax rules! For example, there are some costs that although quite legitimate from an accounting point of view are not allowable as a deduction in arriving at the profit figure for tax purposes.

The object of adjusting the financial accounts is to make sure that:

- the only **income** that is credited is **trading income**
- the only **expenditure** that is deducted is **allowable trading expenditure**

When we adjust profits, we will start with the profit from the financial accounts, and

- deduct any income that is not trading income, and
- add back any expenditure that has already been deducted but is not allowable

This approach is much more convenient than re-writing the whole profit and loss account based on tax rules. It is quite logical, because it effectively cancels out income and expenditure that is not relevant for tax purposes.

example – adjusting the profits

Suppose that we wish to adjust a set of financial accounts (shown here in summary form):

	£'000
Sales	500
less cost of sales	200
Gross trading profit	300
Non-trading income	150
	450
less expenditure	120
Net profit	330

Analysis of the accounts has shown that the cost of sales is entirely allowable, but £40,000 of the £120,000 expenditure is not allowable for tax purposes.

To adjust the profits we would carry out the following computation:

	£'000
Net profit per accounts	330
Less non-trading income	(150)
Add expenditure that is not allowable	40
Adjusted trading profit	220

This provides us with the same answer that we could get by writing out the accounts in full, using only the trading income and allowable expenditure. If we did that it would look as follows. This is shown just for comparison – we won't actually need to rewrite the accounts in this way.

	£'000
Sales	500
Less allowable cost of sales	200
Gross trading profit	300
Less allowable expenditure	80
Net profit	220

We will now look in more detail at adjustments for income, followed by expenditure.

adjusting income

Provided the 'sales', 'turnover' or 'revenue' figure relates entirely to trading, this figure will not need adjusting. Other income may or may not be taxable, but if it is not trading income, then it will need to be adjusted for in the trading profit calculation.

The following are examples of income that are **not assessable as trading income**, and should therefore be adjusted for by **deducting** from the net profit shown in the financial accounts:

■ non-trading interest receivable

- rent receivable
- gains on the disposal of non-current assets (fixed assets)
- dividends received

All these examples should be adjusted by simply deducting the amount that was credited to the financial accounts. There is no need to worry about exactly how the figure was originally calculated. We will then have arrived at what the profit would have been if these items had not been included originally. Items that originate from the trade (eg discounts received) are taxable as part of trading income, and therefore need no adjustment.

Non-trading interest and **rent received** will reappear in the taxable total profits (TTP) computation as investment income and property income respectively. Throughout the examples in this book you can assume that any interest received is non-trading and is therefore dealt with as outlined here unless stated otherwise.

Gains on the disposal of non-current assets could result in chargeable gains. These gains need to be calculated according to special rules before being incorporated into the taxable total profits as we will see in Chapter 4. **Dividends received** from UK companies are not assessable under Corporation Tax at all (since they have been paid out of another company's taxed income), although, as we will see later, they can have an impact on the rate of tax applied.

adjusting expenditure

We will only need to adjust for any expenditure accounted for in the financial accounts profit if it is **not allowable**. We do this by **adding it back** to the financial accounts profit. Expenditure that is allowable can be left unadjusted in the accounts. Although this may seem obvious, it is easy to get confused.

The general rule for expenditure to be allowable in a trading income computation is that it must be:

- revenue rather than capital in nature, and
- 'wholly and exclusively' for the purpose of the trade

Although we will look at how to deal with various specific types of expenditure shortly, these rules are fundamental, and should always be used to guide you in the absence of more precise information. This part of the unit will require a good deal of study, since it is quite complex, and the rules and examples that follow will need to be remembered. The best way to approach this is to continually revise the topic and practice lots of examples.

expenditure that is not allowable

The following are examples of expenditure that is not allowable, and therefore require adjustment. Some clearly follow the rules outlined above, while others may have arisen from specific regulations, or court cases forming precedents (case law).

■ **any capital expenditure**
This follows the normal financial accounting use of the term, to mean expenditure on assets that will have a value to the business over several accounting periods. Capital expenditure includes expenditure to improve non-current assets, and installation costs and legal expenses in connection with acquiring non-current assets.

■ **depreciation of non-current assets**
This is because capital allowances are allowable instead, as HM Revenue & Customs alternative to depreciation, as we will see in the next chapter. Even where there are no capital allowances available, depreciation is still not allowed. Other items which are similar to depreciation (eg amortisation of certain assets, and losses on disposal of non-current assets) are also not allowable.

■ **part of lease rental payments for high emission cars**
When a car with an emission level of more than 130g/km of CO_2 is leased for over 45 days through an operating lease, 15% of the lease rental payment is disallowed, leaving an allowable expenditure of 85% of the payment. If the car has emission levels lower than this then all of the lease rental payment is allowable.

■ **entertaining expenditure**
This relates to business entertaining of customers or suppliers. Entertaining of the businesses' own staff is however allowable (see page 2.9).

■ **gifts to customers**
Virtually all gifts made to customers are not allowable. There is an exception for some low-value items, as we will see shortly.

■ **increases in general bad debt provisions**
Any such increase (that is debited to the income statement) must be added back in the computation, and decreases in general provisions adjusted for by deducting from profits. A general provision could be based on a lump sum, or a percentage of total trade receivables (debtors). Increases in specific provisions and the actual write-off of bad debts are however allowable. Where accounts have been prepared using 'impairment' as a means of calculating the bad debt provision, the provision will be treated in the same way as a specific bad debt provision. This applies as long as objective evidence was used to calculate the amount of impairment. This situation could arise if, for example, the accounts are prepared under International Accounting Standards. See also the additional note on page 2.9.

■ **charitable payments**
These items can be deducted from the total profits of the company in the taxable total profits (TTP) calculation as Gift Aid payments. Where this occurs the expenditure cannot also be deducted in the

calculation of trading profits. We will look a little more closely at gift aid payments in Chapter 5.

■ **fines for law breaking**

Fines imposed on the company itself for lawbreaking (e.g. for breaches of health & safety legislation) are not allowable, nor are the associated legal costs. The costs of tax appeals are also not allowable. Fines for minor motoring offences incurred by employees whilst on business are allowable, but not if the employee is a Director of the company.

■ **certain legal expenses**

Legal expenses incurred on forming a company or acquiring new leases (both long and short leases).

■ **illegal payments**

For example bribes, or payments made in response to threats.

■ **donations to political parties**

These are not for the purpose of 'the trade' and so are not allowable.

■ **writing off non-trade loans**

For example, loans to employees or directors (unless they were incurred in the normal course of trade).

■ **dividends payable**

The payment of dividends is not an allowable expense. However if these occur in the accounts after the net profit that we have used as the starting point for our calculation, there will be no need for an adjustment.

■ **Corporation Tax**

Logically, the tax payment itself is not tax deductible!

expenditure that is allowable

As already stated, revenue expenditure that is 'wholly and exclusively' for the purpose of the trade is allowable. We will now list some illustrative examples, a few of which were referred to above.

■ normal **cost of sales**

■ normal **business expenditure**, for example:
- distribution costs
- administration
- salaries and wages, and employers' NIC
- rent, rates and insurance
- repairs
- advertising
- business travel and subsistence
- accountancy services
- research & development expenditure

- **specifically allowable expenditure**:
  - operating lease rental payments for cars with emission levels of 130g/km or less
  - legal expenses on renewing (but not acquiring) a short (ie 50 years or shorter) lease
  - interest payable on trade loans
  - staff entertaining (eg staff Christmas parties)
  - trade bad debts written off (note, however, that writing off of a loan to an employee is not allowable, since it is not a trade item)
  - increases in specific provisions for trade bad debts and impairment provisions based on objective evidence (see note below). Specific provisions are those based on named debtors
  - gifts to customers that contain a conspicuous advertisement, costing up to £50 per recipient per year – this however does not apply to food, drink, tobacco or gift vouchers, gifts of which can never be allowable – allowable examples would include calendars and diaries
  - gifts of trading stock to educational establishments, charities or registered amateur sports clubs
  - employees' parking fines incurred while on business, but not those of directors

- **capital allowances**

  We will see how to calculate capital allowances in the next chapter. In the exercises in this chapter we will use capital allowance figures that have already been calculated. Because capital allowances will not be recorded in the financial accounts, they will be deducted as a separate item in the adjustment to the accounts.

note regarding trade bad debts and provisions

Whereas a sum written off a trade debt or an increase in a specific provision is allowable, any recovery of amounts previously written off and any decrease in specific provisions is taxable, and no adjustment is needed. This can be a confusing area. The following table summarises the position:

Expenditure	Treatment	Action
Trade Bad Debts Written Off	Allowable	No adjustment
Increases in Specific Bad Debt Provisions	Allowable	No adjustment
Increases in General Bad Debt Provisions	Not allowable	Add back
Income	**Treatment**	**Action**
Trade Bad Debts Recovered	Taxable	No adjustment
Decreases in Specific Bad Debt Provisions	Taxable	No adjustment
Decreases in General Bad Debt Provisions	Not taxable	Deduct

TRADING ALOUD LIMITED: ADJUSTING THE PROFIT

Trading Aloud Limited is a company that specialises in selling acoustic equipment. The unadjusted income statement for the year ended 31/3/2016 is as follows:

	Notes	£	£
Sales			900,000
less cost of sales			530,000
Gross profit			370,000
Rental income			120,000
Dividends received			140,000
			630,000
less expenses:			
Salaries and wages	(1)	95,400	
Depreciation		51,000	
Directors' fees		45,000	
Administration expenses		17,600	
Advertising	(2)	12,600	
Travel and entertaining	(3)	19,500	
Bad debts and provisions	(4)	21,650	
			262,750
Net Profit			367,250

Notes:

(1) Salaries and wages includes £4,350 employers' NIC.

(2) Advertising includes:
  (a) gifts of food hampers to 70 customers £3,250
  (b) gifts of 100 mouse-mats with company logos £500

(3) Travel and entertaining is made up as follows:

	£
Employees' travel expenses	7,400
Employees' subsistence allowances	5,450
Entertaining customers	6,650
	19,500

(4) Bad debts and provisions is made up of:

	£
Trade bad debts written off	13,400
Increase in general bad debt provision	5,000
Increase in specific bad debt provision	3,250
	21,650

Capital allowances for the period have been calculated at £15,000.

required
Adjust the net profit shown to arrive at the trading income assessment for Corporation Tax purposes.

solution
The computation is shown here with notes that explain the rationale behind each adjustment and allowed item. Items that are to be deducted are shown in the left-hand column, and those to be added kept in the main (right-hand) column for clarity.

		£
Net Profit per accounts		367,250
Add Back:		
Expenditure that is shown in the accounts but is not allowable		
Depreciation		51,000
Food Hampers		3,250
Entertaining Customers		6,650
Increase in General Bad Debt Provision		5,000
		433,150
Deduct:		
Income not taxable as trading income	£	
Rental Income	120,000	
Dividends Received	140,000	
Capital Allowances	15,000	
		(275,000)
Trading Income Assessment		158,150

Notes:

- The sales and cost of sales appear to be normal trading items.
- The rental income will be brought into the main Corporation Tax computation as property income.
- The dividends received are not subject to Corporation Tax.
- Salaries and Wages (including employers' NIC) are allowable.
- Depreciation is never allowable.
- Director's fees are treated in the same way as other staff salaries.
- Administration expenses appear to be wholly and exclusively for the trade.
- The advertising costs are allowable, including the mouse-mats that fall under the provision regarding items under £50 per person. The hampers cannot be covered by this rule as they contain food.
- Employees' travel and subsistence costs are allowable, but entertaining customers is never allowable.
- Changes in general provisions for bad debts must always be adjusted for, but specific provision increases and bad debts written off are allowable.
- The capital allowance figure is shown here as a final deduction in arriving at the assessable trading income.

working from published accounts

The principle of adjusting profits for tax purposes is the same when using a published version of financial accounts. The only issue that requires extra care is the choice of profit figure as a starting point from the range of figures available. It makes sense to use the profit figure that will require the least number of adjustments. The best profit figure to use will therefore be profit before tax so that this item will not need further adjustment. We will now use a Case Study to illustrate this procedure. Since you will probably be familiar with the International Accounting Standards (IAS) format, we will use it here.

Case Study

FORMAT COMPANY LIMITED: ADJUSTING PUBLISHED ACCOUNTS

The published accounts of Format Company Limited under IAS for the year ended 31 March 2016 are shown below, together with notes that provide some analysis of the summarised data.

Capital allowances have already been calculated, and amount to £86,400.

	£'000
Revenue	963
Cost of Sales	(541)
Gross Profit	422
Other Income	390
Distribution Costs	(56)
Administrative Expenses	(123)
Finance Costs	(24)
Profit before Tax	609
Tax	(150)
Profit for the Year	459

Notes:

- Cost of Sales includes depreciation of £140,000
- Administrative Expenses include the following:
  - Increase in Bad Debt Provision due to impairment calculation based on objective evidence   £7,700
  - Entertaining Customers   £9,600
- Other Income consists of:
  - Rental Income   £220,000
  - Interest Received from Investments   £60,000
  - Profit on Sale of Non-current Assets   £95,000
  - Dividends Received   £15,000
- Finance Costs relates to bank overdraft interest

required

Calculate the trading income as adjusted for tax purposes.

solution

We will start our computation with the 'Profit before Tax' since the item that follows that figure is not allowable, whereas the items that precede it could be a mixture of allowable and non-allowable.

	£	£
Profit before Tax		609,000
Add Back:		
Expenditure that is shown in the accounts but is not allowable		
Depreciation		140,000
Entertaining Customers		9,600
		758,600
Deduct:		
Income that is not taxable as trading income		
Rental Income	220,000	
Interest Received from Investments	60,000	
Profit on Sale of Non-current Assets	95,000	
Dividends Received	15,000	
Capital Allowances	86,400	(476,400)
Trading Income Assessment		282,200

DEALING WITH ACCOUNTS FOR LONG PERIODS

In Chapter One we saw that a **chargeable accounting period** (CAP – the period that we must use for Corporation Tax purposes) is the same as the period that the accounts have been prepared for, but only if that period is for 12 months or less. Where the company produces its financial accounts for a period exceeding 12 months, this will be divided into two CAPs (and require two Corporation Tax computations):

- one CAP for the first 12 months of the financial accounting period and
- one CAP for the balance of the financial accounting period

For example, if a company produces financial accounts for the 18 month period 1/7/2014 to 31/12/2015, there will be two CAPs:

- a 12 month CAP: 1/7/2014 to 30/6/2015, and
- a 6 month CAP: 1/7/2015 to 31/12/2015

The mechanism for dealing with the two Corporation Tax computations for these periods is:

- the financial accounts for the long period are adjusted in one operation, with the exception of the capital allowances deduction
- the adjusted profits (before the deduction of any capital allowance) are then time-apportioned into the two CAPs
- capital allowances are calculated separately for each CAP (as we will see in the next chapter)
- each CAP's adjusted trading profit is then finalised by deducting the capital allowances that have been calculated for the specific period

We will now use a Case Study to illustrate this principle.

Case Study

THYME LIMITED: ACCOUNTS FOR A LONG PERIOD

Thyme Limited is changing its accounting dates, and to accommodate this has produced one long set of financial accounts, from 1/10/2014 to 31/3/2016.

Capital allowances have already been calculated for each of the two CAPs as follows:

CAP 1/10/2014 to 30/9/2015   £15,000

CAP 1/10/2015 to 31/3/2016   £6,000

The financial accounts for the 18 months to 31/3/2016 are as follows:

	£	£
Sales		237,000
less cost of sales		103,000
Gross profit		134,000
less expenses:		
Salaries and wages	43,500	
Rent, rates, and insurance	8,700	
Depreciation etc	11,000	
Selling expenses	15,780	
General expenses	15,630	
Bad Debts	19,400	
		114,010
Net Profit		19,990

The following information is also provided:

- salaries and wages relate to the two directors, who are the only employees

- depreciation etc is made up as follows:

    - Depreciation   £35,000
    - Loss on sale of motors   £9,500
    - Profit on sale of building   (£33,500)

- selling expenses include:

    - Entertaining customers   £4,700
    - Gifts of wine to customers   £1,000
    - Gifts of calendars to customers £500
      (£10 each, with company advert)

- general expenses include accountancy fees of £2,800

- bad debts are made up of:

    - Increase in specific provision   £8,000
    - Bad debts written off   £23,600
    - Bad debts recovered   (£12,200)

required

1   Adjust the financial accounts for the 18-month period, before deduction of capital allowances.

2   Time-apportion the adjusted profit figure into CAPs.

3   Calculate the trading income assessment for each CAP.

solution

1

	£	£
Net Profit for 18-month period per accounts		19,990
Add back non-allowable expenditure:		
Depreciation		35,000
Loss on sale of motors		9,500
Entertaining customers		4,700
Gifts of wine		1,900
		71,090
Deduct income that is not taxable as trading income		
Profit on sale of building	33,500	
		(33,500)
Adjusted profit before capital allowances		37,590

Notes:

- The profit on the sale of the building is not taxable as trading income, and is therefore deducted. An alternative approach would be to add back the net £11,000 that relates to the three items under the heading of 'depreciation'.

- The calendars are allowable under the gift rules.

- All the items under the bad debts heading are allowable/taxable, and therefore do not require adjustment.

2 The adjusted profit for the 18-month period is time-apportioned as follows:

CAP 1/10/2014 to 30/9/2015   £37,590 x 12/18   = £25,060
CAP 1/10/2015 to 31/3/2016   £37,590 x 6/18   = £12,530

3 Capital allowances are then deducted from the adjusted profit for each CAP:

	1/10/14 – 30/9/15	1/10/15 – 31/3/16
	£	£
Adjusted profit	25,060	12,530
Capital allowances	15,000	6,000
Trading Income	10,060	6,530

DEALING WITH TRADE LOSSES

If, once profits have been tax-adjusted and any capital allowances deducted, the result is a minus figure, a 'trading loss' will have arisen. This will have two implications:

■ the **trading income assessment** for the chargeable accounting period will be **zero** (not the negative profit figure)

■ the amount of the **negative profit figure** will form the **trading loss**, and the company can choose how to deal with it

How does one deal with this situation? The options are as follows:

1   The trading loss can be carried forward to reduce trading income from the same trade in the future. If this option is chosen the loss must be used up as quickly as possible. If the following year's profit from the same trade is less than the loss, then that profit will be reduced to nil and the balance of the loss carried on forward. This will occur as many times as is necessary to offset the whole loss.

2   The trading loss can be used to reduce (or eliminate) all of the taxable total profits (TTP before Gift Aid deduction) in the same CAP that the loss arose. This set off would be against all taxable investment income and chargeable gains for the period, before deducting Gift Aid payments.

3   Only if option (2) above is chosen, the loss can then be carried back against the taxable total profits (TTP before Gift Aid deduction) of the CAP in the 12 months immediately before the one in which the loss occurred. If there were two CAPs partly falling into that 12-month period, then both could be used.

The diagram on the next page illustrates these options, using as an example a company making up accounts to the 31 December each year. A loss arises in the year ended 31/12/2015.

We will discuss Gift Aid in more detail in Chapter 5.

Where option (2) has been used, or option (2) followed by option (3), and the whole loss has still not been offset, any balance will follow option (1).

We can now revise our diagram (see page 2.3) illustrating the Corporation Tax Computation procedures to incorporate possible trading loss set off. The dark boxes are additions to the diagram.

We will now use a Case Study to illustrate these options. We will also return to this topic in later chapters when we have studied the build-up of the taxable total profits (TTP) in more detail.

Case Study

DOWNSEA PANS LIMITED: TRADING LOSS OPTIONS

Downsea Pans Limited has the following tax-adjusted results for the three chargeable accounting periods to 31/12/2016.

CAP	year ended 31/12/14	year ended 31/12/15	year ended 31/12/16
	£000	*£000*	*£000*
Trading Profit/(Loss)	120	(150)	160
Profits from investments	40	50	55
Chargeable gains	75	15	80

The company did not make any Gift Aid payments.

required

State the options available for offsetting the £150,000 trading loss incurred in the CAP year ended 31/12/2015.

Demonstrate the effects on the relevant taxable total profits (TTP) figures by showing Corporation Tax computation extracts.

solution

We will show the options one by one, but with all the three years' details shown in columnar form for reference.

Option One

The trading loss could be carried forward and set against the trading income of y/e 31/12/2016. Since this profit is larger than the loss, the whole loss could be offset in this way. The Corporation Tax computation extract for y/e 31/12/2016 would be affected, and the three years would look as follows:

	y/e 31/12/14	y/e 31/12/15	y/e 31/12/16
	£000	*£000*	*£000*
Trading Income	120	0	160
less **loss relief**			(150)
			10
Profits from Investments	40	50	55
Chargeable Gains	75	15	80
TTP	235	65	145

Option Two

The trading loss could be set against the other profits and chargeable gains of the CAP y/e 31/12/2015 (the CAP in which the loss was incurred). Due to the size of the loss this will not be sufficient to offset the whole loss. The balance of the loss could then be carried back to the CAP y/e 31/12/2014 and set against the TTP in that period as well. This would give the following Corporation Tax computation extracts:

	y/e 31/12/14	y/e 31/12/15	y/e 31/12/16
	£000	£000	£000
Trading Income	120	0	160
Profits from Investments	40	50	55
Chargeable Gains	75	15	80
	235	65	295
less loss relief			
first set off		(65)	
second set off	(85)		
TTP	150	0	295

Note that the loss can only be carried back after the current year set-off has been carried out to its full extent.

Option Three

Following the current year set-off as in option two, the previous year TTP need not be utilised. In that case the balance of the loss would be carried forward under S393(1) against the trading income only of y/e 31/12/2016. This would give the following figures for the three years.

	y/e 31/12/14	y/e 31/12/15	y/e 31/12/16
	£000	£000	£000
Trading Income	120	0	160
less loss relief			(85)
			75
Profits from Investments	40	50	55
Chargeable Gains	75	15	80
	235	65	210
less loss relief		(65)	
TTP	235	0	210

The actual choice of option would depend on factors such as the tax rates that would apply to the levels of TTP in each year. We will examine this issue in Chapter 5.

Chapter Summary

■ The 'taxable total profits' (TTP) include trading income, profits from investments, and chargeable gains. To arrive at the trading income, the profits based on the financial accounts must be adjusted, and capital allowances calculated and deducted from the adjusted profit figure.

■ To adjust the profit based on the financial accounts, any income shown in the accounts that is not taxable as trading income is deducted, and any expenditure that is not allowable is added. The capital allowances that will have been calculated separately are then deducted to arrive at the assessable trading income.

■ To be allowable, expenditure must be revenue (not capital), and wholly and exclusively for the purpose of the trade. There are also detailed rules about whether certain items of expenditure are allowable.

■ Where the financial accounts are prepared for a period exceeding twelve months, the period will form two chargeable accounting periods. One CAP will be for the first twelve months, and the other for the balance of the financial accounting period. To deal with this situation, the financial accounts are adjusted as a whole, apart from the capital allowances. The adjusted profit is then time-apportioned into the two CAPs, and separate capital allowance figures deducted from each to form two trading income assessments.

■ Where the adjusted trading profits (after capital allowances) result in a negative figure, the trading income assessment is zero, and a trading loss is formed that can be relieved in several ways. It may be carried forward and set off against the first available profits of the same trade. It may alternatively be set against the taxable total profits (TTP before any Gift Aid deductions) of the CAP in which the loss was incurred. Where this happens and not all the loss is used up, the balance can be carried back against the taxable total profits (TTP before any Gift Aid deductions) arising in the preceding twelve months.

Taxable Total Profits (TTP)

the figure used as the basis for calculation of Corporation Tax for a limited company. It includes trading profits, profits from investments, and chargeable gains. It is calculated for each chargeable accounting period (CAP) that the company operates in

Chargeable Accounting Period (CAP)

the period for which the taxable total profit (TTP) must be calculated. It is the same as the period for which the company produces financial accounts, unless that period is for more than twelve months. In that case the financial accounting period is divided into two CAPs

Adjusted Trading Profits the trading profits that have been adjusted for tax purposes by excluding income not taxable as trading income, and non-allowable expenditure

Trading Income Assessment

the taxable trading profits for the CAP. It is made up of adjusted trading profits, after deducting any capital allowances

Trading Loss This occurs when the adjusted trading profits after deducting capital allowances produces a negative figure. The negative figure is the trading loss, whilst the trading income assessment is zero.

Loss Relief the offsetting of the trading loss against profits, according to legislation. This may be against future profits from the same trade, or against certain taxable total profits (TTP)

Activities

2.1   The numbered items listed below appear in an income statement (before the net profit figure).

If you are adjusting the trading profit for tax purposes, state whether each item should be:

- added to the net profit
- deducted from the net profit
- ignored for adjustment purposes

1   accountancy fees payable

2   amortisation of lease

3   non–trade interest received

4   dividends received

5   employees' travel expenses payable

6   gain on sale of non-current asset

7   decrease in specific provision for bad debts

8   gifts of cigars (with company adverts) to customers, costing £40 per recipient.

9   increase in general bad debt provision

10   donation to political party

11   employers' National Insurance contributions

12   charitable donation under the Gift Aid scheme

2.2   Ahoy Trading Limited is a company that specialises in selling yachting equipment.
The unadjusted income statement for the accounting year is as follows:

	£
Sales	500,000
less cost of sales	220,000
Gross profit	280,000
Interest received	20,000
Dividends received	70,000
	370,000

less expenses:	£	£
Salaries and wages	99,000	
Depreciation	42,000	
Loss on sale of non-current assets	5,000	
Administration expenses	19,600	
Advertising	18,000	
Interest payable	22,000	
Travel and entertaining	19,100	
Bad debts and provisions	15,000	
		239,700
Net Profit		130,300

Notes:

- Administration includes £350 employees' parking fines incurred while on company business.

- Advertising includes:
    - gifts of chocolates with company logos to 100 top customers £4,900
    - gifts of sailing books with company logos to 200 other customers £5,000

- Travel and entertaining is made up as follows:

	£
- Employees' travel expenses	3,400
- Employees' subsistence allowances	5,600
- Entertaining customers	6,000
- Entertaining staff at Christmas	4,100
	19,100

- Bad debts and provisions is made up of:

	£
- Trade bad debts written off	18,400
- Decrease in general bad debt provision	(5,000)
- Increase in specific bad debt provision	1,600
	15,000

Capital allowances for the period have been calculated at £23,000.

Required:

Adjust the net profit shown to arrive at the trading income assessment for Corporation Tax purposes.

2.3   All I Need Trading Limited has an unadjusted income statement for the accounting year as follows:

	£	£
Sales		770,000
less cost of sales		420,000
Gross profit		350,000
Interest received		40,000
Gains on disposal of non-current assets		50,000
Rental income received		60,000
		500,000
less expenses:		
Discounts allowed	10,000	
Salaries and wages	80,500	
Depreciation	51,000	
Bad debts written off	12,000	
Rates and insurance	12,500	
Postage and stationery	11,050	
Administration expenses	12,600	
Advertising	14,000	
Travel and entertaining	19,750	
		223,400
Net Profit		276,600

Notes:

- Administration includes £2,000 directors' speeding fines incurred while on company business.
- Advertising consists of:
  - gifts of CDs with company logos to 1000 customers £9,000
  - gifts vouchers with company logos to 200 other customers £5,000
- Travel and entertaining is made up as follows:

	£
Employees' travel expenses	6,400
Employees' subsistence allowances	5,600
Entertaining customers	4,000
Entertaining staff on company trip to races	3,750
	19,750

Capital allowances for the period have been calculated at £31,500.

Required:

Adjust the net profit shown to arrive at the trading income assessment for Corporation Tax purposes.

2.4   Mint Limited is changing its accounting dates, and to accommodate this has produced a set of financial accounts over an extended period, from 1/12/2014 to 31/3/2016.

Capital allowances have already been calculated for each of the two CAPs as follows:

CAP 1/12/2014 to 30/11/2015   £8,000

CAP 1/12/2015 to 31/3/2016   £2,500

The financial accounts for the 16 months to 31/3/2016 are as follows:

	£	£
Sales		293,000
less cost of sales		155,000
Gross profit		138,000
add:		
Bad debts recovered		3,100
Discounts received		2,000
		143,100
less expenses:		
Salaries and wages	68,500	
Rent, rates, and insurance	9,200	
Depreciation etc	10,000	
General expenses	15,630	
Interest payable	8,300	
Bad debts written off	12,400	
Selling expenses	15,000	
		139,030
Net Profit		4,070

The following information is also provided:

- depreciation etc is made up as follows:

Depreciation	£45,000
Loss on sale of computer	£19,500
Profit on sale of Building	£54,500

- general expenses include debt recovery fees of £800
- selling expenses include:

Entertaining customers	£1,930
Gifts of diaries to customers	£600
(£6 each, with company advert)	

Required:

- Adjust the financial accounts for the 16-month period, before deduction of capital allowances.
- Time-apportion the adjusted profit figure into CAPs.
- Calculate the trading income assessment for each CAP.

2.5   The published accounts of Doormat Company Limited for the year ended 31 March 2016 are shown below, together with notes that provide some analysis of the summarised data. Capital allowances have already been calculated, and amount to £153,000.

	£000
Revenue	743
Cost of Sales	(302)
Gross Profit	441
Other Income	290
Distribution Costs	(144)
Administrative Expenses	(243)
Finance Costs	(50)
Profit before Tax	294
Tax	(71)
Profit for the Year	223

Notes:

- Cost of Sales includes depreciation of £20,000
- Administrative Expenses include the following:

Loan to employee written off	£8,000
Increase in Specific Bad Debt Provision	£2,800
Increase In General Bad Debt Provision	£7,700
Entertaining Customers	£9,100

- Other Income consists of:

Rental Income	£200,000
Discounts received from trade suppliers	£12,000
Interest Received from Investments	£30,000
Profit on Sale of Non-current Assets	£33,000
Dividends Received	£15,000

- Finance Costs relates to bank overdraft interest.

Required:

- Calculate the trading income assessable figure as adjusted for tax purposes, and the amount of any trading loss.
- State how the trading loss could be relieved without carrying it forward to future periods.

2.6   State whether the following statements are true or false:

(a)	Expenditure on purchasing a second hand van is an example of revenue expenditure	
(b)	Expenditure on purchasing a new van is an example of capital expenditure	
(c)	If a company wishes to carry a loss forward, then it can only set it off against trading profits from the same trade	
(d)	A company can opt to set a trade loss against the taxable total profits (TTP) of the year before the loss whether or not it has first set the loss against the taxable total profits (TTP) relating to the year of the loss	

3 Corporation tax – capital allowances

this chapter covers...

In this chapter we examine in detail the capital allowances that are available on 'plant and machinery' for companies. These allowances are used instead of depreciation on certain non-current assets for Corporation tax purposes.

We start by examining what is classed as 'plant and machinery' for capital allowances purposes, and then go on to see what type of allowances are available.

We will learn about the 'Annual Investment Allowance' and then examine the other (more complicated) capital allowances that can be claimed. We will see how capital allowance computations involve pooling certain assets together while keeping others separate.

The final section is devoted to calculating capital allowances for short chargeable accounting periods, and how the length of period affects some (but not all) allowances.

INTRODUCTION TO CAPITAL ALLOWANCES

As we saw in the last chapter, depreciation of non-current (fixed) assets is not an allowable expense for Corporation Tax purposes, but **capital allowances** are often provided instead.

A **capital allowance** reduces the taxable profit for a chargeable accounting period. It results from the acquisition and use of certain non-current assets.

Capital allowances are not, however, automatically available for any non-current asset owned and depreciated by a company. Although many categories of non-current asset do attract capital allowances, there are some that do not. The company's own depreciation policy is also irrelevant when calculating the amount of capital allowance that can be claimed – the same HM Revenue & Customs rules apply for all companies.

To be eligible for capital allowances, the expenditure on the non-current assets must firstly be defined as **capital expenditure**, rather than revenue. Here the definition of capital is generally the same as in financial accounting – expenditure on assets that will benefit the business over several accounting periods.

Secondly, the expenditure must be on assets that attract specific capital allowances. There are several categories of capital allowances, but in this learning area we will be examining the main rules relating to **Plant and Machinery**.

Capital allowances are claimable for each Chargeable Accounting Period (CAP) separately, based on expenditure incurred in that period and any balances of expenditure brought forward. We will see exactly how this works shortly.

For all expenditure on non-current assets that attract capital allowances, it does not matter how the funding is obtained, whether from:

■ cash reserves and money in the bank

■ a loan

■ hire purchase

■ finance leases of at least 5 years

In all these cases capital allowances are available on the full capital cost as soon as the expenditure is incurred – not when all payments have finally been made. Any interest on loans or hire purchase agreements etc is not capital expenditure, but forms allowable revenue expenditure.

If however an asset is leased on an **operating lease** then no capital allowances are available as the expenditure is treated as **revenue** as we saw in Chapter 2.

WHAT IS 'PLANT AND MACHINERY'?

Plant and machinery capital allowances form a major area of study in this learning area, and a large number of assets come under this category. As we will see, 'plant and machinery' covers not only items that most of us would expect to be classified in this way, but also a number of unexpected types of asset.

The exact definition of 'plant and machinery' has been subject to debate and modification through statute and case law over the years. One idea that may be useful as a starting point is that plant and machinery covers 'apparatus with which' the business operates, rather than assets 'in which' the business operates. This excludes assets which are simply part of 'the setting' of the business (eg buildings) from being plant and machinery. Examples of plant and machinery that we will deal with are listed below. Both new and second-hand items qualify.

- **plant or machinery** in the normal use of the phrase. This includes moveable and fixed items and their installation costs, and ranges from factory conveyor equipment to cement mixers
- **vans, lorries, and other commercial vehicles**. This category also includes tractors, trailers and other specialist vehicles
- **cars** owned by a limited company and used by the employees (including for private use) are included as plant and machinery
- **furniture, carpets and other moveable items**. Equipment such as specialist lighting used for shop displays or to create atmosphere have been classed as plant and machinery
- **computers and other electronic equipment**. This includes 'information and communications technology'. Software is also eligible expenditure where it is a capital purchase

CAPITAL ALLOWANCES FOR PLANT & MACHINERY

Capital allowances for plant and machinery are currently provided in two ways:
- the Annual Investment Allowance (AIA), and
- through other capital allowances, such as First Year Allowances (FYAs) and Writing Down Allowances (WDAs)

Note that capital allowances are not scaled down according to when in the chargeable accounting period (CAP) as asset is bought. If (for example) an asset is eligible for an 18% allowance, the full 18% is claimable whether the asset is bought in the first month of the CAP or the last month.

We will look at each of these two procedures in turn, and see how they work.

Annual Investment Allowance (AIA)

This provides a very simple system for companies to claim capital allowances. The Annual Investment Allowance applies to virtually all plant and machinery **except cars**, and provides an allowance of the whole amount spent on this plant and machinery, up to a total amount of £500,000 per year for CAPs ending on or before 31/12/2015. The limit is £25,000 for CAPs starting on or after 1/1/2016. For CAPs that straddle 31/12/2015 there are special rules that we will examine shortly.

Any acquisitions in a year that exceed the relevant limit are dealt with through the pooled system that we will look at shortly, and will then be eligible for other capital allowances

The key features of the scheme are:

- it applies to the acquisition in the chargeable accounting period of virtually all plant and machinery except cars.

- it is available for the first £500,000 / £25,000 of qualifying expenditure per 12 month CAP.

- the relevant limit is reduced proportionally if the CAP is less than 12 months (e.g. the limit is £375,000 for a 9 month CAP ending on or before 31/12/2015).

- it gives a capital allowance equal to the whole of such expenditure, and this allowance can then be deducted in the calculation of adjusted trading profits.

example

Suppose A Limited had adjusted trading profits (before capital allowances) of £600,000 for the CAP 1/1/2015 to 31/12/2015.

If during the CAP it spent £220,000 on plant and machinery, it could set the whole £220,000 against trading profits, giving a trading income assessment of £380,000.

or

If during the CAP it spent £545,000 on plant and machinery it could set £500,000 (the maximum) against trading profits, giving a trading income assessment of £100,000 before other capital allowances. The remaining £45,000 expenditure would be subject to capital allowance claims through the pooling system.

We will shortly look at how this works and what allowances can be claimed.

In some cases groups of companies may not be entitled to the normal annual limit for each company in the group, but may be required to share the limit between the companies. This could occur if the companies shared premises or had similar activities.

AIA in CAPs straddling 31 December 2015

As noted already the AIA annual limit changed on 31 December 2015 from £500,000 per year to £25,000 per year. Where a CAP straddles 31 December 2015 the maximum AIA for the whole CAP will be based on calculating proportions of each limit that are based on the length of time of each part of the CAP and then adding them together.

For example, the maximum AIA for a CAP for the 12 month period from 1 April 2015 to 31 March 2016 would be calculated as follows:

Period 1/4/2015 – 31/12/2015	£500,000 x 9/12	£375,000
Period 1/1/2016 – 31/3/2016	£25,000 x 3/12	£6,250
Maximum AIA for whole CAP		£381,250

In this situation, any expenditure that took place between 1/1/2016 and 31/3/2016 would also be restricted to a maximum AIA of £6,250. There would be no equivalent restriction in the earlier part of the CAP.

pooled expenditure calculations

There are some situations that fall outside of the AIA. These are:
- balances of unrelieved capital expenditure brought forward from earlier periods
- expenditure during the period on cars
- expenditure on plant and machinery during an accounting period in excess of the AIA limit
- disposals during the period of plant and machinery

These situations require a working involving one or more expenditure 'pools'. Each pool requires a separate calculation (shown in a separate column) in the capital allowance computation that will be used to calculate any capital allowances that are claimable. Separate pools are used for:
- each piece of plant deemed to have a 'short life' – one 'single asset pool' each
- a 'special rate pool' that is used for cars that have high emissions levels (over 130g/km) and is also used for certain long-life assets and 'integral features'
- the general (or 'main') pool for everything else, including cars of 130g/km emissions or less all merged together

The pool workings will carry forward from one period to the next, and keep running totals of unrelieved expenditure.

The capital allowances that can be calculated and claimed through this system are as follows:

- **100% First Year Allowances (FYAs).** These are **only** available for **new low emission cars, new zero emission goods vehicles** and certain **'energy efficient' and 'water efficient' plant**. 'Low emission' cars (also known as 'ultra low emission' cars) are defined as those with emissions not exceeding 75 grams per kilometre of CO_2. This means that the whole cost of a new low emission car can be claimed as a capital allowance. This is separate to, and in addition to any Annual Investment Allowance claimed for other plant. Other cars (that aren't new and / or don't meet the definition of low-emission) are not entitled to 100% First Year Allowances.

- **18% Writing Down Allowance (WDA)** is available on **pool balances, except** single asset pools where the asset has been disposed of before the end of the period, and the special rate pool.

- **8% Writing Down Allowance (WDA)** is available for the pool balance on the special rate pool.

- **Balancing Allowances** (or the opposite – a **balancing charge**) are calculated when a single asset pool is closed because the asset has been disposed of. It can also occur in the general pool if the business ceases.

carrying out a computation using pools

In order to follow logically through the process, it is best to deal with the elements in the following order, using as many pools as necessary:

- **start** with the written down values brought forward from the previous period

- **add** the eligible expenditure on any acquisitions that do not qualify for first year allowances or annual investment allowance. This will be expenditure on 'normal' cars (i.e. not new low-emission) and will need to be analysed into:
  - those over 130g/km (these go into the special rate pool), and
  - those between 75g/km and 130g/km (that go into the general pool)

- **calculate** 100% first year allowances on any new low-emission cars or other qualifying plant

- **calculate** the annual investment allowance on qualifying expenditure. Where the expenditure exceeds the available AIA, add any remaining balance of expenditure into the relevant pool

- **deduct** the proceeds of disposals (limited to the original cost)
- **calculate** the writing down allowances (WDAs) on the pool balances after the above transactions
- **calculate** any balancing allowances or balancing charges
- **calculate** the written down values of each pool to be carried forward to the next chargeable accounting period
- **calculate** the total capital allowances that can be claimed

This is quite complicated, but once a few examples have been looked at it should become clearer. Let us first look at a fairly basic example so that we can get the idea of the way that it works.

---

example

The Simple Company Limited has a chargeable accounting period running from 1 January 2015 to 31 December 2015. At the start of the period there was a brought forward balance of £26,000 in the general (main) pool from the previous year:

During the chargeable accounting period y/e 31/12/2015, the Simple Company Ltd had the following transactions in plant and machinery:

Purchases (cost)

Plant & Machinery	£515,000
Car (emissions 125g/km)	£18,000

Disposals (proceeds)

Plant (main pool)	£5,000

The Simple Company Limited had adjusted trading profits (before capital allowances) for the CAP y/e 31/12/2015 of £750,000.

Required

(a) Calculate the total capital allowances claimable for the CAP.

(b) Calculate the assessable trading profits after deducting capital allowances.

Solution

(a) The capital allowance computation using the pool is built up as follows. The column on the right hand side is to collect and total the allowances. Note that allowances are deducted from the pool balances, but appear as positive figures in the capital allowances column.

	Main Pool	Capital Allowances
	£	£
WDV bf	26,000	
add		
Acquisitions without FYA or AIA:		
Car (125g/km)	18,000	
Acquisitions qualifying for AIA:		
Plant & Machinery 515,000		
AIA Claimed (500,000)		500,000
Balance into main pool	15,000	
less		
Proceeds of Disposals	(5,000)	
	54,000	
18% WDA	(9,720)	9,720
WDV cf	44,280	
Total Capital Allowances		509,720

Note the following important points:

The cost of the car enters the main pool. This is because it has an emission rating of 130g/km or less.

The plant and machinery is entitled to annual investment allowance (AIA) of £500,000. This calculation is carried out next, and the excess of £15,000 is added to the main pool. This £15,000 will form part of the balance of £54,000 that is entitled to 18% writing down allowance (WDA).

The proceeds on disposal are deducted from the pool before the writing down allowance (WDA) is calculated.

The total capital allowance is made up of the AIA and the WDA in this example.

(b) The assessable trading profit can now be calculated:

	£
Adjusted trading profits (before capital allowances)	750,000
Less capital allowances	(509,720)
Assessable trading profit	240,280

'Short-Life' Assets

Short-life assets are those that the company believes it will dispose of within eight years of the end of the current CAP. Any assets that the company choses to categorise in this way are dealt with by entering each asset into a separate short-life asset pool. This will enable balancing allowances to be claimed if the asset is disposed of for a small amount.

Under the annual investment allowance scheme the full value of all plant (including short-life assets) up to £500,000 (or £25,000) per year can be claimed in full, so this arrangement could be useful for assets in excess of the AIA limit. If the asset is not sold within eight years of the end of the CAP in which it was acquired the balance of expenditure brought forward is transferred to the main pool and the short-life asset pool is closed.

We will now use a slightly more complex case study to see how the capital allowance computation works in more detail.

Case Study

SPENDER PLC
PLANT AND MACHINERY CAPITAL ALLOWANCES

Spender plc has a chargeable accounting period running from 1 January 2015 to 31 December 2015. At the start of the period, the following balances were brought forward in its capital allowances computation from the previous year:

General (main) pool	£48,000
Single asset pools:	
Short-life asset	£20,000

During the chargeable accounting period y/e 31/12/2015, Spender plc had the following transactions in plant and machinery:

Purchases (cost)

Equipment	£32,000
Van	£17,000
Lorries	£550,000
New 'Low Emission' Car	£28,000
Car with emissions of 200g/km	£19,000

Disposals (proceeds)

Short-life asset	£13,000
Plant (main pool)	£10,000

Spender plc had adjusted trading profits (before capital allowances) for the CAP y/e 31/12/2015 of £1,000,000.

required

(a) Calculate the total capital allowances claimable for the CAP.

(b) Calculate the assessable trading profits after deducting capital allowances.

solution

(a) Of the expenditure during the CAP, the following items are eligible for AIA, but their total exceeds the annual limit of £500,000.

	£
Equipment	32,000
Van	17,000
Lorries	550,000
	599,000

Note that the expenditure on the cars is not eligible for this allowance.

The expenditure in excess of the AIA allowance will be added to the main pool and be eligible for writing down allowances (WDA) at 18%.

The capital allowance computation using the pools can now be built up (*see table opposite*). We will use one column for each pool, plus a further column on the right hand side to collect and total the allowances.

(b) Following the capital allowances computation shown on the next page, the assessable trading profit can now be calculated:

	£
Adjusted trading profits (before capital allowances)	1,000,000
Less capital allowances	(561,180)
Assessable trading profit	438,820

The notes below explain some of the more complex issues in the capital allowances computation. Make sure that you can understand all the points so that you could build up a similar solution without any template.

(1) The new low-emission car had a 100% first year allowance (FYA). The balance after deducting the allowance from the cost (in this case zero) is notionally added to the main pool. When the car is ultimately sold the proceeds will be deducted from the main pool.

(2) The acquisitions qualifying for AIA exceed the £500,000 limit. The excess is added to the main pool.

(3) The writing down allowances are calculated as
    a. main pool £137,000 x 18% = £24,660.
    b. short-life asset – no WDA since asset has been disposed of.
    c. special rate pool £19,000 x 8% = £1,520. The car was entered into this pool as it has emissions over 130g/km.

(4) The balancing allowance on the short-life asset pool is claimed to close the pool with a zero balance.

(5) The written down values carried forward on the two remaining pools will be used to start the computation for the next period.

	main pool £	short-life asset £	special rate pool £	capital allowances £
WDV bf	48,000	20,000		
add				
Acquisitions				
without FYA or AIA:				
Car (200g/km)			19,000	
Acquisitions				
with 100% FYA:				
Low-emission				
car (1) £28,000				
100% FYA £(28,000)	0			28,000
Acquisitions				
qualifying for AIA (2)				
Equipment £32,000				
Van £17,000				
Lorries £550,000				
£599,000				
AIA £(500,000)				500,000
Excess	99,000			
less				
Proceeds of disposals:	(10,000)	(13,000)		
	137,000	7,000	19,000	
18% WDA (3)	(24,660)			24,660
8% WDA (3)			(1,520)	1,520
Balancing Allowance (4)		(7,000)		7,000
WDV cf (5)	112,340	0	17,480	
Total Capital Allowances				561,180

The reference numbers shown above are linked to the explanation shown on the previous page and this page.

capital allowance computations straddling 31 December 2015

As noted earlier, there are special calculations required for the annual investment allowance (AIA) limit when the CAP straddles 31 December 2015.

The following case study will demonstrate how the calculations that have been explained are used in a computation. It will also reinforce the approach to a computation that we used in the last case study.

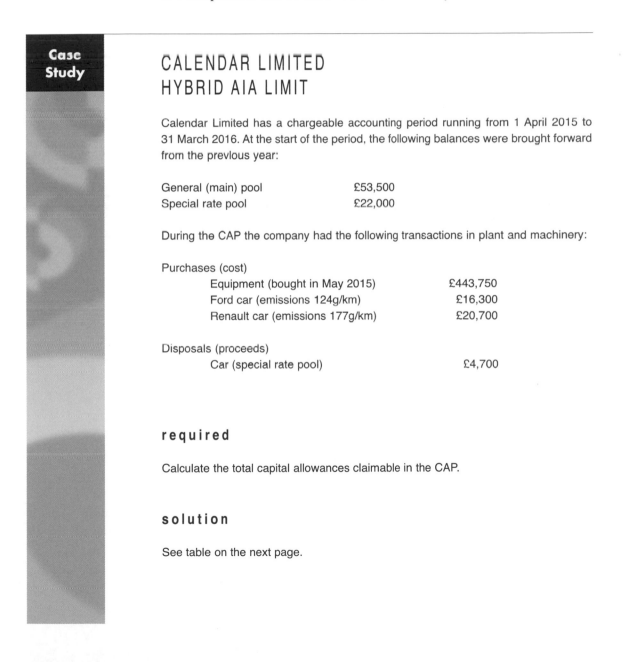

Case Study

CALENDAR LIMITED
HYBRID AIA LIMIT

Calendar Limited has a chargeable accounting period running from 1 April 2015 to 31 March 2016. At the start of the period, the following balances were brought forward from the previous year:

General (main) pool	£53,500
Special rate pool	£22,000

During the CAP the company had the following transactions in plant and machinery:

Purchases (cost)

Equipment (bought in May 2015)	£443,750
Ford car (emissions 124g/km)	£16,300
Renault car (emissions 177g/km)	£20,700

Disposals (proceeds)

Car (special rate pool)	£4,700

required

Calculate the total capital allowances claimable in the CAP.

solution

See table on the next page.

	main pool £	special rate pool £	capital allowances £
WDV bf	53,500	22,000	
add			
Acquisitions without FYA or AIA:			
Ford car	16,300		
Renault car		20,700	
Acquisitions qualifying for AIA:			
Equipment £443,750			
AIA £(381,250)			381,250
Excess	62,500		
less			
Proceeds of disposals:		(4,700)	
	132,300	38,000	
WDA at 18%	(23,814)		23,814
WDA at 8%		(3,040)	3,040
WDV cf	108,486	34,960	
Total Capital Allowances			408,104

Notes:

The AIA limit is £381,250, based on (£500,000 x 9/12) + (£25,000 x 3/12).

As the purchase of equipment for £443,750 was before 31/12/2015 there is no further AIA restriction.

Had equipment been bought between 1/1/2016 and 31/3/2016, the maximum AIA on such expenditure would have been £6,250 (£25,000 x 3/12).

CAPITAL ALLOWANCES FOR SHORT CAPS

So far in this chapter we have examined the way that capital allowances for plant and machinery are calculated for chargeable accounting periods of twelve months.

It is, however, possible to have CAPs for less than twelve months, and this can arise either:

- if the accounts are prepared for a period of less than twelve months, or
- where accounts are prepared for a period exceeding twelve months, and are divided into two CAPs, one for the first twelve months, and another for the balance, which will be for less than twelve months

In each of these situations, the impact on capital allowances for plant and machinery in the short CAP is as follows:

- First Year Allowances, Balancing Allowances and Balancing Charges are unaffected and are calculated as normal.
- Writing Down Allowances are time-apportioned based on the short CAP.
- the Annual Investment Allowance maximum limit is time-apportioned based on the short CAP. This is also based on the limits that apply to the periods before and/or after 31 December 2015.

DEALING WITH THE ACCOUNTS FOR A LONG PERIOD

As we saw in the last chapter, where we have accounts that are prepared for a long period, the procedure is:

- the accounting profits for the long period are adjusted in one computation, before deducting capital allowances
- this adjusted profits figure is then time-apportioned into the two CAPs
- capital allowances are calculated separately for each CAP
- each CAP's adjusted profit is then finalised by deducting the capital allowances that have been calculated for that CAP

We can now examine the issues involved in creating two capital allowance computations, one for each CAP within a long period for which accounts were prepared. The points to note are:

- each acquisition and disposal of assets needs to be allocated to the correct CAP, and incorporated in the appropriate computation
- the written-down values at the end of the first CAP will become the brought forward amounts at the start of the second CAP
- the rules regarding time apportionment of WDAs for short CAPs as described above need to be used in the second CAP

Now that we have seen all the principles explained, we can use a Case Study to illustrate the way they work.

**Case
Study**

CHOPPITT PLC:
DEALING WITH ACCOUNTS FOR A LONG PERIOD

Choppitt plc has produced a set of accounts for the period 1/9/2014 to 31/12/2015. The adjusted trading profit for the 16-month period has already been produced from the accounts, and provides a profit of £960,000, before any capital allowances are taken account of.

The plant and machinery capital allowance computation for the CAP y/e 31/8/2014 provided carried forward written down values as follows:

*   general pool   £50,000

Analysis of the accounts reveals that the following assets were acquired or disposed of during the 16-month period:

1/4/2015	disposal of plant for £2,000 (original cost £20,000).
1/10/2015	acquisition of second-hand BMW car for £17,500 (125g/km).
1/11/2015	acquisition of plant costing £203,334.

required

1   State the periods for the two CAPs.

2   Calculate the Plant & Machinery capital allowances for each of the two CAPs.

3   Calculate the trading income assessments for each of the two CAPs.

solution

1   The CAPs will be:

    1/9/2014 - 31/8/2015   (12 months)
    1/9/2015 - 31/12/2015   (4 months)

2   To calculate the Plant and Machinery capital allowances we will need to prepare two computations, one for each CAP.

    Each one will incorporate the acquisitions and disposals that occur in that CAP.

    Within the CAP for the 12 months ending 31/8/2015 is disposal of plant.

    There are no acquisitions of plant and machinery in this period that can be used to claim annual investment allowance (AIA).

    The capital allowance computation is as follows:

CAP FOR THE 12 MONTHS ENDING 31/8/2015		
	Main Pool	**Capital Allowances**
	£	£
WDV bf	50,000	
Disposals:		
Plant	(2,000)	
Sub Total	48,000	
WDA 18%	(8,640)	8,640
WDV cf	39,360	
Total Capital Allowances		8,640

Within the four-month CAP ending 31/12/2015 are the acquisition of plant, and the BMW car.

The limit for annual investment allowance for this four-month period is £500,000 x 4/12 = £166,667. The amount spent on plant is £203,334, so the maximum of £166,667 AIA is claimed, and the remaining £36,667 joins the main pool.

Note that the annual WDA % for the main pool is 18%. The 18% is reduced to 4/12 since is a short CAP.

CAP FOR THE 4 MONTHS TO 31/12/2015		
	Main Pool	**Capital Allowances**
	£	£
WDV bf	39,360	
add		
Acquisitions without FYA or AIA:		
Car (125g/km)	17,500	
Acquisitions qualifying for AIA:		
Plant £203,334		
AIA claimed £(166,667)		166,667
Excess	36,667	
	93,527	
WDA 18% x 4/12	(5,612)	5,612
WDV cf	87,915	
Total Capital Allowances		172,279

3   Calculation of trading income assessments.

Firstly the adjusted trade profits are time-apportioned:

CAP 1/9/2014 to 31/8/2015   £960,000 x 12/16   = £720,000

CAP 1/9/2015 to 31/12/2015   £960,000 x 4/16   = £240,000

Capital allowances are then deducted from the adjusted profit for each CAP:

	1/9/14 – 31/8/15	**1/9/15 – 31/12/15**
	£	£
Adjusted profit	720,000	240,000
Capital allowances:		
P & M	(8,640)	(172,279)
Trading Income	711,360	67,721

CAPITAL ALLOWANCES WHEN COMPANIES CEASE TRADING

When a company ceases trading the capital allowances in the final CAP are subject to a special approach, as follows:

■ there can be **no** WDA, FYA or AIA in this final CAP

■ all remaining assets will have been disposed of by the company, with any proceeds brought into the computation as normal

■ there can be no written down values to carry forward in **any** pools, so the pools must be closed by using balancing allowances or balancing charges to bring all the pool balances to zero

As the only capital allowances will be balancing allowances or charges the length of the final CAP will not cause any complications. This is because balancing allowances and balancing charges are unaffected by short CAPs as we discussed a little earlier.

Chapter Summary

- Capital allowances are available on certain non-current (fixed) assets, and act for tax computation purposes as an alternative to depreciation, which is never allowable as tax-deductible (set off against tax).

- The main type of capital allowances is for 'plant and machinery'.

- Plant and machinery includes vehicles, computers, and various other assets.

- An annual investment allowance is available for the whole cost of virtually all plant and machinery, except cars, up to a maximum of £500,000 for a 12-month period before 31/12/2015. There are special rules for CAPs that straddle 31/12/2015.

- Allowances include 100% first year allowances for new low emission cars, zero emission goods vehicles, and energy-saving and water-saving plant. There are also writing down allowances at various rates depending on the circumstances.

- Most assets are merged together or 'pooled' in the capital allowance computation, but some need to be kept separately in 'single asset pools'. Single asset pools are used for short-life assets. Balancing allowances and charges occur in single asset pools when the asset has been disposed of, and also in the general pool and special rate pool when the business ceases.

- When capital allowances are calculated for a chargeable accounting period of less than twelve months any writing down allowances are time-apportioned. The AIA limit is also time-apportioned.

- First year allowances and balancing allowances and charges are unaffected by short CAPs. Where the accounts for a company have been prepared for a period of over 12 months, the two CAPs that result will each require a separate capital allowance computation. Non-current asset acquisitions and disposals will need to be allocated to the correct CAP before these capital allowance computations are carried out.

Capital allowance
the term used for allowances that reduce taxable profit for a chargeable accounting period, resulting from the acquisition and use of certain non-current assets

Chargeable Accounting Period (CAP)
the period for which the profits chargeable to Corporation Tax must be calculated. It is the same as the period for which the company produces financial accounts, unless that period is for more than twelve months. In that case the financial accounting period is divided into two CAPs

Plant and Machinery
one of the major non-current asset categories for capital allowance purposes. It includes vehicles and computers

Annual Investment Allowance (AIA)
this is an allowance that can be claimed against the whole cost of most plant and machinery, with the exception of cars. The maximum that can be claimed depends on the dates of the CAP

First Year Allowances
first year allowances are available at 100% for new low-emission cars, zero emission goods vehicles, and energy-saving and water-saving plant

Writing Down Allowances
these allowances (WDA) are available at a percentage of the pool value for plant and machinery. This percentage is time-apportioned for short CAPs

Written Down Value
this term relates to the balance at the end of a CAP that remains in a plant and machinery pool. It represents the part of the pool value that has not yet been claimed as allowances, and is carried forward to the next CAP

Balancing Allowance
this allowance can be claimed when an asset is sold for less than the written-down value (unrelieved expenditure) in a single asset pool. A balancing allowance or balancing charge will also occur in all pools when a company ceases trading

Balancing Charge
this charge is the opposite of an allowance, and occurs when the disposal proceeds of an asset in a single asset pool are more than the written-down value (unrelieved expenditure). It is in effect a reclaiming of excess allowances previously obtained

Activities

3.1   A company has a 12-month CAP from 1/1/2015 to 31/12/2015. At the start of the period the written down value in the main pool was £21,000. There were no single asset pools.

During the CAP the company had the following transactions in plant and machinery:

Acquisitions (Costs)

Car (emissions 125g/km)	£16,000
Plant	£493,000
Van	£10,000

Disposals (Proceeds – less than original cost)

Machinery	£2,000

Required:

Calculate the total capital allowances for the CAP.

3.2   The Capital Company Limited has a twelve month chargeable accounting period running from 1/4/2015 to 31/3/2016. The adjusted trading profit for this CAP has already been calculated at £154,000 before deduction of capital allowances for plant & machinery.

The capital allowance computation for the last CAP closed with written down values as follows:

main pool	£60,000
short-life single asset pool (machine bought in 2013 to use for temporary contract)	£10,000

During the CAP the following assets were acquired and disposed of:

30/4/2015	a new fork-lift truck was bought for £30,000.
31/7/2015	a new BMW car was bought for £24,000 (emissions 115g/km).
31/7/2015	a computer system was bought for £5,000 (not a short-life asset).
31/10/2015	the machine in the short-life pool was sold for £4,000.
31/12/2015	a machine in the main pool was sold for £3,000.

All disposal proceeds were less than original cost.

Required:

- Using a plant and machinery capital allowance computation, calculate the total allowances for the CAP year ended 31/3/2016.

- Calculate the assessable trading income for the CAP year ended 31/3/2016.

3.3 The Middle Company Limited has a 12-month CAP from 1/4/2015 to 31/3/2016. At the start of the period the written down value in the main pool was £10,000, and there was also a special rate pool with a balance of £2,800.

During the CAP the company had the following transactions in plant and machinery:

Acquisitions (Costs) All purchased in January 2016.

Plant	£253,000
Machinery	£12,000

Disposals (Proceeds – less than cost)

Machinery in main pool	£3,500

Required:

Calculate the total capital allowances, assuming the maximum is claimed.

3.4 Solvitt plc has produced a set of accounts for the period 1/4/2014 to 30/6/2015. The adjusted trading profit for the 15-month period has already been computed as £480,000, before any capital allowances are taken account of.

The plant and machinery capital allowance computation for the CAP y/e 31/3/2014 provided carried forward written-down values as follows:

general pool	£60,000
special rate pool	£14,000

Analysis of the accounts reveals that the following assets were acquired or disposed of during the 15-month period.

1/12/2014	Disposal of plant for £4,000 (original cost £30,000)
1/2/2015	Acquisition of second-hand Ford car for £16,000 (emissions 123g/km)
1/5/2015	Acquisition of plant costing £45,000

Required:

- State the periods for the two CAPs that need to be formed.
- Calculate the Plant and Machinery capital allowances for each of the two CAPs.
- Calculate the trading income assessments for each of the two CAPs.

3.5   Tuffwun Limited has produced a set of accounts for the period 1/3/2015 to 31/12/2015. The adjusted trading profit for the 10-month period has already been produced from the accounts, and provides a profit of £510,000, before any capital allowances are taken account of.

Tuffwun Limited's plant and machinery capital allowance computation for the CAP y/e 28/2/2015 provided carried forward written down values as follows:

general pool	£90,000
special rate pool	£13,000

Analysis of the accounts reveals that the following assets were acquired or disposed of during the ten month period:

Acquisition of new 'low emission' car for £20,000

Acquisition of a BMW car for £27,000 (emissions 189g/km)

Disposal of plant for £1,000 (original cost £10,000)

Acquisition of plant costing £440,834

Required:

• Calculate the Plant and Machinery capital allowances for Tuffwun Limited for the CAP to 31/12/2015.

• Calculate the trading income assessment for Tuffwun Limited for the CAP to 31/12/2015.

4 Corporation tax – chargeable gains

this chapter covers...

In this chapter we learn about how chargeable gains (and the opposite – capital losses) are calculated. These gains then form part of the taxable total profits (TTP) for a limited company.

We start by examining the basis of assessment, including what constitutes the disposal of an asset, and list the main exempt assets. We then learn how to calculate gains using the basic format, before going on to look at some special situations.

The situations that we examine further are:

- *part disposals*
- *improvement expenditure*
- *special rules for chattels*
- *matching rules for shares*
- *bonus and rights share issues*

Finally we examine a deferral relief that can be opted for when a company buys assets in certain categories within a defined time of disposing of an asset. This 'rollover relief' has the effect of postponing the impact of the gain on the first asset.

INTRODUCTION TO CHARGEABLE GAINS

A chargeable gain (or its opposite – a capital loss) occurs when a company disposes of certain assets that it has previously acquired. The gain is then brought into the Corporation Tax computation. It does not apply to a trading situation, where items are regularly bought and sold to make a profit. Such profits would be assessed as trading income, as we have already seen. The assets that can form chargeable gains will often be non-current (fixed) assets or investments that the company has acquired outside of its trading activities. A chargeable gain often applies to the sale of an asset that may have been owned for quite some time.

In addition to applying to the business assets of companies, chargeable gains can also arise for individuals who are subject to capital gains tax on the disposal of both personal assets and business assets. In this book, however, we are only going to examine how disposals of business assets are taxed. In this chapter we will examine the way that companies' chargeable gains are subject to Corporation Tax, and later in this book we will look at how Capital Gains Tax applies to the disposal of business assets by individuals.

Gains on the disposal of personal assets are dealt with in Osborne Books' *Personal Tax*.

a note for those familiar with Capital Gains Tax for individuals

Although there are similarities between Capital Gains Tax for individuals and the treatment of chargeable gains for companies under Corporation Tax, there are also **significant differences**. If you have already studied personal taxation you should be very careful to study the way in which the gains of companies are taxed. Do not be lulled into a false sense of security by the similarities to the system that you have already studied.

The following main differences between Capital Gains Tax for individuals and chargeable gains for companies will now be highlighted in advance so that you can appreciate their impact. In calculating the chargeable gains of companies

- there is no annual exempt amount
- there is an indexation allowance, claimed up to the date of disposal
- the matching rules for shares are different from those for individuals

These are important differences, and can cause confusion.

basis of assessment

Chargeable gains are calculated according to the same Chargeable Accounting Periods (CAPs) as are used for the rest of the Corporation Tax computation. The basis of assessment is the chargeable gains less capital losses arising from disposals that occur during the CAP. We will look at how losses are dealt with a little later in this chapter. The main issue to understand at this point is that the chargeable gain that is brought into the Corporation Tax computation is based on the total (or aggregate) of gains that have occurred during the CAP, and that a gain can only arise when a disposal has taken place.

disposals

A disposal arises when an asset is

- sold (or part of it is sold), or
- given away, or
- lost, or
- destroyed

Most of the situations that we will deal with will be based on the sale of an asset.

CHARGEABLE AND EXEMPT ASSETS

For a chargeable gain or capital loss to arise, the asset that has been disposed of must be a 'chargeable' asset. Disposals of exempt assets cannot form chargeable gains or capital losses. Instead of there being a long list of the assets that are chargeable, there is a fairly short list of assets that are exempt. The simple rule is that if an asset is not exempt, then it must be chargeable!

Chargeable business assets that are popular in tasks include:
- land and buildings
- shares

You must remember that these are only examples – all assets are chargeable unless they are exempt.

exempt assets

The following is a list of the main **exempt assets** that relate to companies:
- trading inventory (as discussed earlier, this is part of the trading profit)
- cars

- chattels bought and sold for £6,000 or less (chattels are tangible moveable property)
- Government Securities (also known as 'Gilts', these are a form of investment)
- animals (for example racehorses)

CHARGEABLE GAINS AND CORPORATION TAX

Where, during a CAP, there are several disposals that result in chargeable gains, these are aggregated and the result brought into the Corporation Tax computation. This total chargeable gain then forms part of the 'taxable total profits' (TTP) along with trading profits as Trading Income and any income from investments. The Corporation Tax is then calculated on the total profits, as we will see in the next chapter.

If any disposals result in capital losses, then these are set against any chargeable gains relating to the same CAP. Provided the net result is a chargeable gain, this amount is brought into the Corporation Tax computation as described above. If the losses exceed the chargeable gains of the same CAP, then the result is that:

- no chargeable gains are brought into the TTP computation, and
- the net capital loss is carried forward to be set against the chargeable gain that arises in the next CAP (and so on if necessary until all the loss is utilised)

Note that **capital losses cannot be set against any other profits** (eg from trading or investment) in the Corporation Tax computation, but must be carried forward against future chargeable gains.

We must now turn our attention to how to calculate the chargeable gain or loss on each separate disposal.

THE COMPUTATION OF EACH GAIN

Each disposal of a chargeable asset requires a calculation to determine the amount of any gain or loss. This computation follows a standard format that is in effect a 'mini' statement of profit or loss (income statement) for the item disposed of.

There are some minor variations to this format in particular circumstances, as we will see later. The basic format is shown on the next page:

computation of a chargeable gain	
	£
Proceeds on disposal	X
less	
Incidental costs of disposal	(x)
Net proceeds	X
less:	
Original cost	(x)
Incidental costs of acquisition	(x)
Unindexed gain	X
less	
Indexation allowance	(x)
Chargeable Gain	X

We will now look at the components of the individual gain computation in more detail.

proceeds on disposal

This normally refers to the amount that the asset was sold for, ie the selling price. However there are some special situations where the figure used is different:

- if the asset is given away, or sold to a connected company or person at less than the market value, the market value is used in the computation instead of the actual amount received. Companies under the same control are connected with each other and with the person(s) controlling them

- if the asset is lost or destroyed then the asset will have been disposed of for zero proceeds, and zero will be used in the computation. The exception to this would be if an insurance claim had been made, in which case the claim proceeds would be used

incidental costs of disposal

These are the costs incurred by the company in selling the asset. Examples include advertising expenses, auction costs, or estate agent's fees for selling a property.

original cost, and incidental costs of acquisition

These relate to the amount paid to acquire the asset in the first place, plus any other costs incurred to buy it. Examples of these costs include legal fees and auction costs. We will examine later on in this chapter how to deal with expenditure that is incurred after purchase to improve the asset.

indexation allowance

This is a deduction that is used to compensate for the impact of inflation on the value of the asset. It works by using figures from the Retail Price Index (RPI) to calculate an inflation factor to multiply by the original cost and any other acquisition costs. This allows for general inflation of the cost between the date of acquisition and the date of disposal.

The indexation factor is calculated as:

$$\frac{(RPI\ at\ the\ date\ of\ disposal - RPI\ at\ the\ date\ of\ acquisition)}{RPI\ at\ the\ date\ of\ acquisition}$$

The result of this fraction is rounded to three decimal places before being multiplied by the **historical cost figure.**

A common error is to multiply the indexation factor by the unindexed gain instead of the cost. This is illogical.

If the fraction calculation produces a negative figure, because the RPI at disposal is lower than the RPI at acquisition, then no indexation is applied. This would occur if there was deflation occurring between the two dates. This means that indexation can never increase a gain.

Note also that the indexation allowance cannot either

■ turn an unindexed gain into a loss, or

■ increase the amount of an unindexed loss

This means that the indexation allowance cannot be a larger amount than the unindexed gain that it follows in the computation. If the figure before indexation is applied is a loss, then there can be no indexation allowance at all.

We will now use a Case Study to show how the computation is carried out.

Note that the RPI figures are shown in the Tax Data section at the beginning of this book. The figures that we need in this Case Study are, however, repeated here for convenience. **You will normally be provided with the indexation factor itself** in an assessment.

THE SIMPLE COMPANY LIMITED: CALCULATING A CHARGEABLE GAIN

The Simple Company Limited bought a retail shop in August 1990. The company paid £59,000 for the shop, and also paid legal fees of £1,000 at the same time to arrange the purchase. The shop was sold in April 2015. The company prepares its accounts annually to 31 December, and the sale of the shop was the only chargeable disposal that the company made in 2015. It had no capital losses brought forward.

We will assume three different selling prices for the sale of the shop. In each case the estate agent's fees for the sale were £3,000, and the company incurred further legal fees of £2,000.

1   Assume that the company sold the shop for £240,000

2   Assume that the company sold the shop for £75,000

3   Assume that the company sold the shop for £58,000

required

Using the RPI figures of 128.1 for August 1990 and 258.0 for April 2015, calculate the chargeable gain or capital loss resulting from the disposal of the shop (to the nearest £) for each of the situations 1, 2 and 3.

Also state the amount of chargeable gain to be brought into the TTP for the CAP year ended 31/12/2015 for each situation, and explain how any capital loss should be dealt with.

solution

Option 1

	£
Proceeds on disposal	240,000
less:	
Incidental costs of disposal	(5,000)
Net proceeds	235,000
less:	
Original cost	(59,000)
Incidental costs of acquisition	(1,000)
Unindexed gain	175,000
less:	
Indexation allowance*	(60,840)
Chargeable Gain	114,160

* the indexation factor is calculated as:

$$\frac{(258.0 - 128.1)}{128.1} = 1.014 \text{ (rounded to 3 decimal places)}$$

The indexation factor is multiplied by the costs incurred in August 1990 of £59,000 + £1,000 = £60,000:

1.014 x £60,000 = £60,840

The chargeable gain of £114,160 would form part of the TTP for the CAP for the year ended 31/12/2015.

Option 2

	£
Proceeds on disposal	75,000
less:	
Incidental costs of disposal	(5,000)
Net proceeds	70,000
less:	
Original cost	(59,000)
Incidental costs of acquisition	(1,000)
Unindexed gain	10,000
less:	
Restricted indexation allowance*	(10,000)
Chargeable Gain	Nil

*Here the indexation allowance that would be calculated as £60,840 (as in option 1) is restricted to the amount of the unindexed gain of £10,000, so that it will not turn an unindexed gain into a loss.

Since there is neither a gain nor a loss, there is no figure to form part of the TTP for the CAP for the year ended 31/12/2015.

Option 3

	£
Proceeds on disposal	58,000
less:	
Incidental costs of disposal	(5,000)
Net proceeds	53,000
less:	
Original cost	(59,000)
Incidental costs of acquisition	(1,000)
Unindexed loss	(7,000)
less:	
Indexation allowance*	Nil
Capital Loss	(7,000)

*Here there is no indexation allowance since there is an unindexed loss that cannot be increased through indexation.

Since there is a capital loss, and no chargeable gains in the CAP to set it against, there is no figure to form part of the TTP for the CAP y/e 31/12/2015. The capital loss of £7,000 will be carried forward to set against chargeable gains in the next CAP.

links with capital allowances

As we saw in the last chapter, capital allowances are available for 'Plant and Machinery'. The following rules apply to the disposal of non-current assets where capital allowances have been claimed on the asset:

- where the asset is sold for less than it cost, the only tax implication is through plant and machinery capital allowance computations. A capital loss will not arise

- where a chattel is sold for more than it cost, a chargeable gain can only arise if the proceeds exceed £6,000. If the proceeds do exceed £6,000 then a chargeable gain can arise, subject to the special chattel rule that we will look at shortly. This situation is rare, since items in this category do not usually appreciate in value.

DEALING WITH PART DISPOSALS

We saw earlier in the chapter that a disposal can relate to all or part of an asset. Although part disposal will not apply to many assets that are not divisible, it could apply, for example, to a piece of land.

If an asset was acquired as a whole, and then part of it is sold while the rest is retained we need to compute the gain (or loss) on the part that was disposed of. The difficulty is that although we know how much the proceeds are for that part of the asset, we probably do not know how much of the original cost of the whole asset relates to that portion.

The solution to this problem is to value the remaining part of the asset at the time of the part disposal. The original cost can then logically be apportioned by using these figures.

The formula for working out the cost of the part disposed of is:

$$\text{Original cost of whole asset} \quad \times \quad \frac{A}{(A + B)}$$

where   A = proceeds (or market value) of the part disposed of

        B = market value of the part retained

The following example will illustrate this type of calculation.

example of a gain computation involving part disposal

Fielding and Company Limited bought a piece of land for £4,000 in January 1991 to use as a car park. In February 2015 the company sold a part of the land for £3,000. At the same time the remainder of the land was valued at £9,000.

The indexation factor from January 1991 to February 2015 is 0.972.

The portion of the original cost relating to the part of the field that was sold can be calculated as:

$$£4,000 \quad \times \quad \frac{£3,000}{(£3,000 + £9,000)} \quad = \quad £1,000$$

The computation would then be carried out in the normal way:

	£
Proceeds	3,000
less cost (as calculated above)	(1,000)
indexation allowance:	
0.972 x £1,000	(972)
Chargeable Gain	1,028

IMPROVEMENT EXPENDITURE

Where expenditure after acquisition is used to enhance an asset, and the asset is then disposed of in this improved condition, the improvement expenditure forms an allowable cost in the computation.

The expenditure must be of a 'capital' nature, and examples of this could include extending a building or having an antique professionally restored. The improvement expenditure will also attract indexation allowance. This would run from the date the improvement expenditure was incurred until the date of disposal. A situation would therefore arise where two (or more) indexation allowances were deducted in the computation, each with different start dates, but all with the same end date. This is shown in the diagram that follows on the next page.

The following example illustrates how this works in practice:

example: chargeable gain involving improvement expenditure

Ledger and Company Limited bought an office building for £60,000 in September 1984. In January 1990 the company spent £40,000 extending the property. The company sold the building in February 2015 for £300,000.

The indexation factors are:

September 1984 to February 2015	1.849
January 1990 to February 2015	1.148

The calculation is as follows:

	£
Proceeds	300,000
less:	
original cost	(60,000)
improvement expenditure	(40,000)
Unindexed gain	200,000
less:	
indexation allowance on original cost	
1.849 x £60,000	(110,940)
indexation allowance on extension	
1.148 x £40,000	(45,920)
Chargeable Gain	43,140

SPECIAL RULES FOR CHATTELS

Chattels are tangible, moveable items such as furniture, portable equipment, works of art and vans.

Apart from the exemptions for all cars, and chattels bought and sold for less than £6,000, there are also some special rules about the amount of gain or loss that can occur when chattels are disposed of. Although these rules are not particularly complicated, they do need to be understood and remembered.

chattels sold at a gain for over £6,000

In this situation the gain is limited to an amount of:

$$5/3 \text{ (Proceeds} - £6,000)$$

Note that in this formula both the fraction of 5/3 and the amount of £6,000 are stated in the tax legislation and will be the same in all these calculations.

'Proceeds' here refers to the gross proceeds – before the deduction of any incidental costs of disposal.

This restriction may, or may not, affect the chargeable gain. To give an illustration, suppose that gains (after any indexation) had been calculated on disposals in the following two examples:

Disposal A   Proceeds £9,000,   Gain £7,500

Disposal B   Proceeds £9,000,   Gain £2,500

In the case of Disposal A, the gain would be restricted to:

$$5/3 \text{ (£9,000} - £6,000) \quad = \quad £5,000$$

£5,000 would therefore be used as the chargeable gain figure. Using the same formula for Disposal B the gain would also be restricted to £5,000, but since the calculated gain is only £2,500 the restriction would be irrelevant and have no effect.

chattels sold at a loss for less than £6,000

If the chattel had been bought for less than £6,000 the transaction would be exempt from CGT, as both the cost and proceeds are less than £6,000.

If the chattel had cost more than £6,000 then the loss would be limited by using the figure of £6,000 in the gains computation **instead of the actual proceeds**. This will mean that the allowable capital loss is smaller than the actual loss incurred.

We use the phrase 'deemed proceeds' to describe substituting the actual proceeds with another figure. £6,000 is always used as the 'deemed proceeds' where the actual proceeds are less than £6,000, but the chattel was bought for more than £6,000.

For example a chattel, such as a painting that was displayed in the Boardroom, bought for £8,000 and sold for £3,000 would result in a loss calculated as:

	£
Deemed proceeds	6,000
less actual cost	(8,000)
Loss	(2,000)

Make sure that you understand the logic of this, and remember that it is the proceeds that are deemed to be £6,000. This is an area where it is easy to get confused if you are not careful.

We will now present a Case Study to consolidate an understanding of the main issues that we have covered in this chapter so far.

Case Study

INN CREASE LIMITED: USING SPECIAL RULES

Inn Crease Limited runs a chain of hotels and pubs. During the CAP y/e 31/12/2015 the company made the disposals listed below.

The company has capital losses brought forward from the previous CAP of £20,000.

disposals:

- The company sold an antique dresser in January 2015 for £7,500. The dresser had cost £2,500 when purchased in January 1996.

- The company sold part of a plot of land for £100,000 in February 2015. It had bought the whole plot in January 1990 for £80,000. In February 2015 the market value of the remaining part of the plot of land was £300,000.

- The company sold an office building in March 2015 for £200,000. The building was bought in September 1995 for £60,000, and extended in June 2000 at a cost of £40,000.

- The company sold ten identical shoe-cleaning machines from its hotels for £100 each in January 2015. The machines had been bought for £500 each in January 1996, and plant & machinery capital allowances had been claimed on them through the main pool.

- The company sold 1,000 ordinary shares in Gloxxo plc for a total of £15,000 in March 2015. The shares had been bought for £6.00 each in September 1995. These had been the only shares that it owned in Gloxxo plc.

indexation factors

The indexation factors have been calculated as follows:

January 1990 - February 2015	1.148
September 1995 - March 2015	0.707
January 1996 - January 2015	0.700
June 2000 - March 2015	0.503

required

- Calculate the chargeable gain or capital loss on each applicable disposal.

- Calculate the total chargeable gain that will be used in the taxable total profits computation for the CAP y/e 31/12/2015.

solution

Antique Dresser

	£
Proceeds	7,500
less cost	(2,500)
less indexation (0.700 x £2,500)	(1,750)
Chargeable Gain	3,250

but gain restricted to:

5/3 (£7,500 − £6,000) = £2,500

Land

Proceeds	100,000
less apportioned cost:	
£80,000 x £100,000 / £400,000	(20,000)
less indexation:	
1.148 x £20,000	(22,960)
Chargeable gain	57,040

Office building

	£
Proceeds	200,000
less cost	(60,000)
Improvement expenditure	(40,000)
less:	
indexation on cost	
£60,000 x 0.707	(42,420)
indexation on improvement	
£40,000 x 0.503	(20,120)
Chargeable gain	37,460

Shoe cleaning machines

The shoe cleaning machines are sold at a loss, and are therefore dealt with entirely through the Plant and Machinery capital allowances computation.

Shares

Proceeds	15,000
less cost	(6,000)
less indexation (0.707 x £6,000)	(4,242)
Chargeable Gain	4,758

calculation of chargeable gain for taxable total profits computation

We can now bring the chargeable gains together, and deduct the capital loss brought forward.

	£
Antique dresser	2,500
Land	57,040
Office building	37,460
Shares	4,758
	101,758
Less capital loss brought forward	(20,000)
Chargeable gain to be used in taxable total profits computation	81,758

MATCHING RULES FOR SHARES

In the Case Study on the previous pages, shares are shown as chargeable assets, and the computation for the acquisition and subsequent disposal of a block of shares is the same as for other assets.

A complication can arise when various quantities of the same type of share in the same company are bought over a period of time and then sold. The problem faced is similar to that in any inventory valuation situation – how to determine which of the shares that were bought are deemed to be the ones that were sold.

The problem is solved in this situation by the application of strict **matching rules**, in other words, matching up the shares that have been sold with the shares originally held.

When shares are sold the **matching process** is carried out by working through, in order, the following categories of acquisition, missing out any that do not apply, until all the shares sold have been matched. A separate chargeable gains computation is then used for each separate match.

■ firstly, any shares bought on the **same day** that the disposal occurs are matched with that disposal

■ secondly, any shares bought in the **nine days before the disposal** are matched with those disposed of. When this occurs no indexation allowance is available

■ finally any remaining shares not yet matched are deemed to have come from the **'FA 1985 pool'** of shares. This is a device for merging and indexing shares. ('FA 1985' stands for the 'Finance Act 1985' which established this procedure, explained on the next page)

The matching process is a little complicated, but forms a possible examination task. The most likely questions will involve shares matched to the FA 1985 pool because there are no very recent acquisitions.

Note that these matching rules for companies are different from the ones that relate to individuals that you may have studied and which are covered in Chapter 8 of this book.

Remember that this matching process only applies where there have been several purchases of the same type of shares in the same company. It does not apply to a mixture of different companies' shares, nor is it needed where a shareholding is bought and sold intact.

using the 'FA 1985 pool'

This device was introduced in the 1985 Finance Act, and merges (or 'pools') shares in the same company and of the same type together, and applies indexation allowances at the same time. As explained on the last page, it forms the last of the matching rules, and is used to calculate the cost of shares acquired earlier than nine days before disposal.

The pooling process is similar to the calculation of weighted average inventory valuations (as you have probably studied in Costing), but with the additional complication of indexation allowance.

The 'pool' needs to record accurate data:

■ the number of shares in each transaction

■ actual costs

■ indexed costs

These form the three main columns of the pool working.

The pool commences with the first shares bought. The cost of these is then indexed up to the time when other shares are bought (or sold). These are added in, and the cumulative indexed cost is then re-indexed up to the date of the next share purchase or sale. This process is repeated as often as necessary, with the last indexation occurring up to the disposal date of the shares for which we are working out the gain. The indexed balance in the pool is then used to calculate the cost of shares from the pool that are sold, by apportionment based on the number of shares.

We will now demonstrate how this works, using a numerical example.

example: using the FA 1985 pool

On 1/1/2015 Jay Limited sold 10,000 ordinary shares in WyeCo Ltd for £15 each, from its shareholding of 25,000. The shareholding had been built up as follows:

>   1/1/1988 bought 17,000 shares for £5.00 each
>   1/1/1993 bought 8,000 shares for £7.00 each

The relevant indexation factors are:

January 1988 to January 1993	0.335
January 1993 to January 2015	0.852

Since there are no acquisitions on the day of disposal, nor the nine days before that, the whole of the disposal of 10,000 shares will be matched with the pool. The pool will be built up as follows, with the disposal deducted as the latest transaction:

	Number	Cost	Indexed Cost
		£	£
1/1/1988 Purchase	17,000	85,000	85,000
Indexation to Jan 1993: £85,000 x 0.335			28,475
			113,475
1/1/1993 Purchase	8,000	56,000	56,000
			169,475
Indexation to January 2015: £169,475 x 0.852			144,393
Pool Totals:	25,000	141,000	313,868
Less Disposal	(10,000)	(56,400)	(125,547)
Pool Balance after disposal	15,000	84,600	188,321

You should examine these workings carefully, and note the following:

• Indexation is applied to consecutive periods based on transaction dates. Here the periods were:
  - January 1988 to January 1993
  - January 1993 to January 2015

• Purchases at cost are added to the cumulative indexed cost figure, and the combined amount is then re-indexed to the date of the next transaction.

• The cost figures for the disposal are a proportional amount of the pool costs before disposal, based on the number of shares.

(eg £313,868 x 10,000 / 25,000 = £125,547)

The computation for the disposal will now be as follows:

	£
Proceeds (10,000 x £15)	150,000
less cost	(56,400)
less indexation (£125,547 – £56,400)	(69,147)
Chargeable Gain	24,453

The cost and indexation figures are shown here separately, but would total the indexed cost amount shown in the pool workings (£56,400 + £69,147 = £125,547). This is shown this way in case the indexation needs to be restricted to avoid creating a loss.

If at some future date there was another disposal of shares from the pool then the pool balances remaining (indexed as appropriate) would be used to determine the cost of the shares in the further disposal.

BONUS AND RIGHTS ISSUES

dealing with bonus shares

Bonus shares are additional shares given free to shareholders, based on their current shareholding. This is sometimes called a 'scrip issue' and this process may be carried out as part of a capital restructuring of a company.

For chargeable gains purposes, the bonus shares are treated as if they were acquired at the same time as the original shares that generated the issue. For example a company that owned 1,000 shares that were bought in January 2001 would be entitled to a further 200 shares if there were a bonus issue of 'one for five' shares. The total of 1,200 shares would be treated as bought in January 2001 for the amount paid for the 1,000 shares.

Bonus shares are added to the pool when they are received. Since no payment is made, there is no adjustment to the cost or indexed cost figures. The bonus share transaction date is not relevant for indexation purposes.

dealing with rights issues

A rights issue is when additional shares are sold to existing shareholders, usually at a special discounted price. For matching purposes, the shares that are bought in this way are treated as if they were bought with the original shares. However, any indexation that applies to rights issue shares will only apply from the date that they were paid for. Rights issue shares will join the pool and be treated like any other share purchase. Their cost will be added into the pool, and the date they were bought will be treated as a date to index to and from as usual.

Dealing with share transactions is one of the most complicated areas of study in this learning area, yet it is a likely assessment task. We will therefore use a further Case Study to consolidate understanding.

CHER THYME LIMITED:
MATCHING AND POOLING SHARES

Cher Thyme Limited has acquired the following quoted ordinary shares in AbCo Plc:

1/5/1985	1,000 shares at £4.00 each	£4,000
1/1/1990	Bonus issue of 1 for 4	
1/1/1992	1,750 shares at £4.20 each	£7,350
1/1/1995	Rights issue of 1 for 2 at £4.10 each	
1/12/2001	1,800 shares at £5.10 each	£9,180

On 8/12/2001 the company sold 1,000 of its shareholding of AbCo Plc

On 15/3/2015 the company sold a further 2,500 ordinary shares in AbCo Plc for £10.00 each.

required

1   Identify which shares would have already been matched against the disposal that took place on 8/12/2001.

2   State how the disposal of shares on 15/3/2015 will be matched against the acquisitions.

3   Calculate the total gain arising from the sale of shares that took place on 15/3/2015.

Indexation factors have already been calculated, and are as follows:

May 1985 - Jan 1992	0.424
Jan 1992 - Jan 1995	0.077
Jan 1995 - Dec 2001	0.188
Dec 2001 - March 2015	0.483

solution

1   The disposal of 1,000 shares on 8/12/2001 would have been matched with 1,000 of the 1,800 shares that were bought on 1/12/2001 for £5.10 each. This leaves 800 of that purchase to join the pool at that time.

2   Matching of the 15/3/2015 disposal of 2,500 shares will be against the pool, since there are no acquisitions on the same day, or any in the previous nine days.

3   To carry out the computation we must first build up the FA 1985 pool:

	Number	Cost	Indexed Cost
		£	£
1/5/1985 Purchase	1,000	4,000	4,000
1/1/1990 Bonus Issue	250		
Indexation May 1985 to Jan 1992:			
£4,000 x 0.424			1,696
	1,250	-	5,696
1/1/1992 Purchase	1,750	7,350	7,350
	3,000	11,350	13,046
Indexation Jan 1992 to Jan 1995			
£13,046 x 0.077			1,005
1/1/1995 Rights issue 1 for 2	1,500	6,150	6,150
	4,500	17,500	20,201
Indexation Jan 1995 to Dec 2001:			
£20,201 x 0.188			3,798
1/12/2001 Purchase (Balance)	800	4,080	4,080
	5,300	21,580	28,079
Indexation Dec 2001 to March 2015:			
£28,079 x 0.483			13,562
Pool Totals	5,300	21,580	41,641
Less Disposal	(2,500)	(10,179)	(19,642)
Pool Balance after disposal	2,800	11,401	21,999

	£
Proceeds (2,500 x £10)	25,000
Less cost	(10,179)
Less indexation (£19,642 – £10,179)	(9,463)
Chargeable Gain	5,358

ROLLOVER RELIEF

Rollover relief applies when one business asset is sold, and another is bought. It is a deferral relief, which means that it postpones the impact of a chargeable gain. Since a gain can be deferred more than once, provided the rules don't change in the future, gains can sometimes be postponed almost indefinitely.

Where one business asset is replaced with another, then the gain of the first may be rolled over (deferred) into the second, so that any eventual gain on the replacement asset would include the gain deferred from the first asset.

For example, suppose a qualifying asset, such as a warehouse, is sold for £200,000, incurring a gain of £50,000. Another qualifying asset is then bought for £220,000, and the gain on the first asset is rolled over into the second, which means no tax is payable on the gain at this time.

If the second asset is sold some time later, and incurs a 'normal' chargeable gain of £100,000, the deferred gain from the first asset will increase the total chargeable gain to £150,000.

Full deferral can only occur when all the proceeds of the first asset are invested in the replacement asset(s). Any part of the proceeds that are not reinvested in the second asset will form a chargeable gain immediately.

The replacement asset must be acquired between one year before and three years after the sale of the first asset.

Both assets must be in the categories listed below, but do not have to be like-for-like replacements for each other, nor even in the same category.

This is an abbreviated list based on the type of assets involved:

- land & buildings
- immovable plant & machinery
- ships, aircraft & hovercraft

A company could, for example, sell an aircraft, and invest the proceeds in an office building and roll over the gain.

A possible assessment task involves rollover relief relating to land and buildings. You may be expected to recognise that rollover relief would benefit a company in a given situation, and calculate the position accordingly.

Companies can choose whether or not to use rollover relief.

The example on the next page illustrates how the system works.

example: rollover relief

Rollo and Company Limited purchased an office building in January 1992 for £300,000. The company sold the building in January 2015 for £800,000. A shop had been purchased for £950,000 in August 2014.

The indexation factor from January 1992 to January 2015 is 0.883.

The chargeable gain on the office building would be calculated as follows (initially ignoring any rollover relief).

	£
Proceeds	800,000
less cost	(300,000)
less indexation	
0.883 x £300,000	(264,900)
Chargeable Gain	235,100

Using rollover relief, all of this gain of £235,100 can be deferred, because all of the proceeds were invested in the shop – the shop was bought for more than £800,000. This means that there is no gain on the office building chargeable in the current CAP.

The deferral works by deducting the deferred gain of £235,100 from the purchase cost of the shop in the chargeable gains computation when the shop is ultimately disposed of.

This would make the revised 'cost' figure (£950,000 – £235,100) = £714,900. Any gain at disposal of the shop would therefore consequently be greater than if rollover relief had not been used.

If the shop had been purchased for less than £800,000, not all of the gain on the office building could have been deferred. For example, if the shop had been bought for £700,000 only £135,100 of the gain could be deferred and a £100,000 gain would be chargeable immediately.

Chapter Summary

■ Chargeable gains for companies are part of the taxable total profits (TTP). Such gains arise when chargeable assets are disposed of during the chargeable accounting period (CAP). A disposal usually takes the form of the sale of the asset. All assets are chargeable unless they are exempt. Exempt assets include cars, government securities (gilts), and certain chattels.

■ Each disposal uses a separate computation that compares the proceeds or market value with the original cost of the asset. Indexation allowance is also deductible based on inflation from the time of acquisition up to disposal. Losses are set off against gains before bringing the net figure into the taxable total profits computation. Where the net result is a capital loss, the amount is carried forward to set against chargeable gains arising in the next CAP. Where capital allowances have been claimed on an asset that is disposed of, capital losses cannot arise.

■ The cost of a part disposal is calculated by apportioning the cost of the whole asset. This is carried out by using the proceeds of the part disposed of as a proportion of the value of the whole asset at the time of disposal.

■ Improvement expenditure that is reflected in the asset when disposed of is an allowable cost. It also attracts indexation allowance from the date of expenditure up to the date of disposal.

■ Chattels that are acquired and sold for under £6,000 are exempt. Where they are sold at a gain for over £6,000 the gain is restricted to 5/3 of the proceeds minus £6,000. Where sold at a loss for under £6,000, the loss is restricted by substituting £6,000 for the actual proceeds in the computation.

■ When shares of the same type in the same company are bought and sold at different times matching rules are used to identify the shares disposed of. Firstly shares bought on the day of disposal are matched. Secondly those bought in the 9 days before disposal are matched. Thirdly acquisitions are pooled (including indexation) and matched. This is known as the FA 1985 (Finance Act 1985) pool.

■ Bonus and rights issues are treated as acquired at the time of the shares that they are derived from for matching purposes. They can both appear as part of the FA 1985 pool.

■ Rollover relief relates to certain categories of assets. It can defer a chargeable gain where the company reinvests all or part of the proceeds of disposal in further assets. The full deferral of a gain can only occur when all of the proceeds are reinvested.

Key Terms	**Chargeable Gains**	these can arise when companies dispose of chargeable assets. Chargeable Gains form part of the taxable total profits (TTP)
	Capital Loss	this is effectively a negative chargeable gain. It results when the allowable costs of an asset exceed the sale proceeds (or market value). Indexation cannot be used to increase a loss. A capital loss is used by setting it against a gain in the same CAP, or if this is not possible, by carrying it forward to set against chargeable gains in the next available CAP
	Disposal	a disposal for Capital Gains Tax purposes is the sale, gift, loss or destruction of an asset
	Chargeable Asset	this term is used to describe assets, the disposal of which can result in a chargeable gain or capital loss. All assets are chargeable unless they are exempt
	Exempt Asset	this is an asset that is not a chargeable asset. Exempt assets include cars, Gilts, and some chattels
	Chattel	a tangible, moveable asset
	Net Proceeds	the proceeds from the sale of an asset, less any incidental costs of selling the asset
	Unindexed Gain	the net proceeds (or market value in some situations) less the original cost of the asset and any other allowable costs incurred. It is the subtotal of the gain computation before indexation allowance is deducted
	Indexation Allowance	an amount that is deductible in the gain computation that compensates for the effect of inflation on the asset between acquisition and disposal. It uses the Retail Price Index to calculate a factor that is multiplied by the historical cost of the asset

Part Disposal   this occurs when part of an asset is disposed of, but the remainder is retained

Improvement Expenditure

this term relates to capital expenditure that enhances an asset. If the enhancement is still evident at disposal then the improvement expenditure is an allowable cost

Matching Rules for Shares

these rules determine which acquisitions of shares are identified with each disposal

Bonus Shares   shares issued at no cost to shareholders, the number of shares being based on their current shareholding

Rights Issue   shares issued by a company to its existing shareholders at a special price

Rollover Relief   a deferral relief available to businesses (including companies). It has the effect of postponing a chargeable gain when the proceeds of disposal have been reinvested in further assets

Activities

4.1   Analyse the following list of assets into those that are chargeable assets and those that are exempt.

(a)   Antique painting sold for £10,000

(b)   An office block

(c)   Shares in CIC plc

(d)   An industrial building

(e)   A portable machine, sold at a profit for under £6,000

(f)   A plot of land

(g)   A car

(h)   Government securities

(i)   Trading stock

4.2   April Limited bought an office block in May 1995 for £600,000 and sold it in January 2015 for £1,300,000. The company had no other disposals in the CAP y/e 31/12/2015. April Limited had a capital loss brought forward from the previous CAP of £15,000.

The indexation factor from May 1995 to January 2015 is 0.707.

Calculate the chargeable gain that will form part of the taxable total profits for April Limited for the CAP y/e 31/12/2015.

4.3   Cee Limited bought 200 ordinary shares in Zedco plc in August 1998 for £50,000 and sold them in March 2015 for £145,000. It had no other disposals in the CAP y/e 31/12/2015.

Cee Limited had a capital loss brought forward from the previous CAP of £25,000.

The indexation factor from August 1998 to March 2015 is 0.571.

Calculate the chargeable gain that will form part of the taxable total profits for Cee Limited for the CAP.

4.4 Aye Limited made the following disposals in March 2015. These were its only disposals during CAP y/e 31/12/2015.

It sold a factory for £500,000 that had been used since it was bought new for £300,000 in September 1986.

It sold part of a piece of land for £30,000 that it had bought in January 1992. The whole piece of land had cost £50,000 at that time. At the time of the sale the remaining land was valued at £120,000.

Required:

Calculate the total chargeable gains arising from the two disposals.

The relevant indexation factors are:

September 1986 to March 2015   1.615

January 1992 to March 2015   0.896

4.5 Dee Limited made the following disposals in its CAP y/e 31/12/2015.

It sold 10,000 of its ordinary shares in Zydeco Ltd on 30/03/2015 for £60,000 in total. The shareholding in this company had been built up as follows:

1/1/1992   Bought 3,000 shares for £3.00 each.

1/1/1995   Bought 12,000 shares for £3.50 each

1/1/1999   Received bonus shares on the basis of 1 for 5

1/1/2000   Sold 5,000 shares

It sold a portable antique machine to a local museum for £6,900 on 31/3/2015. The machine had been bought for £3,000 in January 2000, and capital allowances had been claimed on it since through the main pool.

Required:

•   Calculate any chargeable gain made on

   - the disposal of shares in March 2015, and

   - the disposal of the machine in March 2015.

•   State how the disposal of the machine will be dealt with for capital allowances.

The relevant indexation factors are:

January 1992 to January 1995   0.077

January 1995 to January 2000   0.141

January 2000 to March 2015   0.543

4.6 For each statement, tick the appropriate box.

	Chargeable Asset	**Exempt Asset**
Vintage car	☐	☐
Antique vase	☐	☐
Greyhound	☐	☐

4.7 Trevor Ltd sold a valuable picture for £12,000 in April 2015. This was bought for £4,000 in August 2000. The indexation factor from August 2000 to April 2015 was 0.513.

Complete the following computation:

£

Proceeds	☐
Cost	☐
Indexation allowance	☐
Gain	☐
Chattel restriction on gain	☐

State whether the chattel restriction will have any effect on the original gain.

4.8   Practice Ltd bought 5,000 shares in Luncheon Ltd for £15,500 in October 2001. A rights issue of 1 for 50 shares was bought in July 2003 for £2 per share. In April 2015, Practice Ltd sold all the shares for £9 per share.

Indexation factors were: October 2001 to July 2003: 0.114; July 2003 to April 2015: 0.123

What is the gain made on these shares?

	No. Shares	Cost £	Indexed Cost £

Proceeds	£
Indexed Cost	£
Gain	£

Corporation tax – calculating the tax

this chapter covers...

In this chapter we bring together all the results of our studies of Corporation Tax in chapters 1 to 4, and learn how to calculate the Corporation Tax itself. To do this we start by reviewing the components of the computation, including an examination of deductions for gift aid.

We then go on to study how Corporation tax is calculated in Financial Years 2015 and 2014.

We will then see how to tackle situations where chargeable accounting periods straddle financial years that have different tax rates applying.

We will then review the process and options for offsetting various losses, and consider the issues that can affect the choice of optimum loss set-off. We will also review the division of profits from all sources when dealing with an accounting period of over 12 months.

The next section is concerned with completing the short version of the CT600 tax return for companies.

The chapter is completed with sections on interest and penalties and record keeping.

THE CORPORATION TAX COMPUTATION

structure of the computation

As discussed in earlier chapters, the Corporation Tax computation starts with a summary of profits from various sources that are chargeable to Corporation Tax. The computation then goes on to calculate the amount of Corporation Tax that is payable.

A separate computation will need to be carried out for each Chargeable Accounting Period (CAP), which will result in a tax liability for the period. A separate CT600 return form will also need to be completed for each CAP. A simple version of this computation is repeated here:

Trading Income		X
+	Profits from Investments	X
+	Chargeable Gains	X
=	Taxable Total Profits	X
	Corporation Tax on taxable total profits	X

Note that 'taxable total profits' were previously known as 'profits chargeable to Corporation Tax' (PCTCT).

revision – what we have covered so far

In Chapters 2 and 3 we examined in detail how the 'Trading Income' figure is calculated, including the calculation of capital allowances for plant & machinery. In Chapter 4 we saw how chargeable gains are calculated on individual chargeable disposals and combined ready for inclusion in the Corporation Tax computation.

where we go from here

In this chapter we will be looking at the final stage of the Corporation Tax computation – bringing all the income together and working out the Corporation Tax liability. We will then see how the tax return is completed and the dates for payment. Finally we will look briefly at the sort of records that should be kept to show how the figures in the computation have been arrived at.

You may recall the summary diagram from Chapter 2, reproduced at the top of the next page. We have now looked in detail at the elements in the first three of the boxes along the top of the diagram, and will now follow the rest of the procedures over the next few pages.

profits from investments

You will see from the above diagram that profits from investments need to be identified so that they can be incorporated into the computation. These profits could include:

- **interest received from non-trade investments**

  The gross amount of any interest receivable (ie on an **accruals basis**) during the CAP forms an investment income assessment that is brought into the main computation. Examples of the sources of interest include bank and building society deposits, debentures and Government securities ('gilts'). You can assume that any such interest in an examination task is non-trade, and should therefore be treated in this way.

- **profits from renting out property**

  The tax-adjusted profits from rental income are assessed as 'property income' on an accruals basis. You would not be expected to carry out adjustments to such figures, and would just need to incorporate the profit figure into the main computation. A little later in this chapter we will see how to deal with any losses that may arise from this type of income.

You should note that **dividends received** from other UK companies are **not** brought into the Corporation Tax computation, and are not taxed. This is because the profits from which they derive have already been taxed through the other company's computation. However, prior to 1 April 2015 such dividends received can have an impact on the rate of Corporation Tax that is applied, as we shall see shortly.

gift-aid payments

Companies are entitled to make gifts to charities under the gift-aid scheme, and obtain tax relief on their payments. This operates simply by allowing the company to deduct the amount of the payment from the total profits in the Corporation Tax computation. This is carried out as the final stage in the calculation of the taxable total profits. The **payment date determines which CAP** the gift-aid payment falls into, for example if the payment was made during a 'long' accounting period. Unlike the gift-aid scheme for individuals (that you may have come across in 'personal tax'), the company makes the payment to the charity as a gross amount, with no adjustment for tax. As we saw in Chapter 2, the company cannot use a gift-aid payment as an allowable deduction in the calculation of Trading Income profits, since this would form a duplication of tax relief.

If there are insufficient total profits to set a gift-aid payment against in the final calculation of taxable total profits, then the tax relief on the balance of the payment is lost, since it cannot be carried forward. Where trading losses are set against the taxable total profits, (as outlined in Chapter 2) this is carried out in priority to gift-aid payments, so again there is a possibility of losing the tax relief on the gift-aid payment.

We will now use a Case Study to demonstrate how the various elements are combined into a Corporation Tax computation, before looking at the tax calculation itself.

Case Study

THE BASIC COMPANY LIMITED: CALCULATING THE TTP

The Basic Company Limited has produced accounts for the year ended 31/3/2016. The accounts have been adjusted for tax purposes, and the following figures have been established:

	£
Adjusted Trading Profit (before capital allowances)	1,000,000
Capital Allowances – Plant & Machinery	163,000
Payment to Charity under Gift-Aid scheme	28,000

	£
Non-Trade Interest Receivable	55,000
Dividends Received from UK Company	90,000
Chargeable Gains	34,000
Rental Income	48,000

required

Using a Corporation Tax Computation, calculate the taxable total profits for the CAP y/e 31/3/2016.

solution

In order to complete the computation, the trading income assessment must first be established:

	£
Adjusted Trading Profits	1,000,000
less Plant & Machinery capital allowances	(163,000)
Trading Income assessment	837,000

Building on the outline computation shown at the start of this chapter, we can now combine the figures that make up the taxable total profits.

Corporation Tax Computation

	£
Trading Income	837,000
Profits from Investments:	
Non-Trade Interest Receivable	55,000
Property Income	48,000
Chargeable Gains	34,000
	974,000
less Gift-Aid payments	(28,000)
Taxable total profits	946,000

Note the structure of the computation, since you will need to use this without further guidance. Note also that the dividends received of £90,000 are left out of the calculation entirely.

In the next section we will see how the tax itself is calculated.

CALCULATING THE CORPORATION TAX LIABILITY

The calculation of Corporation Tax liability is different, depending on whether the CAP

- ■   falls entirely into the Financial Year 2015, or
- ■   falls wholly or partly into an earlier Financial Year.

While the calculation of Corporation Tax in the first situation is very straightforward, you will also need to deal with the more complex situation relating to earlier CAPs.

Financial Year 2015 calculations

The only rate of Corporation Tax that applies to CAPs that fall entirely into FY 2015 is 20%. This rate is applied to the taxable total profits and the result is the Corporation tax liability.

This applies to any CAP that starts on or after 1st April 2015, regardless of whether it is for 12 months or a shorter period.

For example, using the data from the Basic Company Limited case study on pages 5.5 and 5.6, the Corporation Tax would be simply:

Taxable total profits £946,000 x 20% = Corporation tax £189,200

Financial Year 2014 calculations

In order to carry out calculations of Corporation Tax for CAPs that fall partly into the FY2014 and partly into the FY2015 (i.e. those that 'straddle' 1st April 2015) we first need to see how the calculations are carried out for CAPs entirely within FY2014.

Unfortunately, this is much more complicated that the single Corporation Tax rate that applies to FY2015, and involves first establishing which 'band' the company falls into.

The tax rate to be applied, and any further calculation will depend on the size of the company – decided by a special 'augmented profit' figure. We will use the tax rates that apply to the financial year 2014 (the period 1 April 2014 to 31 March 2015).

The 'augmented profits' figure referred to above is calculated as:

	£
Taxable total profits for the CAP (as calculated)	X
add the amount of any dividends received from UK companies plus the associated tax credit	X
'Augmented Profits' for the purpose of determining the tax rate	X

The dividends received plus the associated tax credit is also known as **Franked Investment Income** (FII). The tax credit is equal to 10/90 of the dividend amount itself, and therefore the FII figure can be calculated as:

$$\text{Dividend} + (10/90 \times \text{Dividend})$$

or simply as $\quad\quad 100/90 \times \text{Dividend}$

This is the same calculation that is carried out for individuals when working out the amount of dividend income that is assessable to Income Tax.

Corporation Tax 'bands' and marginal relief (FY2014)

There are currently three 'bands' for Corporation Tax purposes, and the first step is to establish into which band the 'augmented profits' figure falls. This will determine the rate of tax that will be applied to the taxable total profits, and whether there is any **marginal relief** available. Marginal relief is a deduction in the calculation of the Corporation Tax amount. It is calculated by formula and has the effect of smoothing the transition from one tax rate to the next.

For those who have already studied Income Tax you will find that, unlike Income Tax, the Corporation Tax calculation does not involve working up through the bands, nor does the taxable total profits have to be analysed into different categories of income.

The table below shows the bands and the tax rates that apply within each band, based on a twelve month CAP.

Corporation Tax rates

'Augmented Profit' band	Corporation Tax 1/4/2014 – 31/3/2015	Corporation Tax 1/4/2015 – 31/3/2016
£0 – £300,000	Small Profits Rate (20%)	⌐
£300,001 – £1,500,000	Main Rate (21%) less marginal relief	⊢ Main Rate (20%)
£1,500,001 and over	Main Rate (21%)	⌐

Note that the 20% rate for FY2015 is the same as the small profits rate for FY2014.

calculations without marginal relief (FY2014)

Where there is no marginal relief available, the Corporation Tax is calculated simply by multiplying the taxable total profits by the appropriate percentage. Note that it is the taxable total profits that we are using here, not the 'augmented profits' figure that was used to determine the band.

For example, suppose a company has the following results for a twelve month CAP (Chargeable Accounting Period) to 31/3/15:

	Taxable total profits	£200,000
+	Franked Investment Income (FII)	£20,000
=	'Augmented Profits'	£220,000

The 'augmented profits' figure falls into the small profits rate band of £0 to £300,000 (see table on the previous page) and therefore the Corporation Tax will be calculated as:

$$£200,000 \times 20\% = £40,000.$$

calculations using marginal relief (FY2014)

Marginal relief is a deduction in the calculation of the Corporation Tax amount. It is calculated by formula. It has the effect of smoothing the transition from the small profits rate of 20% to the main rate of 21%. Where **marginal relief** is available, the tax is calculated by firstly multiplying the TTP by 21%, and then deducting the marginal relief, which is calculated using the following formula.

Marginal Relief Fraction x (Upper Limit of Band – Augmented Profits) x (Normal TTP / Augmented Profits)

This formula is sometimes abbreviated to:

$$\text{Fraction} \times (U - A) \times (N / A)$$

where

U = **U**pper Limit of Band (normally £1,500,000)

A = '**A**ugmented Profits'

N = **N**ormal Taxable Total Profits

In the financial year 2014 the fraction is **1/400**.

If there are no dividends received, then the final fraction in the formula will equal 1 (taxable total profits = augmented profits). This will make the calculation easier. Note also that this fraction can never exceed 1 since taxable total profits will never be greater than 'Augmented Profits'.

You would be advised to learn the formula in a form that you can use.

We will now use a Case Study to demonstrate how the tax calculation is carried out.

Case Study

THE PREVIOUS COMPANY LIMITED: CALCULATING THE CORPORATION TAX (FY2014)

The Previous Company Limited has produced a Corporation Tax computation for the CAP year ended 31/3/2015.

This shows taxable total profits of £990,000. The company received dividends from another UK company of £90,000 during the CAP.

required

Calculate the Corporation Tax liability of the Basic Company Limited for the CAP y/e 31/3/2015.

solution

The first stage is to calculate the 'augmented profits' figure, that will determine the rate of tax and whether marginal relief is available.

		£
	Taxable total profits for the CAP	990,000
add	the amount of any dividends received from UK companies plus the associated tax credit (£90,000 x 100/90)	100,000
	'Augmented Profits' for the purpose of determining the tax rate	1,090,000

Using the table (on page 5.8) we can see that the Basic Company Limited will pay Corporation Tax at the main rate of 21%, less marginal relief for this CAP. The calculation is as follows:

		£
	Taxable total profits at main rate: £990,000 x 21%	207,900
less	marginal relief:	
	1/400 x (£1,500,000 – £1,090,000) x (£990,000 / £1,090,000)	(931)
	Corporation Tax Liability	206,969

Note:

The marginal relief calculation is best carried out in stages:

- the contents of the first bracket is calculated as £410,000
- this is divided by 400 to give £1,025
- this is multiplied by 990 and divided by 1090 to give the final result (the three zeros can be omitted from both parts of the final fraction like this to avoid exceeding the capacity of the calculator)

Note again that the Corporation Tax is calculated on the taxable total profits, not on the 'augmented profits' figure.

DEALING WITH ASSOCIATED COMPANIES (FY2014)

Where a company is either one of a group of companies, or one of a number of companies that are all controlled by the same person, then the companies are said to be 'associated' for tax purposes. The impact of this is that the limits of £1,500,000 and £300,000 for each band are scaled down, by dividing them by the total number of associated companies.

Therefore a company that was one of three associated companies (itself and two others) would pay Corporation Tax at the full rate if its 'augmented profits' were over £1,500,000 / 3 = £500,000. The same would apply to each of the other two associated companies, and the other band limit of £300,000 would also be similarly scaled down. This would also mean that if marginal relief were available the band upper limit in the formula would also be the scaled down figure. The 'augmented profits' in this situation only include dividends from companies that are not associated.

The example below will demonstrate how this works.

example: computations for associated companies

One of Three Limited has two associated companies. Its taxable total profits for the CAP for the year ended 31/3/2015 is £250,000. It also received dividends during the CAP of £45,000 from another UK company (not an associate).

As there are three associated companies in total, the band limits are scaled down by dividing by three. The 'augmented profits' would be £250,000 + (£45,000 x 100/90) = £300,000. This is between the scaled down limits of

- £1,500,000 / 3 = £500,000, and

- £300,000 / 3 = £100,000

Therefore the company pays Corporation Tax at main rate, less marginal relief.

The Corporation Tax calculation would be:	£
Taxable total profits at main rate: £250,000 x 21%	52,500
less marginal relief:	
1/400 x (£500,000 – £300,000) x (£250,000 / £300,000)	(417)
Corporation Tax Liability	52,083

DEALING WITH SHORT CHARGEABLE ACCOUNTING PERIODS (FY2014)

Where the CAP is less than twelve months the band limits are time-apportioned. This has the same impact as the scaling down of bands to deal with associated companies.

For example, if the CAP were for nine months, the limits would become:

- £1,500,000 x 9/12 = £1,125,000
- £300,000 x 9/12 = £225,000

The limit figure used in the marginal relief formula would also be the time-apportioned one.

If there were a situation where there were both

- associated companies, and
- a short CAP

then the limits would be scaled down twice.

For example a company with one associate, and a four-month CAP would have an upper limit of:

- (£1,500,000 / 2) x 4/12 = £250,000

DEALING WITH FINANCIAL YEARS WITH DIFFERENT TAX RATES

So far we have only dealt with CAPs that either fall entirely into FY2015 (when there is only one rate of tax) or entirely into FY2014 (where the tax rate and application of marginal relief depends on the tax band).

Now we must deal with periods which straddle 1 April 2015 and fall partly into FY2014 and partly into FY2015. Although this can be complicated, tasks based on this scenario are very likely in your examination.

This means that we must be particularly careful if the CAP for a company falls partly into the financial year 2014 and partly into the financial year 2015. If the CAP does straddle the 1 April 2015, this is the general procedure that we should adopt:

- time apportion the taxable total profits into the part falling into the FY 2014 and that falling into the FY 2015
- calculate the Corporation Tax for the part falling into the FY 2015 using the rate of 20%
- the part falling into the FY 2014 will be liable at either the main rate of 21%, or at 21% less marginal relief, or at the small profits rate of 20%.

Carry out the appropriate calculation depending on the band into which the 'augmented profit' figure falls

■ add together the Corporation Tax figures for FY 2015 and for FY 2014 to arrive at the Corporation Tax figure for the CAP

If the company is to pay tax in FY2014 at main rate less marginal relief then the limits used in the formulas will need to be time-apportioned based on the length of that part of the CAP.

If the company is in the 'small profits' band then the above procedure will not need to be followed to work out the tax as the tax rate in both years will be 20%. However, the tax figures for each financial year will be needed if you are required to complete a tax return.

We will now use a Case Study to demonstrate the technique in full.

Case Study

THE COMPLEX PRACTICE: DEALING WITH DIFFERENT FINANCIAL YEARS

situation

The Complex Practice specialises in producing tax computations for limited company clients. There are currently four (unconnected) clients with adjusted tax data as follows:

• the Alpha Company Limited has a twelve month CAP running from 1 January 2015 to 31 December 2015. It has TTP for this period of £2,100,000, and did not receive any dividends

• the Beta Company Limited has a twelve month CAP running from 1 November 2014 to 31 October 2015. It has TTP for this period of £120,000, and received dividends from UK companies of £54,000

• the Delta Company Limited has a twelve month CAP running from 1 February 2015 to 31 January 2016. It has TTP for this period of £1,200,000, and received dividends from UK companies of £108,000

• the Gamma Company Limited has a ten month CAP running from 1 September 2014 to 30 June 2015. It has TTP for this period of £500,000, and received dividends from UK companies of £9,000

required

Calculate the Corporation Tax for each of the four companies.

solution

• The Alpha Company Limited has an 'augmented profits' figure of £2,100,000 (the same as the TTP since there are no dividends received). This means that the company will pay Corporation Tax for this CAP at the main rate.

We must therefore time-apportion the TTP, and calculate the main rate tax for each financial year.

FY 2014:	TTP	1/1/2015 - 31/3/2015
		£2,100,000 x 3/12 = £525,000
	Corporation Tax	£525,000 x 21% = £110,250

FY 2015:	TTP	1/4/2015 - 31/12/2015
		£2,100,000 x 9/12 = £1,575,000
	Corporation Tax	£1,575,000 x 20% = £315,000

Total Corporation tax for CAP   £110,250 + £315,000 = £425,250

- The Beta Company Limited has an 'augmented profits' figure for the CAP of £120,000 + (£54,000 x 100/90) = £180,000. As this figure is below £300,000 the small profits rate of Corporation Tax is payable for the CAP in FY2014.

  Since the rate is 20% for both the financial years 2014 and 2015 there is no need to carry out any time-apportionment.

  The Corporation Tax for the whole CAP is £120,000 x 20% = £24,000.

- The Delta Company Limited has an 'augmented profits' figure for the CAP of £1,200,000 + (£108,000 x 100/90) = £1,320,000.

  As this figure is between £300,000 and £1,500,000 the company must pay Corporation Tax at the main rate less marginal relief in FY2014. Since we will be using the marginal relief formula for the FY2014 part of the CAP, we will have to calculate both the TTP and the 'augmented profits' figures relating to this financial year, as well as the time-apportioned band maximum of £1,500,000.

Financial Year	Time Apportionment	TTP	Augmented Profits	Max of Band
2014	2/12	£200,000	£220,000	£250,000
2015	10/12	£1,000,000	N/A	N/A

The tax calculation for each part of the CAP is then:

Financial Year 2014:   £

Corporation Tax at Main Rate   £200,000 x 21% =   42,000
Less marginal relief
            1/400 x (£250,000 − £220,000) x (£200,000 / £220,000)   (68)
                                                                                              41,932

Financial Year 2015:

Corporation Tax at Main Rate   £1,000,000 x 20% =   200,000

The total Corporation Tax for the CAP is:
£41,932 + £200,000 = £241,932.

- The Gamma Company Limited has an 'augmented profits' figure for the CAP of £500,000 + (£9,000 x 100/90) = £510,000. Since this is a ten-month CAP we must compare this figure with 10/12 of the normal limits. The 'augmented profits' figure falls between the time-apportioned limit figures of 10/12 x £300,000 = £250,000 and 10/12 x £1,500,000 = £1,250,000. This confirms that the company will pay tax for the FY2014 part of this CAP at main rate less marginal relief. The calculation will therefore be similar to the Delta Company Limited, although we must take care with the time-apportionment calculations.

The data that we will need is as follows:

Financial Year	Time Apportionment	TTP	Augmented Profits	Max of Band
2014	7/10	£350,000	£357,000	£875,000
2015	3/10	£150,000	N/A	N/A

The tax calculation for each part of the CAP is then:

Financial Year 2014:   £

Corporation Tax at Main Rate   £350,000 x 21% =   73,500
Less marginal relief
         1/400 x (£875,000 – £357,000) x (£350,000 / £357,000)   (1,270)
                                                                                          72,230

Financial Year 2015:

Corporation Tax at Main Rate   £150,000 x 20% =   30,000

The total Corporation Tax for the CAP is:
£72,230 + £30,000 = £102,230.

The tax calculations in this case study have become progressively more difficult with each example. Make sure that you can follow the logic and carry out the calculations yourself.

DEALING WITH A VARIETY OF LOSSES

Over the last few chapters we have seen how different sorts of losses can be relieved against profits.

- in Chapter 2 we saw that trading losses can be
  - carried forward against future trading profits, or
  - set against the current period taxable total profits before Gift Aid payments, and if this has been done,
  - then set against the taxable total profits before Gift Aid payments of the previous twelve months

- in Chapter 4 we saw that capital losses on a disposal are first set against chargeable gains arising in the same CAP, and then carried forward against chargeable gains in the future

- rental losses can be set against the current period taxable total profits and any amount not used carried forward and set against future taxable total profits before Gift Aid payments

We must therefore be careful if presented with a variety of losses to deal with each one correctly. Although the above rules are fairly straightforward, they must be learnt, since it would be easy to get confused.

We will use a Case Study now to illustrate how to deal with a variety of losses.

Case Study

LOSER PLC:
DEALING WITH DIFFERENT LOSSES

Loser plc has the following adjusted results for the CAPs y/e 31/3/2015, and y/e 31/3/2016.

	CAP y/e 31/3/2015	CAP y/e 31/3/2016
	£	£
Trading Profit / (Loss)	(300,000)	500,000
Rental Profit / (Loss)	(15,000)	45,000
Non-Trade Interest Receivable	425,000	210,000
Chargeable Gains / (Capital Loss)	(50,000)	120,000

The company has not received dividends from other UK companies. The company did not make any Gift Aid payments.

Note that tax rates for the financial year 2014 are different to the single rate for the financial year 2015.

required

1 Explain how the rental losses and capital losses must be offset, and describe the alternative ways in which the trading loss could be offset.

2 Calculate the Corporation Tax liability for the CAPs y/e 31/3/2015 and y/e 31/3/2016, based on each alternative.

3 Recommend how the trading loss should be offset, based on the amount of tax payable.

solution

1 The rental loss of £15,000 is set against the taxable total profits for the year ended 31/3/2015, giving a net figure of £410,000. The capital loss must be carried forward to the next CAP, to reduce the Chargeable Gains amount. This will give a chargeable gains assessment of £120,000 – £50,000 = £70,000 in the CAP to 31/3/2016.

The trading loss could either be:

(a) set against the taxable total profits of the CAP y/e 31/3/2015; since the only profits in that period are from interest receivable less the rental loss, the trade loss would reduce the taxable total profits of the CAP to £410,000 – £300,000 = £110,000. In this situation there is no opportunity to carry the loss back to the year before, since there is sufficient taxable total profits in the y/e 31/3/2015 to utilise all the loss.

(b) carried forward and set against the trading profits of the CAP y/e 31/3/2016; this would reduce the trading income amount for that period to £500,000 – £300,000 = £200,000

2 The tax computations are as follows:

Option (a)

	CAP y/e 31/3/2015	CAP y/e 31/3/2016
	£	£
Trading Income	0	500,000
Property Income	0	45,000
Interest Receivable	425,000	210,000
Chargeable Gains	0	70,000
Less Loss on Property Income	(15,000)	-
Less Trading Loss of the year	(300,000)	-
Taxable total profits	110,000	825,000
Corporation Tax	[1] 22,000	[2] 165,000

Corporation Tax Workings:

		£
(1)	Taxed at small profits rate:	
	£110,000 x 20% =	22,000
(2)	Taxed at main rate:	
	£825,000 x 20% =	165,000

Option (b)

	CAP y/e 31/3/2015	CAP y/e 31/3/2016
	£	£
Trading Income	0	500,000
Less trading loss bf	-	(300,000)
		200,000
Property Income	0	45,000
Interest Receivable	425,000	210,000
Chargeable Gains	0	70,000
Less Loss on Property Income	(15,000)	-
Taxable total profits	410,000	525,000
Corporation Tax	(1) 83,375	(2) 105,000

Corporation Tax Workings:

		£
(1)	Taxed at main rate, less marginal relief	
	£410,000 x 21% =	86,100
	1/400 (1,500,000 – 410,000)	(2,725)
		83,375
(2)	Taxed at main rate:	
	£525,000 x 20% =	105,000

3   By adding together the tax liabilities for each CAP under each option, we can
    see which produces the lower amount.

Option (a)	£22,000 + £165,000 =	£187,000
Option (b)	£83,375 + £105,000 =	£188,375
Difference		£1,375

Option (a) – setting against the current year TTP – produces the lower total tax amount.

This is because in this situation option (a) reduces the TTP in the year ended 31/3/2015, which means it is taxed at the small profits rate, whereas option (b) means this year is taxed at the full rate minus the marginal relief, a higher rate than 20%.

SPLITTING ALL PROFITS FOR LONG ACCOUNTING PERIODS

In Chapter 2 we learned how to deal with the split of trading profits when a long period of account needs to be divided into two chargeable accounting periods. Now that we have also looked at the other components of taxable total profits, it is a good time to review this technique and see how other profits are split.

trading profits (before deducting capital allowances)

As discussed earlier, the trading profits for the whole long period are adjusted, and the resulting adjusted trading profit is then time apportioned.

capital allowances

Separate capital allowance computations are carried out for each CAP. The capital allowances are then deducted from the time-apportioned trading profits that were described above.

interest from non-trade investments

This income is calculated on an accruals basis, and is split based on how much relates to each period (the amount arising).

profits from renting out property

The profits from renting out property are also calculated on an accruals basis. These are split based on how much relates to each period (the amount arising).

chargeable gains

Chargeable gains are allocated to each period based on when each disposal takes place.

taxable total profits

The taxable total profits for each CAP is calculated by adding together the above elements. Any gift aid payments are deducted from the relevant figure based on the date of payment.

franked investment income (FII) and 'augmented profits' (FY2014)

Dividends received plus the associated tax credits are known as FII, and are not part of the taxable total profits, but are taken into account in the calculation of the 'augmented profits' figure for establishing the tax band and calculating any marginal relief in FY2014. The FII for the chargeable accounting period is added to the taxable total profit that has been calculated as described above. The 'augmented profit' figure that results then determines the rate of tax for that CAP by comparing it with the tax band limits.

WHEN TO PAY CORPORATION TAX

As we noted in Chapter 1, Corporation Tax is payable nine months and one day after the end of the chargeable accounting period to which it relates, unless payments by instalment are necessary.

Whether instalment payments need to be made depends on the amount of the 'augmented profits'. Only companies with 'augmented profits' of £1,500,001 and over for a twelve month CAP may need to pay by instalments (assuming no associates or group companies). If there are associated or group companies then the limit of £1,500,000 will be divided by the number of companies in the group (as we saw in determining the band in FY2014).

For CAPs beginning on or after 1 April 2015 the associated companies rule is replaced by a '51% group test'. The £1,500,000 limit is divided by the number of related 51% group companies plus one (in other words including the company that we are working out the payments for).

A '51% subsidiary' is shorthand for a company where more than 50% of its ordinary share capital is beneficially owned (directly or indirectly) by another company.

The 51% group test provides these examples:

Company A is a related 51% group company of company B if:

■ A is a 51% subsidiary of B, or

■ B is a 51% subsidiary of A, or

■ A and B are both 51% subsidiaries of the same other company.

This rule is quite similar to the previous 'associated companies' rule and will usually produce the same result.

Even when a company's augmented profits exceed the £1,500,000 limited (after adjustment if necessary under the associated companies or 51% group test rules) it will **not** need to pay by instalments if **either:**

■ The current corporation tax liability is below an annual rate of £10,000, **or**

■ Provided its current augmented profits are below £10 million, if in the **previous 12 months**

– it didn't exist, or didn't have a CAP, or

– had a CAP ending that had either

• augmented profits below the limit of £1,500,000 (or other limit), or

• corporation tax below £10,000 per year

These rules effectively provide a brief exemption from paying by instalments when a company has seen a rapid rise in its profits.

payment by instalments

For 'large' companies that exceed the above limits, all of the company's estimated Corporation Tax liability must be paid in the following 4 instalments (25% in each instalment). The first instalment is due on day 14 of month 7 within the CAP. The next three instalments follow at 3 monthly intervals. Any remaining balance of Corporation Tax (since the instalments were based on an estimate) will be payable at the normal due date, nine months and one day after the end of the CAP.

---

example: payment of Corporation Tax by instalment

Largos Limited has an estimated TTP of £2,000,000 in the CAP y/e 31/3/2016.

The estimated Corporation Tax would be:

£2,000,000 x 20% = £400,000.

This would be payable in four instalments of £100,000 each on 14/10/2015, 14/1/2016, 14/4/2016 and 14/7/2016. Any remaining balance would be due on 1/1/2017.

The following 'time-line' diagram illustrates this:

COMPLETION OF THE COMPANY TAX RETURN

The company tax return (the 'CT600') must be returned online by twelve months after the end of the company's accounting period from which the CAP was derived. This will be the same date as twelve months after the CAP, unless the accounting period is over twelve months long, and had to be divided into two CAPs.

There is a full version of the CT600, and a shorter version - the 'short tax return form'. We only need to be able to complete the 'short tax return form'.

This short version can be used for CAPs starting on or before 31 March 2015. Any assessment tasks involving completion of the form will therefore be consistent with this cut-off point.

The form consists of four pages, and is shown on pages 5.24 to 5.27. The first page is for company information, with boxes to tick if appropriate, many of which won't apply to us. The second page is the company tax calculation which is important in our studies.

We will now look at the company tax calculation to see what is required, before using a Case Study to demonstrate how to complete the form.

the company tax calculation

This page of the return is reproduced on page 5.26. It generally follows the same logic and order as a Corporation Tax computation, and is therefore relatively easy to fill in.

Notes on the completion of the main boxes in which you will need to make entries are set out below.

Boxes that are simply sub-totals have been excluded from these notes. Make sure that you read the instructions on the form relating to all the boxes carefully, so that you don't miss filling in any of the numerous sub-totals.

The top part of the page is a summary of the items making up the taxable total profits.

The lower section of the page summarises the Corporation Tax itself.

Page 2 Boxes

Box 1   Total turnover from trade or profession. Enter the sales figure here.

Box 3   Trading and professional profits
The trading income amount will be inserted here.

Box 4   Trading losses brought forward claimed against profits
This is only for trading losses that are brought forward from an earlier period to be set against profits from the same trade.

Box 6   Bank, building society or other interest, and profits and gains from non-trading loan relationships
This is for non-trade interest receivable.

Box 11   Income from UK land and buildings. This is for property income.

Box 16   Gross chargeable gains
The total of chargeable gains on disposals in the CAP.

Box 17   Allowable losses . . .
Insert here any capital losses from the current CAP or previous CAPs to be offset against the above gains.

Box 30   Trading losses....
This is where a trading loss is set against the whole taxable total profits

Box 35   Charges paid. Gift aid payments are inserted here.

Box 37   Profits chargeable to Corporation Tax
This is the final taxable total profits figure.

Box 38   Franked investment income
This is for UK dividends received, multiplied by 100/90

Box 39   The number of companies associated in this period. Note that this number of companies does not include the company itself.

Box 42   Marked with an 'X' if any rate less than the main rate is applicable.

Boxes 43-63   Corporation Tax chargeable
This is for tax before any marginal relief is deducted. It needs to be time-apportioned into financial years where the CAP crosses 1 April.

Box 64   Marginal rate relief
This is for the total marginal relief that is to be deducted from the tax above, where it occurs in FY2014.

Box 66   Underlying rate of corporation tax.
This is calculated by dividing the tax (after marginal relief) by the taxable total profits. It is shown to 2 decimal places as a %.

Box 70   Corporation tax chargeable.

HM Revenue & Customs

Page 1

Company - Short Tax Return form
CT600 (Short) (2008) Version 2
for accounting periods ending on or after 1 July 1999

Your company tax return

If we send the company a *Notice* to deliver a company tax return (form *CT603*) it has to comply by the filing date, or we charge a penalty, even if there is no tax to pay. A return includes a company tax return form, any Supplementary Pages, accounts, computations and any relevant information.

Is this the right form for the company? Read the advice on pages 3 to 6 of the Company tax return guide (the *Guide*) before you start.

The forms in the CT600 series set out the information we need and provide a standard format for calculations. Use the *Guide* to help you complete the return form. It contains general information you may need and box by box advice.

Company information

Company name

Company registration number

Tax Reference as shown on the CT603

Type of company

Registered office address

Postcode

About this return

This is the above company's return for the period

from (dd/mm/yyyy)   to (dd/mm/yyyy)

Put an 'X' in the appropriate box(es) below

A repayment is due for this return period

A repayment is due for an earlier period

Making more than one return for this company now

This return contains estimated figures

Company part of a group that is not small

Disclosure of tax avoidance schemes

Notice of disclosable avoidance schemes

Transfer pricing

Compensating adjustment claimed

Company qualifies for SME exemption

Accounts
I attach accounts and computations

• for the period to which this return relates

• for a different period

If you are not attaching accounts and computations, say why not

Supplementary Pages
If you are enclosing any Supplementary Pages put an 'X' in the appropriate box(es)

Loans to participators by close companies, form *CT600A*

Charities and Community Amateur Sports Clubs (CASCs), form *CT600E*

Disclosure of tax avoidance schemes, form *CT600J*

HMRC 09/08

CT600 (Short) (2008) Version 2

Page 2

Company tax calculation

Turnover

1	Total turnover from trade or profession	**1** £

Income

3	Trading and professional profits	**3** £
4	Trading losses brought forward claimed against profits	**4** £
5	Net trading and professional profits	box 3 minus box 4 **5** £
6	Bank, building society or other interest, and profits and gains from non-trading loan relationships	**6** £
11	Income from UK land and buildings	**11** £
14	Annual profits and gains not falling under any other heading	**14** £

Chargeable gains

16	Gross chargeable gains	**16** £
17	Allowable losses including losses brought forward	**17** £
18	Net chargeable gains	box 16 minus box 17 **18** £
21	**Profits before other deductions and reliefs**	sum of boxes 5, 6, 11, 14 & 18 **21** £

Deductions and Reliefs

24	Management expenses under S75 ICTA 1988	**24** £
30	Trading losses of this or a later accounting period under S393A ICTA 1988	**30** £
31	Put an 'X' in box 31 if amounts carried back from later accounting periods are included in box 30	**31**
32	Non-trade capital allowances	**32** £
35	Charges paid	**35** £
37	**Profits chargeable to corporation tax**	box 21 minus boxes 24, 30, 32 and 35 **37** £

Tax calculation

38	Franked investment income	**38** £
39	Number of associated companies in this period **or**	**39**
40	Associated companies in the first financial year	**40**
41	Associated companies in the second financial year	**41**
42	Put an 'X' in box 42 if the company claims to be charged at the starting rate or the small companies' rate on any part of its profits, or is claiming marginal rate relief	**42**

Enter how much profit has to be charged and at what rate of tax

Financial year (yyyy)	Amount of profit	Rate of tax	Tax
43	**44** £	**45**	**46** £ p
53	**54** £	**55**	**56** £ p

63	Corporation tax	total of boxes 46 and 56 **63** £ p
64	Marginal rate relief	**64** £ p
65	Corporation tax net of marginal rate relief	**65** £ p
66	Underlying rate of corporation tax	**66** • %
67	Profits matched with non-corporate distributions	**67**
68	Tax at non-corporate distributions rate	**68** £ p
69	Tax at underlying rate on remaining profits	**69** £ p
70	**Corporation tax chargeable**	See note for box 70 in CT600 Guide **70** £ p

CT600 (Short) (2008) Version 2

Page 3

79	Tax payable under S419 ICTA 1988	**79** £	p
80	Put an 'X' in box 80 if you completed box A11 in the Supplementary Pages CT600A	**80**	
84	Income tax deducted from gross income included in profits	**84** £	p
85	Income tax repayable to the company	**85** £	p

86 **Tax payable - this is your self-assessment of tax payable**

total of boxes 70 and 79 minus box 84

86 £   p

Tax reconciliation

91 Tax already paid (and not already repaid)   **91** £   p

box 86 minus box 91

92 Tax outstanding   **92** £   p

box 91 minus box 86

93 Tax overpaid   **93** £   p

Information about capital allowances and balancing charges

Charges and allowances included in calculation of trading profits or losses

		Capital allowances	Balancing charges
172	Annual investment allowance	**172** £	
105 - 106	Machinery and plant - special rate pool	**105** £	**106** £
107 - 108	Machinery and plant - main pool	**107** £	**108** £
109 - 110	Cars	**109** £	**110** £
111 - 112	Industrial buildings and structures	**111** £	**112** £
113 - 114	Other charges and allowances	**113** £	**114** £

Charges and allowances not included in calculation of trading profits or losses

		Capital allowances	Balancing charges
173	Annual investment allowance	**173** £	
115 - 116	Other non-trading charges and allowances	**115** £	**116** £
117	Put an 'X' in box 117 if box 115 includes flat conversion allowances	**117**	

Qualifying expenditure

118	Expenditure on machinery and plant on which first year allowance is claimed	**118** £
174	Designated environmentally friendly machinery and plant	**174** £
120	Machinery and plant on long-life assets and integral features	**120** £
121	Other machinery and plant	**121** £

Losses, deficits and excess amounts

122	Trading losses Case I	calculated under S393 ICTA 1988 **122** £	124	Trading losses Case V	calculated under S393 ICTA 1988 **124** £
125	Non-trade deficits on loan relationships and derivative contracts	calculated under S82 FA 1996 **125** £	127	Schedule A losses	calculated under S392A ICTA 1988 **127** £
129	Overseas property business losses Case V	calculated under S392B ICTA 1988 **129** £	130	Losses Case VI	calculated under S396 ICTA 1988 **130** £
131	Capital losses	calculated under S16 TCGA 1992 **131** £	136	Excess management expenses	calculated under S75 ICTA 1988 **136** £

CT600 (Short) (2008) Version 2

Page 4
Overpayments and repayments

Small repayments

If you do not want us to make small repayments please either put an 'X' in box 139 or complete box 140 below. 'Repayments' here include tax, interest, and late-filing penalties or any combination of them.

Do not repay £20 or less `139`   Do not repay sums of `140` £ _____ or less. *Enter whole figure only*

Bank details (for person to whom the repayment is to be made)

Repayment is made quickly and safely by direct credit to a bank or building society account.
Please complete the following details:

Name of bank or building society   Branch sort code

`149` _____   `150` ☐☐ ☐☐ ☐☐

Account number   Name of account

`151` ☐☐☐☐☐☐☐☐   `152` _____

Building society reference

`153` ☐☐☐☐☐☐☐☐☐☐☐☐☐☐☐☐☐

Payments to a person other than the company

Complete the authority below if you want the repayment to be made to a person other than the company.
I, as *(enter status - company secretary, treasurer, liquidator or authorised agent, etc.)*

`154` _____

of *(enter name of company)*

`155` _____

authorise *(enter name)*

`156` _____

(enter address)

`157`

                               Postcode

Nominee reference

`158` _____

to receive payment on the company's behalf.

Signature

`159`

Name *(in capitals)*

`160` _____

Declaration

Warning - Giving false information in the return, or concealing any part of the company's profits or tax payable, can lead to both the company and yourself being prosecuted.

Declaration
The information I have given in this company tax return is correct and complete to the best of my knowledge and belief.

Signature

Name *(in capitals)*   Date *(dd/mm/yyyy)*

                                               ☐☐☐☐☐☐☐☐

Status

CT600 (Short) (2008) Version 2

We will now use a Case Study to show how the short calculation is completed.

Case Study

COMPLETION PLC:
FILLING IN THE SHORT CT600

Completion plc has the following Corporation Tax computation for the year ended 31 December 2015. It has no associated/group companies. It received dividends of £144,000.

	£	£
Adjusted Trading Profits	600,000	
Less trading loss brought forward	(50,000)	
Assessable Trading Income		550,000
Property Income		120,000
Interest Receivable		110,000
Chargeable Gains	175,000	
Less capital loss brought forward	(35,000)	
		140,000
Taxable total profits		920,000

Augmented profits £920,000 + (£14,000 x 100/90) = £1,080,000

Corporation Tax:

FY2014: (3 months)

£230,000 x 21%		48,300
Less marginal relief:		
1/400 x (375,000 − 270,000) x (230,000 / 270,000)		(224)
		48,076
FY2015		
£690,000 x 20%		138,000
Total Corporation Tax		186,076

required

Complete page 2 of the short company tax return form CT600 for Completion plc for the CAP y/e 31/12/2015.

solution

The completed form is shown on the next page.

Company tax calculation

Turnover

1	Total turnover from trade or profession	(not provided in this case study)	**1** £

Income

3	Trading and professional profits	**3** £600,000	
4	Trading losses brought forward claimed against profits	**4** £50,000	
5	Net trading and professional profits		box 3 minus box 4 **5** £550,000
6	Bank, building society or other interest, and profits and gains from non-trading loan relationships		**6** £110,000
11	Income from UK land and buildings		**11** £ 120,000
14	Annual profits and gains not falling under any other heading		**14** £ -

Chargeable gains

16	Gross chargeable gains	**16** £175,000	
17	Allowable losses including losses brought forward	**17** £35,000	
18	Net chargeable gains		box 16 minus box 17 **18** £140,000
21	**Profits before other deductions and reliefs**		sum of boxes 5, 6, 11, 14 & 18 **21** £ 920,000

Deductions and Reliefs

24	Management expenses under S75 ICTA 1988	**24** £	
30	Trading losses of this or a later accounting period under S393A ICTA 1988	**30** £	
31	Put an 'X' in box 31 if amounts carried back from later accounting periods are included in box 30	**31**	
32	Non-trade capital allowances	**32** £	
35	Charges paid	**35** £	
37	**Profits chargeable to corporation tax**		box 21 minus boxes 24, 30, 32 and 35 **37** £920,000

Tax calculation

38	Franked investment income	**38** £ 160,000	
39	Number of associated companies in this period or	**39** 0	
40	Associated companies in the first financial year	**40**	
41	Associated companies in the second financial year	**41**	
42	Put an 'X' in box 42 if the company claims to be charged at the starting rate or the small companies' rate on any part of its profits, or is claiming marginal rate relief	**42** X	

Enter how much profit has to be charged and at what rate of tax

Financial year (yyyy)	Amount of profit	Rate of tax	Tax	
43 2 0 1 4	**44** £ 230,000	**45** 21%	**46** £48,300	p
53 2 0 1 5	**54** £ 690,000	**55** 20%	**56** £138,000	p
			total of boxes 46 and 56 **63** £ 186,300	p

63	Corporation tax		
64	Marginal rate relief	**64** £ 224	p
65	Corporation tax net of marginal rate relief	**65** £ 186,076	p
66	Underlying rate of corporation tax	**66** 20.23 %	
67	Profits matched with non-corporate distributions	**67**	
68	Tax at non-corporate distributions rate	**68** £	p
69	Tax at underlying rate on remaining profits	**69** £	p
70	**Corporation tax chargeable**	See note for box 70 in CT600 Guide **70** £ 186,076	p

CT600 (Short) (2008) Version 2

COMPLETING THE REMAINDER OF THE CT600

The Case Study on the last few pages has explained how page 2 of the CT600 is completed. The top part of page 3 (shown on the next page) is a continuation of the tax amount calculation on page 2, and is self-explanatory. We will now describe the completion of the sections on page 3 dealing with capital allowances and losses.

capital allowances and balancing charges

The following are the boxes that you are most likely to need to use.

You may notice that the numbering of boxes on the form has become a little strange as extra boxes have been inserted by HMRC to cope with legislation changes.

Where capital allowances and / or balancing charges have been included in the calculation of the trading profit (as we would normally do) box 172 plus boxes 105 to 114 will be used for the data, as follows:

Box 172   is for the annual investment allowance being claimed

Box 105   is for the writing down allowance for cars over 130 g/km (and some other assets) that appear in the special rate pool

Box 107   is for the writing down allowance for the main pool.

Boxes 106 and 108 will be used where a balancing charge applies to the relevant pool.

You should not need to use boxes 173, or 109 – 117.

Boxes 118 to 121 are for information on **expenditure** on plant and machinery in various categories.

losses, deficits and excess amounts

This section is for completion where losses have been incurred in the CAP to which the return relates (and which exceed any profits that they can be set against). The only boxes that we may need to complete are:

Box 122   Trading losses

Box 127   Property Income losses ('Schedule A Losses')

Box 131   Capital losses

Page 3

79 Tax payable under S419 ICTA 1988	79	£	p

80 *Put an 'X' in box 80 if you completed box A11 in the Supplementary Pages CT600A*   80 ☐

84 Income tax deducted from gross income included in profits	84	£	p

85 Income tax repayable to the company	85	£	p

total of boxes 70 and 79 minus box 84

86 **Tax payable - this is your self-assessment of tax payable**	86	£	p

Tax reconciliation

91 Tax already paid (and not already repaid)	91	£	p

box 86 minus box 91

92 Tax outstanding	92	£	p

box 91 minus box 86

93 Tax overpaid	93	£	p

Information about capital allowances and balancing charges

Charges and allowances included in calculation of trading profits or losses

		Capital allowances	Balancing charges
172	Annual investment allowance	172 £	
105 - 106	Machinery and plant - special rate pool	105 £	106 £
107 - 108	Machinery and plant - main pool	107 £	108 £
109 - 110	Cars	109 £	110 £
111 - 112	Industrial buildings and structures	111 £	112 £
113 - 114	Other charges and allowances	113 £	114 £

Charges and allowances not included in calculation of trading profits or losses

		Capital allowances	Balancing charges
173	Annual investment allowance	173 £	
115 - 116	Other non-trading charges and allowances	115 £	116 £
117	*Put an 'X' in box 117 if box 115 includes flat conversion allowances*	117 ☐	

Qualifying expenditure

118 Expenditure on machinery and plant on which first year allowance is claimed	118	£
174 Designated environmentally friendly machinery and plant	174	£
120 Machinery and plant on long-life assets and integral features	120	£
121 Other machinery and plant	121	£

Losses, deficits and excess amounts

122 Trading losses Case I	*calculated under S393 ICTA 1988* 122 £	124 Trading losses Case V	*calculated under S393 ICTA 1988* 124 £
125 Non-trade deficits on loan relationships and derivative contracts	*calculated under S82 FA 1996* 125 £	127 Schedule A losses	*calculated under S392A ICTA 1988* 127 £
129 Overseas property business losses Case V	*calculated under S392B ICTA 1988* 129 £	130 Losses Case VI	*calculated under S396 ICTA 1988* 130 £
131 Capital losses	*calculated under S16 TCGA 1992* 131 £	136 Excess management expenses	*calculated under S75 ICTA 1988* 136 £

INTEREST AND PENALTIES

interest

Where tax is paid after the due date (or a lower amount is paid than is due) interest is charged. This applies both to large companies that need to pay by instalments, and other companies that should pay nine months and one day after the end of the CAP. The interest rates are laid down by HM Revenue & Customs. The rates charged are currently 1.5% for underpaid quarterly instalments and 3% on late final payments.

If a company overpays its Corporation Tax (or pays early) interest is payable to the company (although the interest rates are generally lower than amounts charged on overdue tax – it is currently 0.5%). Interest that is paid to the Company is taxable, but interest payable is an allowable deduction against non-trading interest.

penalties for not telling HMRC your company is liable for Corporation Tax

HMRC must be made aware that the company is liable to pay tax (for example if the company has just started trading). This must be done within three months of the start of business activities. This is usually done on a 'new company details' form.

If HMRC are not informed, then a penalty can arise. The penalty will be based on a percentage of the 'potential lost revenue' which is the Corporation tax that would be due. The penalty ranges from 0% (if 'reasonable care was taken) to 100% (if the act was deliberate and concealed) of the potential lost revenue.

This is the same system that applies to errors in tax returns and is explained on the next page.

late return penalties

There are also penalties for failure to submit a Corporation Tax Return on time. These are divided into flat amount and percentage penalties:

■ the initial penalties are £100 for submitting up to three months late and £200 for submitting more than three months late. These can increase for repeated occurences

■ in addition 10% of the Corporation Tax relating to the return period can be charged where the return is 6-12 months late, increasing to 20% for over 12 months

penalties system for errors in tax returns and documents

A system for penalties applies for incorrect information stated in tax returns and documents. This is based on a percentage of the extra tax due, depending on the behaviour that gave rise to the error. If the error is:

- due to **lack of reasonable care**, the penalty will be between 0% and 30% of the extra tax due

- **deliberate**, the penalty will be between 20% and 70% of the extra tax due, and if

- **deliberate and concealed**, the penalty will be between 30% and 100% of the extra tax due

The percentage can be reduced if the taxpayer tells HMRC about the error(s), helps them work out the extra tax, and gives HMRC access to check the figures.

If the taxpayer made an error despite taking 'reasonable care' then no penalty will arise.

This system also applies to Income Tax.

failure to keep records

There can be a penalty for not keeping the required records for the correct length of time of up to £3,000 per chargeable accounting period for companies.

KEEPING RECORDS

general principles

Accounting records must be retained by a business, including a company, or its agent (for example an accountant) for at least six years after the end of the accounting period. This period is extended if an enquiry is taking place.

A business will normally archive appropriate accounting records automatically for six years to satisfy the requirements of a variety of statutes, including the Companies Acts and the Limitation Act (which allows legal action to be brought on a contract for up to six years after a breach of that contract). Documents such as invoices, for example, are evidence of contracts of sale.

These records will need to be made available for a number of interested parties – and particularly in the unfortunate event of an inspection or investigation being made:

- auditors (when an audit is required)
- HM Revenue & Customs for both Corporation taxes and VAT
- Department of Work & Pensions

Typical records include:

- ledger accounts and daybooks - manual or computerised
- financial documents, eg invoices, credit notes, bank statements, cheque book stubs
- payroll records
- VAT records

records relating to tax computations

A company will need to keep for at least six years, as part of the general archiving process, a number of records which specifically relate to Corporation Tax matters. These include:

- statements of profit or loss (income statements) and statements of financial position (balance sheets)
- taxation working papers, including capital allowance computations
- copies of tax returns
- invoices relating to allowable expenses and the acquisition of non-current (fixed) assets
- details of non-trade income
- non-current asset schedules

time limits for assessments and claims

Where a company discovers an error in a previous year's tax return and wants to adjust the return (perhaps to claim a tax repayment) the time limit is four years from the end of the tax year.

The same four year limit applies to HMRC when they discover errors in returns (as discussed earlier), provided the company has taken reasonable care. If the errors are the result of careless behaviour by the company the time limit is six years, and if the behaviour was deliberate the time limit is twenty years.

Chapter Summary

- The Corporation Tax computation for a chargeable accounting period (CAP) involves combining profits from various sources, and deducting any payments made to charity under the gift aid scheme.

- For CAPs falling entirely within FY2015 a single rate of Corporation Tax of 20% applies to the taxable total profits (TTP).

- For CAPs falling wholly or partly into FY2014, an 'augmented profits' figure is calculated by adding UK dividends (x 100/90) to the taxable total profits (TTP). Where this figure is £1,500,001 or over for a 12 month period Corporation Tax is payable at the main rate. Where it is below this figure, a different rate or marginal relief applies, according to which band the 'augmented profit' figure falls into.

- The band limits are scaled down where there are associated companies, and where the CAP is for less than 12 months.

- Property income losses are initially set against the taxable total profits of the current period, with any remaining balance carried forward to be set against the first available taxable total profit. Capital losses can only be carried forward to offset against income of the same type. There are various options for dealing with trade losses. Since the marginal rate of Corporation Tax has the highest effective rate, profits within this band should be reduced by losses when possible.

- Corporation Tax is payable a maximum of nine months and one day after the end of the CAP. For 'large' companies, instalments may need to be paid, based on the estimated tax payable.

- The company tax return (CT600) is due to be submitted twelve months after the end of the accounting period.

- Appropriate records must be kept for at least six years from the end of the accounting period.

**Key
Terms**

Taxable total profits (TTP)

this is the figure used as the basis for calculation of Corporation Tax for a limited company. It includes trading income, profits from investments, and chargeable gains, and is charged after gift-aid payments have been deducted. It is calculated for each chargeable accounting period (CAP) within which the company operates

Chargeable Accounting Period (CAP)

this is the period for which the TTP must be calculated. It is the same as the period for which the company produces financial accounts, unless that period is for more than twelve months. In that case the financial accounting period is divided into two CAPs

Gift-Aid

a system which allows payments that companies have made to charity to be deducted in the final calculation of taxable total profits. This provides the company with tax relief on the payment

Franked Investment Income (FII)

this non-taxable income is calculated by multiplying UK dividends received by 100/90. The FII amount is added to the taxable total profits to arrive at the 'augmented profits' figure that is used to establish the rate of Corporation Tax that is payable in FY2014

'Augmented Profits'

this figure is the taxable total profits plus FII. It is used to establish the size of the company, which in turn determines the rate of Corporation Tax that is payable in FY2014

Marginal Relief

a deduction from Corporation Tax calculated at the full rate that applies at some 'profit' levels in FY2014

Associated companies

companies are associated for Corporation Tax purposes when they are part of a group of companies, or are all controlled by the same person. The Corporation Tax band limits in FY2014 are divided by the number of associated companies

CT600

the self-assessment Corporation Tax return for limited companies. One form must be completed for each CAP

Activities

5.1 The Management Company Limited has produced accounts for the year ended 31/3/16. The accounts have been adjusted for tax purposes, and the following figures have been established.

	£
Adjusted Trading Profit (before capital allowances)	1,120,000
Capital Allowances – Plant & Machinery	83,000
Payment to Charity under Gift-Aid scheme	45,000
Non-Trade Interest Receivable	60,000
Dividends Received from UK Company	90,000
Chargeable Gains	48,000
Rental Income	23,000

Required:

Using a Corporation Tax Computation, calculate the taxable total profits for the CAP, and the Corporation Tax payable.

Carry out all calculations to the nearest £.

5.2 The Resource Company Limited has produced accounts for the year ended 31/3/15. The accounts have been adjusted for tax purposes, and the following figures have been established.

	£
Adjusted Trading Profit (before capital allowances)	1,420,000
Capital Allowances – Plant & Machinery	205,000
Payment to Charity under Gift-Aid scheme	8,000
Non-Trade Interest Receivable	12,000
Dividends Received from UK Company	27,000
Chargeable Gains	88,000
Capital Loss brought forward from previous year	18,000
Rental Income	92,000

Required:

Using a Corporation Tax Computation, calculate the taxable total profits for the CAP, and the Corporation Tax payable.

Carry out all calculations to the nearest £.

5.3 The Quick Company Limited has the following tax-adjusted results for the CAP y/e 31/12/15.

	£
Trading Loss	120,000
Chargeable Gains	90,000
Non-trade Interest Receivable	40,000
Rental Income	35,000
Gift-Aid Payment	10,000

The company also has capital losses brought forward of £8,000, and rental losses brought forward of £13,000.

The company wishes to obtain any relief for the offset of its trading loss as quickly as possible, and will therefore set it against the TTP of the current CAP.

Required:

Using a Corporation Tax Computation, calculate the taxable total profits for the CAP, and the Corporation Tax payable.

Carry out all calculations to the nearest £.

State an alternative option that may be available to this company for offsetting its trading loss.

5.4 Trade Trader Ltd has an unadjusted income statement for the year ended 30/9/2015 as follows:

	£	£
Sales		720,000
less cost of sales		400,000
Gross profit		320,000
Interest receivable		50,000
Profit on disposal of non-current assets		50,000
Rental income receivable		40,000
		460,000
less expenses:		
Discounts allowed	11,000	
Salaries and wages	70,000	
Depreciation	41,000	
Bad debts written off	12,000	
Rates and insurance	13,000	
Postage and stationery	10,000	
Administration expenses	14,000	
Advertising	18,000	
Travel and entertaining	20,000	
		209,000
Net Profit		251,000

Notes:

- Administration includes £1,000 directors' speeding fines incurred while on company business.

- Advertising consists of:
    - gifts of CDs with company logos to 1000 customers totalled £8,000
    - gifts of food hampers with company logos to 400 other customers totalled £10,000

- Travel and entertaining is made up as follows:

	£
Employees' travel expenses	7,400
Employees' subsistence allowances	3,600
Entertaining customers	6,000
Entertaining staff on company trip to theme park	3,000
	20,000

The interest receivable is non-trade.

The profit on sale of non-current assets resulted in a chargeable gain of £41,000.

The rental income is assessable as Property Income, and the figure in the accounts can be used for tax purposes.

Capital allowances for the period have been calculated at £11,000.

Required:

1   Adjust the net profit shown to arrive at the trading income assessment for Corporation Tax purposes.

2   Calculate the taxable total profits.

3   Calculate the Corporation Tax payable.

4   Complete page 2 of tax return CT600.
     (A blank form is reproduced in the Appendix of this book or may be downloaded from the Student Resource pages of www.osbornebooks.co.uk or from www.hmrc.gov.uk)

Carry out all calculations to the nearest £.

5.5   Mastermind Limited is changing its accounting dates, and to accommodate this has produced one long set of financial accounts, from 1/4/2014 to 31/7/2015.

Capital allowances have already been calculated for each of the two CAPs as follows:

CAP 1/4/2014 to 31/3/2015	£8,000
CAP 1/4/2015 to 31/7/2015	£2,500

The financial accounts for the 16 months to 31/7/2015 are as follows:

	£	£
Sales		293,000
less cost of sales		155,000
Gross profit		138,000
add		
bad debts recovered		3,100
discounts received		2,000
		143,100
less expenses:		
Salaries and wages	68,500	
Rent, rates, and insurance	9,200	
Depreciation etc.	10,000	
General expenses	15,630	
Interest payable	8,300	
Bad debts written off	12,400	
Selling expenses	15,000	
		139,030
Net Profit		4,070

The following information is also provided:

- depreciation etc is made up as follows:

– Depreciation	£45,000
– Loss on sale of computer	£19,500
– Profit on sale of Building	£54,500

- general expenses include debt recovery fees of £800

- selling expenses include:

  - Entertaining customers   £1,930

  - Gifts of diaries to customers   £600
    (£6 each, with company advert)

The profit on the sale of the building resulted in a chargeable gain of £45,000 on 1/6/2015.

There were no other chargeable gains in either CAP.

Required:

- Adjust the financial accounts for the 16-month period, before deduction of capital allowances.

- Time-apportion the adjusted profit figure into CAPs.

- Calculate the trading income assessment for each CAP.

- Calculate the taxable total profits for each CAP.

- Calculate the Corporation Tax payable in respect of each CAP.

Carry out all calculations to the nearest £.

5.6   Tick the appropriate box for each of the following statements:

	True	False
(a) If a company is five months late in submitting their tax return, they will receive a fixed penalty of £200.		
(b) Penalties for errors made by companies in their tax return vary from 20% to 100%.		
(c) If a company fails to keep records for the appropriate period of time, they can be fined £3,000.		
(d) A company with a period of account ending on 30 April 2015 must keep their records until 30 April 2021.		

5.7 A company has the following information for the year ended 31 December 2015:

- Taxable total profits £625,000

- Dividends received (net amount) £49,500

- The company has one associated company.

Complete the following table to calculate the Corporation Tax payable;

	Financial Year 2014 £	Financial Year 2015 £
Taxable total profits		
Augmented profits		
Max of band		
Tax at main rate		
Marginal Relief		
Tax re Financial Year		
Total Corporation Tax for CAP		

6 Income tax – trading profits

this chapter covers...

In this chapter we turn our attention to the trading profits of sole traders and partnerships – these are taxed under Income Tax. Some of the treatment of these profits is similar to those examined under Corporation Tax, but there are many important differences.

We start by learning about what is considered 'trading' and therefore come under the rules that we are going to study. The factors that help determine that a business is being carried out are called the 'badges of trade'.

We then go on to examine the normal basis of assessment for trading income, and also learn about allowable and non-allowable expenditure for sole traders and partners and see where it differs from the situation for limited companies.

Next we examine the calculation of capital allowances, and see the similarities and important differences compared with Corporation tax.

Finally we will look at offset of trading losses for sole traders and partnerships. Here again there are similarities, but also important differences between the Income tax rules and those for Corporation tax.

INTRODUCTION TO BUSINESS TAXATION OF INDIVIDUALS

In this book so far we have provided an introduction to the taxes that apply to business in the UK, and looked in detail at the way that Corporation Tax is applied to various types of profits of limited companies.

In the remaining chapters of this book we are going to examine how the trading profits and gains of business are subject to Income Tax and Capital Gains Tax. This applies to organisations that have not been formed as limited companies, but are operated by individuals who are sole traders or partners.

The business activities of these individuals are not legally separate from their personal financial interests, and therefore they are subject to Income Tax and Capital Gains Tax on their income and gains from all sources. The learning area 'Personal Tax' (covered in Osborne Books' *Personal Tax* text) examines how Income Tax and Capital Gains Tax is calculated. In this book we will examine the impact of these taxes on individuals' **business** profits and gains.

WHAT IS TRADING?

In order to appreciate the way that Income Tax applies to those who operate a trade, we must first understand exactly what constitutes **trading** from a tax point of view. Nearly all of us buy and sell things from time to time (for example we may change our cars regularly), but we usually wouldn't think of ourselves as traders. It is important to distinguish between a trading and non-trading situation, since

- trading carried out by an individual is assessable to Income Tax as 'Trading Income'
- non-trading activities may be subject to Capital Gains Tax, or may be outside the scope of all taxation

HM Revenue & Customs use several tests known as 'the badges of trade' to help decide whether they believe an activity should be classed as trading. The result of each of these tests will provide evidence in one direction or the other, and the final decision will be judged on the overall weight of evidence. These tests are described below.

the badges of trade

- **profit motive**

    Where profit is clearly the driving force behind the activity, then this is a strong indicator that the activity may constitute trading.

- **subject matter of the activity**

  Where the items bought and sold are of no personal use to the individual then this is further evidence of trading, and this case is strengthened if the individual already works in a situation where such items are traded. Where, however the items are used by the individual or can provide personal pleasure then this would be evidence that the activity is not trading.

- **length of ownership**

  Where items are sold shortly after acquisition then this is an indicator of trading. Where they are held for a long period it may provide evidence that it is not trading.

- **frequency of transactions**

  Where there is a series of similar transactions, then this indicates trading. A single transaction is less likely to be considered as trading.

- **supplementary work**

  Where the individual carries out work on the items (eg repairs) to make them more saleable, this is evidence of trading.

- **reasons for acquisition and sale**

  An intentional purchase and planned sale will provide evidence of trading. An item that was given to the individual, or one that was sold quickly to raise money to pay personal debts is less likely to constitute trading.

These tests will also apply (as far as possible) when considering whether the provision of a service amounts to a business.

We will now illustrate the use of these indicators with a Case Study.

Case Study

DAN THE BANGER MAN: BADGES OF TRADE

Dan works as an assistant accountant, but in his spare time will often be found working on one of his cars in his garage. He usually owns a couple of cars at the same time – one to drive around in and one that he is repairing. He goes to a car auction about once every six weeks and buys a car that needs a little work, provided it is at a good price. After he has repaired the car he usually keeps it for a few weeks to use, before advertising it in his local paper and selling it, so that he can obtain the best price. Dan regards this activity as his hobby.

required

Using the badges of trade, identify:
- the points that indicate that Dan is trading
- the points that suggest non-trading

Explain what conclusion you would reach from the balance of evidence.

solution

The badges of trade can be interpreted as follows:

- **Profit motive**

  Dan seems to deliberately buy and sell at a profit. He buys only at auction, and sets his own selling price through his adverts. This indicates trading.

- **Subject matter**

  Dan gets personal use from the cars that he buys, and this could indicate that he is not trading. The fact that he is not employed in the car trade helps this argument.

- **Length of ownership**

  After repairing the cars, Dan only keeps them for a few weeks. Such a short time indicates trading.

- **Frequency of transactions**

  The buying and selling of cars seems to be a regular activity, with purchases being made about every six weeks. This indicates trading.

- **Supplementary work**

  Repairing the cars counts as supplementary work, and Dan deliberately buys cars that need work carrying out. This indicates trading.

- **Reason for acquisition and sale**

  Acquisition appears to be planned with the ultimate sale in mind. This indicates trading.

In conclusion . . .

Overall, nearly all indicators point to trading. The only point that indicates the opposite is that Dan uses the cars before sale. The fact that he views his activity as a hobby is not relevant in the face of such evidence.

It is likely that HM Revenue & Customs would wish to assess his income from this activity as Trading Income.

notification of starting trading

When an individual starts trading he/she must notify HM Revenue and Customs. The time limit is within 6 months of the end of the tax year for Income Tax and NIC purposes. HMRC will then arrange to tax the income as 'Trading Income' under the self-assessment system as described in the next section.

THE BASIS OF ASSESSMENT OF TRADING PROFITS

Trading profits (both for sole traders and those in partnership) and professional profits are assessed to Income Tax as 'Trading Income'.

The trading income assessment for a sole trader will form part of his/her income that is taxable under Income Tax, and will be incorporated into the personal Income Tax computation. We examined this briefly in Chapter 1, and you may also have studied it in the 'personal tax' learning area.

The assessable trading profits of a partnership are divided between the partners according to the partnership agreement, and each partner's share then forms part of their individual Income Tax computation.

basis period for assessment

Sole traders and partnerships can produce their annual accounts up to any date in the year that they choose. Once the business is established, most accounting years will consistently follow the same pattern.

Income Tax is assessed based on tax years (6 April to the following 5 April), so that all income (both business and personal) can be brought together and the tax calculated. This means that a link must be established between the profits that are generated in an accounting period and a particular tax year. This mechanism is part of the basis of assessment, and is known as the **basis period**.

For a continuing business this link is very straightforward. The normal basis of assessment for trading income is the adjusted profits for the accounting period that ends in the tax year. So for a business that produces its accounts each year to 31 December, the basis period for the tax year 2015/16 would be the accounting period 1/1/2015 to 31/12/2015.

The term 'adjusted profits' refers to profits (on an accruals basis) that have been adjusted for tax purposes, and incorporate any capital allowances. This procedure is very similar to the one that we studied in Chapters 2 and 3 in connection with Corporation Tax for limited companies.

The procedure that we need to use is summarised in the diagram on the next page. This diagram will also be useful later on, when we examine the more complicated basis of assessments that apply to businesses when they are starting trading or ceasing trading.

ADJUSTING THE TRADING PROFITS OF AN ACCOUNTING PERIOD

The procedure for adjusting profits for sole traders and partnerships is very similar to the one used for companies in Chapter 2. This means that you can use a lot of the knowledge gained in that area and apply it to this situation. We will firstly review the way that the procedure works, and then identify the main differences that you will encounter when dealing with trading under Income Tax rules in comparison with Corporation Tax.

review of adjusting profits

The object of adjusting the financial accounts is to make sure that:

■ the only income that is credited is trading income

■ the only expenditure that is deducted is allowable trading expenditure

When we adjust profits, we will start with the profit from the financial accounts, and

■ deduct any income that is not trading income, and

■ add back any expenditure that has already been deducted but is not allowable

adjusting income

Provided that the 'sales' amount relates entirely to trading, this figure will not need adjusting. Other income may or may not be taxable, but if it does not fall under trading income, then it will need to be adjusted for in the trading profit calculation. The following examples of non-trading income that were given in Chapter 2 are also valid in this situation:

■ non-trading interest receivable

■ rent receivable

■ gains on the disposal of non-current (fixed) assets

■ dividends received

adjusting expenditure

We will only need to adjust for any expenditure accounted for in the financial accounts profit if it is not allowable. We do this by adding it back to the financial accounts profit. Expenditure that is allowable can be left unadjusted in the accounts.

The general rule for expenditure to be allowable in a trading income computation is that it must be:

■ revenue rather than capital in nature, and

■ 'wholly and exclusively' for the purpose of the trade

Expenditure that has a 'dual purpose' is therefore strictly speaking not allowable in its entirety (for example travel expenses for a trip combining a business conference and a holiday). However expenditure that can be divided into a part that was wholly business and a part that is wholly private could be apportioned and have the business portion allowed. This could apply to motoring expenses.

Members of the sole trader or partner's family are sometimes employed in their business – for example spouses or children. This will be an allowable expense provided the amount paid is reasonable for the work carried out. For example, paying a son or daughter £40,000 per year for occasional help in the office would not be an allowable deduction (but £5,000 may be). If a relative is employed then PAYE would need to be applied to their earnings in the normal way.

adjusting accounts of companies and individuals

■ **issues not arising for sole traders and partnerships**

The following items will not appear in the accounts that we will be adjusting for Income Tax purposes:

- dividends payable

- Corporation Tax

- payments to directors

■ **issues arising only for sole traders and partnerships**

- private expenditure of the owner(s) – this is non-allowable expenditure.

This could arise where entirely private expenditure had been paid through the business accounts (eg a personal electricity bill), or where certain expenditure needs to be apportioned between business and personal use. This latter situation is possible for expenditure such as motor expenses where business and private mileage could be used to apportion the total cost. As we will see later, there is a similar adjustment that is made to capital allowances on items with some private use.

- drawings of the owner(s) – these are not allowable deductions.

If the accounts have been produced following normal good accounting practice, then drawings will not appear before the net profit figure, and therefore no adjustment will be necessary. However some accounts may have been prepared to include drawing in the profit calculation, possibly under the heading of 'wages' and here the figure must be added back in the adjustment.

- taking trading goods out of the business for private use – this is also non-allowable, but requires particular care.

In contrast to normal accounting practice, these goods need to be accounted for tax purposes at their normal selling price. This means that any profit that would have been made by selling the goods normally through the business is still assessable. If there is no other specific information to guide you, the normal mark-up profit percentage (from the accounts) should be added to the cost price when adjusting the accounts.

We will now summarise some common expenditure items that are allowable and non-allowable in the form of a table. We will then illustrate the points by means of a Case Study.

Allowable Expenditure	Non-Allowable Expenditure
Revenue expenditure wholly & exclusively for trade	Capital expenditure and private revenue expenditure
Cost of sales	Goods for private use
Staff salaries & wages (including relatives if amount paid is in line with work carried out). (including employers' NIC)	Drawings of owner(s), (including self-employed NIC, pension payments and Income Tax). Excessive payments for employing relatives.
Entertaining staff	Entertaining customers or suppliers
Certain gifts to customers (up to £50 each p.a., not food, drink, tobacco or vouchers)	All other gifts to customers
Trade bad debts written off	Non-trade bad debts written off
Increases in specific bad debt provisions	Increases in general bad debt provisions
Staff fines for minor motoring offences (e.g. parking)	All other fines for lawbreaking (owners and staff)
Capital allowances	Depreciation

<table>
<tr><td>**Case Study**</td></tr>
</table>

THE SOLE TRADER:
ADJUSTING TRADING PROFITS

Rachel Sole is a fishmonger, operating under the trade name of 'The Sole Trader'.

Her draft accounts for the year are as follows:

	£	£
Sales		64,000
less cost of sales:		
Opening inventory (stock)	6,000	
Purchases	30,000	
	36,000	
less closing inventory (stock)	4,000	
		32,000
Gross profit		32,000
add: building society interest rec'd		600
		32,600
less expenses:		
Rent, Rates & Insurance	1,500	
Part Time Employee's Wages	5,500	
Employers' NIC for Part Time Employee	112	
Depreciation on Fittings	1,250	
Increase in General Provision for Bad Debts	550	
General Expenses	1,450	
Purchase of new Freezer Cabinet	1,000	
Wages drawn for self	15,100	
Personal pension contribution for self	400	
		26,862
Net Profit		5,738

Notes:

1   Rachel pays the combined electricity bill for the shop and her private flat out of her personal bank account. The amount relating to the shop is calculated at £250.

2   Rachel took fish from her shop throughout the year to eat at home. The purchases figure in the accounts of £30,000 is after deducting the £1,000 cost price of this fish. Rachel's normal mark-up is 100% on cost.

3   Capital allowances have been calculated at £2,500 for the accounting period.

required

Calculate the trading income assessment for Rachel.

solution

	£
Net Profit per accounts	5,738

Add Back:

Expenditure that is shown in the accounts but is not allowable

Depreciation	1,250
Increase in General Bad Debt Provision	550
Capital expenditure (freezer)	1,000
Drawings	15,100
Personal pension contributions	400
Adjustment to reflect profit in goods taken for own use	1,000
	25,038

Deduct:

Income that is not taxable as trading income	£	
Building Society Interest Received	600	
Allowable expenditure not shown in accounts		
Electricity for business	250	
Capital Allowances	2,500	
		(3,350)
Trading Income Assessment		21,688

Note:

The adjustment for notional profit on the fish taken out of inventory is based on the normal mark up of 100% of cost. This increases the value of the fish taken out of the business to its normal selling price. The mark up could also have been calculated from the accounts, where gross profit/cost of sales = 100%.

If the transaction deducting the fish at cost from the purchases had not been recorded in the accounts already, a total adjustment of £2,000 would have been required.

CAPITAL ALLOWANCES UNDER INCOME TAX

You will be relieved to learn that the calculation of capital allowances for plant & machinery under Income Tax is nearly identical to the system under Corporation Tax. Before you study this section, you may find it useful to revise capital allowances as they apply to Corporation Tax.

There are three main issues that are important regarding the capital allowances for a sole trader or partnership.

- Capital allowances are calculated for the accounting period, and are treated as allowable expenditure. If the accounting period is for less than 12 months, or between 12 months and 18 months, writing down allowances only are time apportioned. This is consistent with the treatment under Corporation Tax, although you will recall that CAPs over 12 months long do not exist under that system.

- The same annual investment allowance (AIA) that is available to limited companies is also available to sole traders and partnerships for acquisitions of plant and machinery. The limits of £500,000 or £25,000 or a hybrid figure for a 12-month period (time-apportioned for shorter or longer accounting periods) is also the same as for companies.

- Assets that have some private use by the owner(s) of the business are treated in a special way for plant & machinery capital allowances purposes, since only the business proportion of any allowance can be claimed. The general rule is that any asset with part private use must be held in a 'single asset pool', and the initial calculations of the allowances and balances carried forward are carried out as normal. However, only the business proportion of all allowances and charges that apply to that asset can be claimed. So, a car with part private use would need to enter its own single asset pool. The writing down allowance on the car would be calculated as normal, but only the business proportion of the allowance would be claimed as a capital allowance.

If an asset with part private use (other than a car) was acquired then it would be entitled to the Annual Investment Allowance (AIA). However only the business proportion of the AIA could be claimed. For the purpose of determining whether expenditure breaches the AIA limit, the whole of the expenditure on assets with part private use is counted – not just the business proportion. However the taxpayer can choose which assets to claim AIA on if the total expenditure is over the limit.

This is the main practical difference between preparing capital allowances under income tax and corporation tax, and can cause confusion. Remember that companies do not have private use, and therefore no private use adjustment applies.

The AIA limit change from £500,000 to £25,000 occurred on 1 January 2016 for income tax payers (self-employed and partners) – the same date as for limited companies. The rules to calculate hybrid AIA limits will apply to accounting periods straddling this point and should therefore be carried out in exactly the same way as we saw earlier in the book. Note that it is the accounting period dates that are important here to determine any time-apportionment, not the dates of the tax year that the accounting period relates to.

We will now use a Case Study to illustrate some of the issues that we have discussed. When you are reading it, make sure, in particular, that you can understand how the private use of assets by the partners (or sole traders) affects the computation.

Case Study

CAPITOL IDEAS:
CAPITAL ALLOWANCES

Capitol Ideas is the trading name of a partnership owned and run by James and Jo Capitol. The business produces accounts to 31 March each year. The adjusted trading profit for the accounting period of 12 months to 31/3/2016 has already been calculated at £84,000 before deduction of capital allowances for plant & machinery.

The capital allowance computation for the last accounting period closed with written down values as follows:

* main pool   £30,000

* single asset pool for car (a BMW) with 25% private use by Jo   £15,000

During the accounting period the following assets were acquired and disposed of:

* a new pick-up truck was bought for £20,000. This was to have 20% private use by James, and was bought in January 2016

* the BMW was sold for £14,000

* a used Audi car was bought for £25,000. This was to replace the BMW, and also had 25% private use by Jo. Emissions level is 120g/km

* a machine in the main pool was sold for £2,000

* a computer system was bought for £5,000 in February 2016

* a Ford car for staff use was bought for £11,000. Emissions level is 115 g/km

All disposal proceeds were less than original cost.

required

* Using a plant & machinery capital allowance computation, calculate the allowances for the accounting period y/e 31/3/2016.

* Calculate the adjusted trading profits for the accounting period (after capital allowances), and state for which tax year these will form the trading income assessable profits.

solution

The capital allowance computation is shown below. The notes that follow provide explanations.

	Main Pool	Car (BMW) 25% private	Car (Audi) 25% private	Pick-up Truck 20% private	Capital Allowances
	£	£	£	£	£
WDV bf	30,000	15,000			
add					
Acquisitions					
without FYA or AIA:					
Ford Car (115g/km)	11,000				
Audi Car (120g/km)					
(25% private use)			25,000		
Acquisitions qualifying for AIA:					
Computer 5,000					
AIA claimed (5,000)	0				5,000
Pick up truck 20,000					
AIA claimed (1,250) x 80%				18,750	1,000
less					
Proceeds of Disposals:					
Machine	(2,000)				
BMW		(14,000)			
	39,000	1,000	25,000	18,750	
WDA 18%	(7,020)		(4,500) x 75%	(3,375) x 80%	13,095
Balancing Allowance		(1,000) x 75%			750
WDV cf	31,980	0	20,500	15,375	
Total Capital Allowances					19,845

Notes:

- The only additions that do not attract AIA or FYAs are the two cars. The Audi has 25% private use so is kept separate, while the Ford joins the main pool. Both cars have emission levels of 130g/km or less and so are entitled to 18% writing down allowances.

- The limit of AIA on purchases in 2016 is £6,250. The £5,000 cost of the computer can be claimed in full, leaving only £1,250 of the cost of the truck eligible for AIA. The £1,250 is then restricted for the 20% private use.

- The disposal proceeds of the machine are deducted from the main pool.

- The WDA on the Audi is £4,500 x 75% business use. Note that the full £4,500 is used to calculate the WDV carried forward.

- The disposal of the BMW was for less than the WDV brought forward. There is therefore a balancing allowance, but this is restricted to the business use of 75%. If a balancing charge had arisen it would also have been restricted to the proportion of business use.

Calculation of trading income assessment:	£
Adjusted trading profits (before capital allowances)	84,000
Capital allowances (as above)	(19,845)
Trading income assessment for tax year 2015/16	64,155

This amount will be then divided between the partners.

DEALING WITH TRADING LOSSES

In Chapters 2 and 5 we saw how trading losses for a limited company can be offset to reduce the amount of Corporation Tax that is payable. We will now examine the equivalent rules that apply to sole traders and partnerships under Income Tax. You will need to take particular care with loss provisions, since some rules under Income Tax and Corporation Tax are similar but not identical, and this can lead to confusion.

In this section we will examine losses that occur in continuing businesses that are using normal twelve month accounting periods. If, once profits for an accounting period have been tax-adjusted and any capital allowances deducted, the result is a minus figure a '**trading loss**' will have arisen. This will have two implications:

- the trading income assessment for the relevant tax year will be zero (not the negative profit figure). This is the tax year in which the accounting period ends – ie the basis period
- the amount of the negative profit figure will form the trading loss, and the individual can choose how to set it off

The choices available are as follows:

1   The trading loss can be carried forward to reduce profits from the same trade in the future. If this option is chosen the loss must be used up as quickly as possible. If the following year's profit from the same trade is less than the loss, then that profit will be reduced to nil and the balance of the loss carried on forward. This will occur as many times as is necessary to offset the whole loss.

2   The trading loss can be used to reduce (or eliminate) the total taxable income in the tax year of the loss. This set-off would be against taxable income from all sources for the relevant tax year.

2(a)   If the trading loss has been set off against total taxable income for the year of the loss, the taxpayer can then set any remaining loss against capital gains of the same year. This extension of the claim is optional.

3   Whether or not option (2) above is chosen, the loss can be carried back against the total taxable income from all sources in the tax year preceding the tax year of the loss. If the tax payer has sufficient loss and wishes to set against both these tax years, he/she can choose which year to set-off the loss first.

3(a)   If the trading loss has been set off against the total taxable income for the year preceeding the loss, the taxpayer can opt to extend the claim to set the loss against any capital gains for that year.

The set off against capital gains in 2(a) and 3(a) is before the annual exempt amount is deducted (see Chapter 8).

Note that one important difference between Income Tax loss set-off and the rules under Corporation Tax is that under Income Tax the order of options 2 and 3 are entirely the taxpayer's choice.

Since the set offs under all the options take place before the personal allowance (currently £10,600) is deducted, there is a danger that this tax-free amount will be wasted in some situations.

The following diagram illustrates the main options using as an example a sole trader making up accounts to the 31 December each year. A loss arises in the year ended 31/12/2014, which forms the basis period of the tax year 2014/15.

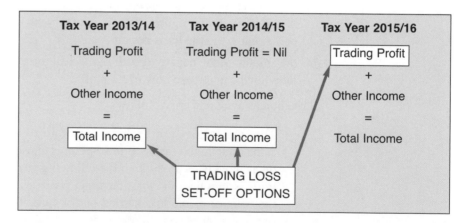

'Other Income' could include property income, employment income, savings income, and dividend income.

Case Study

DOWNHILL TRADING: TRADING LOSS OPTIONS

Downhill Trading is a business operated by Dawn Hill, who sells skiing equipment. The business has the following tax-adjusted trading results for the three twelve month accounting periods to 31/12/2016. Dawn also has other taxable income for the tax years 2014/15 - 2016/17 as stated below.

Accounting periods	y/e 31/12/14	y/e 31/12/15	y/e 31/12/16
	£	£	£
Trading Profit/(Loss)	12,000	(15,000)	16,000
Tax Years	**2014/15**	**2015/16**	**2016/17**
	£	£	£
Other Income	4,000	5,000	5,500

Dawn does not have any capital gains.

required

State the options available for offsetting the £15,000 trading loss incurred in the y/e 31/12/2015. Demonstrate the effects on the relevant total income figures, and comment briefly on the implications of each option.

solution

The tax year of the loss will be 2015/16, since the accounting period y/e 31/12/2015 ends in (i.e. is the basis period for) this tax year. The other two accounting periods (y/e 31/12/2014 and y/e 31/12/2016) form the basis periods for 2014/15 and 2016/17 respectively.

We will show the options one by one, but with all the three tax years' details shown in columnar form for reference. There are four options in this situation.

Option A

The trading loss could be carried forward and set against the trading income assessment of 2016/17. Since this profit is larger than the loss the whole loss could be offset in this way. The three years would look as follows:

	2014/15	2015/16	2016/17
	£	£	£
Trading Profits	12,000	0	16,000
less loss relief			**(15,000)**
			1,000
Other Income	4,000	5,000	5,500
Total Income	16,000	5,000	6,500

An advantage of this option is that there is sufficient total income in each tax year to utilise at least some of Dawn's personal allowances. However Dawn would have to wait until the tax for 2016/17 was payable until she felt the tax benefit of the loss in cash saved.

Option B

The trading loss could be set against the other income of the tax year of the loss (2015/16). Due to the size of the loss this will not be sufficient to offset the whole loss. The balance of the loss could then be carried back to the previous tax year and set against the total income. This would give the following figures.

	2014/15	2015/16	2016/17
	£	£	£
Trading Profits	12,000	0	16,000
Other Income	4,000	5,000	5,500
	16,000	5,000	1,500
less loss relief	**(10,000)**	**(5,000)**	
Total Income	6,000	-	21,500

A disadvantage of this approach would be that the personal allowance in 2015/16 is wasted, since there is no income in that tax year. However, Dawn would get a tax refund for 2014/15 almost immediately, assuming that she had already paid Income Tax based on total income of £16,000.

Option C

The trading loss could be set against the other income of the tax year of the loss (2015/16), as in option B. The balance of the loss could then be carried forward to the next tax year and set against the profits of the same trade only. This would give the following figures.

	2014/15	2015/16	2016/17
	£	£	£
Trading Profits	12,000	0	16,000
less loss relief			**(10,000)**
			6,000
Other Income	4,000	5,000	5,500
	16,000	5,000	11,500
less loss relief	-	**(5,000)**	
Total Income	16,000	-	11,500

A disadvantage of this approach would be that the personal allowance in 2015/16 is wasted, since there is no income in that tax year. Dawn would pay no tax for that year, but would have to wait to feel any further tax effect of the loss until payment of the 2016/17 tax.

Option D

The trading loss could be set against the other income of the previous tax year (2014/15). This would accommodate the whole loss. This would give the following figures:

	2014/15	2015/16	2016/17
	£	£	£
Trading Profits	12,000	0	16,000
Other Income	4,000	5,000	5,500
	16,000	5,000	21,500
less loss relief	**(15,000)**	-	
Total Income	1,000	5,000	21,500

A disadvantage of this approach would be that most of the personal allowance in 2014/15 is wasted, since there is only £1,000 of income in that tax year. However Dawn would get a tax refund for the tax paid for that year almost immediately, assuming she had already paid Income Tax based on a total income of £16,000.

Chapter Summary

■ Trading profits of sole traders and partners are subject to Income Tax, and are included in their computations along with personal income. Evidence indicators called 'badges of trade' are used to establish whether an individual is trading or not.

■ The normal basis of assessment for the trading income of a business is the adjusted profits (after capital allowances) of the accounting period that ends in the tax year. The accounts of sole traders and partnerships are tax-adjusted in a similar way to those of a limited company. Specific expenditure that is non-allowable in arriving at trading profit includes owners' drawings, private expenditure, and trading goods taken from the business for private use.

■ Capital allowances for plant & machinery can be claimed by the self-employed in a similar way to companies. Cars that have a private use element by the business owners need to be kept in a single asset pool, and only the business proportion of the capital allowances can be claimed. The business use part of other assets bought can form a claim for AIA or FYA.

■ Where the adjusted trading profits (after capital allowances) result in a negative figure, the trading income assessment is zero, and a trading loss is formed that can be relieved in several ways. It may be carried forward and set-off against the first available profits of the same trade. It may alternatively be set against the total income of the tax year in which the loss was incurred, and / or the previous tax year. Claims against total income of year of loss and previous tax years can also be extended against capital gains.

Key Terms

Badges of Trade	indicators that are used to determine whether an activity constitutes trading, and should therefore be taxed as such
Basis Period	the term that describes the link between accounting periods and tax years. For a continuing business, the basis period for a particular tax year is the 12-month accounting period that ends in that tax year
Adjusted Trading Profits	trading profits that have been adjusted for tax purposes by excluding income not taxable as trading income and non-allowable expenditure

Trading Income Assessment

the taxable trading profit for the tax year. It is made up of adjusted trading profits for the basis period, after deducting any capital allowances

Plant & Machinery	one of the major non-current asset categories for capital allowance purposes. It includes vehicles and computers

Annual Investment Allowance (AIA)

this is an allowance that can be claimed against the whole cost of most plant and machinery, with the exception of cars. The maximum that can be claimed is £500,000 or £25,000 or a hybrid amount for a 12-month period. This limit is reduced for shorter periods

First Year Allowances	100% First Year Allowances are available on new low-emission cars in the CAP in which the acquisition takes place
Writing Down Allowances	allowances are available at 18% of the pool value for plant and machinery. This figure relates to 12-month accounting periods, and is time-apportioned for shorter periods and longer periods up to 18 months. 8% writing down allowances are available on the balance on the 'special rate pool'

Written Down Value (Plant & Machinery)

this term relates to the balance at the end of an accounting period that remains in a plant & machinery pool. It represents the part of the pool value that has not yet been claimed as allowances, and is carried forward to the next accounting period

Balancing Allowance (Plant & Machinery)

this allowance can be claimed when an asset is sold for less than the written down value (unrelieved expenditure) in a single asset pool

Balancing Charge (Plant & Machinery)

this is the opposite of an allowance, and occurs when the disposal proceeds of an asset in a single asset pool are more than the written down value (unrelieved expenditure). It is in effect a reclaiming of allowances previously obtained

Trading Loss

this occurs when the adjusted trading profits after deducting capital allowances produces a negative figure. The negative figure is the trading loss, whilst the trading income assessment is zero

Loss Relief

the offsetting of the trading loss against profits or total income etc (plus capital gains if elected), according to legislation. This may be against future profits from the same trade, or against total income of the current and / or previous tax year

Activities

6.1 Michelle Flatley has moved home seven times in the last five years, and currently lives in a house valued at £500,000. Her first property was a small studio apartment that she was left by her uncle. It was valued at £40,000. After carrying out some renovations she moved in, and stayed three months before selling the property for £60,000 and investing the proceeds in her next flat. She has continued this procedure with all the properties that she has owned, always renovating with a view to a prospective buyer, and always making a profit by timing the sale carefully.

Required:

Using each of the 'badges of trade', explain the issues that provide evidence that she is trading, and those that point to non-trading.

6.2 The following items appear in a sole trader's income statement (profit and loss account), before the net profit figure. You are calculating an adjusted trading profit for tax purposes. State in each case whether:

- the item should be added to the net profit, or

- the item should be deducted from the net profit, or

- the item should be ignored

1 depreciation of vehicles

2 loss on sale of non-current assets

3 building society interest received

4 dividends received

5 owner's drawings

6 profit on sale of non-current asset

7 increase in general provision for bad debts

8 gifts of food hampers (with company adverts) to customers, costing £45 per recipient.

9 decrease in specific bad debt provision

10 owner's self-employed national insurance contribution

11 employers' national insurance contributions regarding employees

12 owner's private expenses

6.3 Vikram Singh is in business as a sole trader. The unadjusted income statement for the year ended 31/1/2016 is as follows:

	£	£
Sales		700,000
less cost of sales		420,000
Gross profit		280,000
Bank interest received		12,000
Rental income		10,000
		302,000
less expenses:		
Salaries and wages	78,000	
Depreciation	22,000	
Loss on sale of non-current assets	4,000	
Administration expenses	11,600	
Advertising	8,000	
Overdraft interest payable	2,000	
Travel and entertaining	10,000	
Pension contributions	7,400	
Bad debts and provisions	15,000	
		158,000
Net Profit		144,000

Notes:
- Salaries and wages include £18,000 drawn by Vikram.
- Advertising includes:
  - gift-vouchers given to 100 top customers £3,000
  - gifts of diaries with company logos to 200 other customers £1,000
- Travel and entertaining is made up as follows:

	£
Employees' travel expenses	2,000
Vikram's business travel expenses	3,500
Entertaining customers	4,500
	10,000

- Pension contributions consist of:

Contribution regarding employees	5,000
Contribution regarding Vikram	2,400
	7,400

- Bad debts and provisions is made up of:

Trade bad debts written off	10,400
Increase in specific bad debt provision	4,600
	15,000

- Capital allowances for the accounting period have been calculated at £23,000.

Required:

Adjust the net profit shown to arrive at the trading income assessment for the tax year 2015/16.

6.4 Candies & Cakes is the trading name of a shop owned and run by John Candy. The business produces accounts to 31 March each year. The adjusted trading profit for the accounting period of twelve months to 31/3/2016 has already been calculated at £12,000 before deduction of capital allowances for plant & machinery.

The capital allowance computation for the last accounting period closed with written down values as follows:

• main pool	£25,000
• single asset pool for car with 40% private use by John	£10,000

During the accounting period the following assets were acquired and disposed of:

- a new 'low emission' car was bought for £26,000. This was to have 40% private use by John
- the original car used partly privately by John was sold for £4,000
- a computer system was bought for £2,000
- a food processor was sold for £200
- a new shop counter was bought for £3,000

All disposal proceeds were less than original cost.

Required:

- Using a plant & machinery capital allowance computation, calculate the allowances for the accounting period y/e 31/3/2016.
- Calculate the adjusted trading profit or loss for the accounting period (after capital allowances).
- Explain any alternative options that are available to John, following the results of the last task.

6.5 Stan and Anne have run their partnership manufacturing business for many years, producing accounts up to the 31 March each year. At the start of April 2015 the following written down balances were brought forward for Plant & Machinery capital allowance purposes:

Main Pool	£66,300
Electronic Machine (short life asset)	£2,000
Car (80% business use BMW)	£16,000

The income statement for the year ended 31/3/2016 was as follows:

	£	£
Sales		1,200,000
less cost of sales:		
Raw materials	300,000	
Direct labour	450,000	
Factory overheads	200,000	
		950,000
Gross profit		250,000
less:		
Administration salaries	50,000	
Selling & distribution expenses	15,000	
Depreciation etc	40,000	
General expenses	35,000	
		140,000
Net profit		110,000

Notes:

- The direct labour relates to 20 employees of the partnership, and includes £5,000 employers' national insurance contributions.

- The administration salaries include £20,000 drawn by Stan, and £25,000 drawn by Anne. All private motor expenses are included in these drawings.

- The 'depreciation etc' figure is made up as follows:

	£
Depreciation on plant & cars	32,000
Loss on sale of BMW car sold for £12,000	3,000
Depreciation on Factory	6,000
Gain on sale of Vauxhall car, sold for £4,000	(1,000)

- A used Range Rover (80% business use) was bought for £28,000 to replace the BMW. It has emissions of 200 g/km.

- A Ford Focus was bought to replace the Vauxhall. It had 100% business use and cost £19,000. It has emissions of 125 g/km.

- There were no other acquisitions or disposals of non-current assets.

- General expenses include the following items:

	£
Bad Debts written off	3,000
Reduction in General Bad Debt Provision from £12,000 to £8,000	(4,000)
Office Party for all 20 employees	1,500
Entertaining customers	2,000

Calculate:

- The Plant & Machinery Capital Allowances for the accounting period.

- Trading Income assessment for the partnership for 2015/16, after incorporating the above capital allowances.

6.6 Mr Chang is a sole trader. His business has the following income statement:

	£	£
Sales		1,210,210
less Cost of sales:		808,480
Gross profit		401,730
less:		
Wages and salaries	125,778	
Rent, rates and insurance	59,221	
Repairs to plant	8,215	
Advertising and entertaining	19,077	
Accountancy and legal costs	5,710	
Motor expenses	53,018	
Telephone and office costs	14,017	
Depreciation	28,019	
Other expenses	92,460	405,515
Loss		(3,785)

Notes:

- Wages and salaries include:

	£
Mr Chang	30,000
Mr Chang's wife, who works in the marketing department	18,000

- Advertising and entertaining includes:

	£
Gifts to customers:	
Bottles of wine costing £15 each	2,250
40 diaries carrying the business's logo	400
Staff Christmas party for 20 employees	1,485

- Motor expenses include those relating to:

	£
Delivery vans	10,403
Sales manager's car	6,915
Mr Chang's car expenses (the car is only used for private mileage)	5,700

- Other expenses include:

	£
Cost of staff training	3,550
Subscription to a golf club for Mr Chang	220

- Capital allowances have already been calculated at £9,878

Required:

Complete the adjusted trading profits computation.

7 Income tax – further issues

this chapter covers...

In this chapter we examine some of the more complex issues connected with the income of sole traders and partnerships.

We commence with the rules regarding basis of assessment for these organisations when trading starts. The initial tax years do not use the normal rules, but instead special rules apply which must be learnt. A further set of rules apply in the final tax year when trading ceases.

The chapter then looks specifically at partnerships, and the rules for dividing the profits of the partnership between the partners is explained and illustrated. These include the rules that apply when partners join or leave a partnership.

The next sections are concerned with National Insurance for sole traders and partners, followed by payment dates for Income Tax and a summary of penalties for non-compliance.

Finally we examine the relevant tax forms for sole traders and partnerships, and illustrate their completion.

WHEN BUSINESSES START TRADING

In the last chapter we saw that the basis of assessment that applies when businesses have been trading for some time is the profits of the twelve month accounting period that ends in the tax year. This normal basis is known as the 'current year basis'. We now need to examine the special rules that operate before the normal basis can apply – in the first years of a new business. These rules apply to both sole traders and partnerships, and are designed so that all the profits throughout the life of a business are certain to be assessed in at least one particular tax year. We do not have an equivalent situation for limited companies, since under Corporation Tax each chargeable accounting period is assessed separately, with no need for basis periods.

A major issue to note is that right from the start of the business, accounts will be produced for the accounting periods that the business owners decide upon. These accounts will then be adjusted for tax purposes, including calculating capital allowances for the accounting period. Only when that has been carried out does the procedure relating to basis periods that we will now examine come into play.

We must initially determine which is the tax year in which the new business will first be assessed to Income Tax. The rule for this is straightforward – the first tax year in which a new business' profits are assessed is the tax year in which the business starts. Starting with this tax year, there are rules about exactly what profits from what period of time will be assessed in each of the first tax years. Because different businesses will have different accounting periods we will need to apportion the tax-adjusted trading profits (after capital allowances) to match these basis periods.

basis periods in the opening years

In the following summary that covers the majority of situations, 'accounting date' refers to a date up to which accounts are produced.

	tax year	basis period
1	the tax year in which the business starts	from the start date to the next 5 April
2	the next (second) tax year	the 12 month period that ends on the accounting date in the second tax year
		or (if that's impossible because the accounting period isn't long enough)
		the first 12 months of the business
3	the third tax year	normal 'current year basis' - the 12 month accounting period that ends in the third tax year

For example, if a new business starts trading on 1 January 2013, and produces annual accounts each year to 31 December, the following would apply.

The first tax year – the tax year in which business starts – is 2012/13.

The basis period for the tax year 2012/13 will be 1/1/2013 - 5/4/2013.

The second tax year will be the next year, 2013/14.

The basis period for the tax year 2013/14 will be the 12 months to 31/12/2013.

This is the 12-month period ending on the accounting date in the second tax year.

The third tax year will be the next year, 2014/15.

The basis period for the tax year 2014/15 will be the 12 months to 31/12/2014.

This is the normal 'current year' basis – the 12-month accounting period that ends in the third tax year.

This is demonstrated on the following time-line diagram.

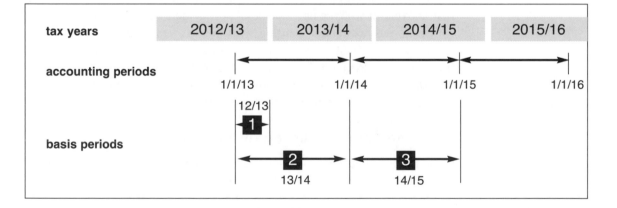

You can see that in this example there is a period of time that relates to two basis periods: the period 1/1/2013 to 5/4/2013 forms the basis period for 2012/13, but is also part of the year ended 31/12/2013 that forms the basis period for 2013/14. This is a common occurrence, and is known as an overlap period. The profits arising in that period are known as overlap profits. These profits are effectively assessed twice – once in each tax year. Only when the business ceases trading can such overlap profits reduce the final trading income assessment.

The rules and examples used so far will enable you to deal with the vast majority of situations for a new business. The only exception occurs when a business starts in one tax year and then produces a long first set of accounts that end in the third tax year. Since there is no accounting end date in the second tax year the previous summary does not apply. Instead, this is dealt with as follows:

■ the basis period for the second tax year is 6 April to 5 April – i.e. the actual tax year

■ the basis period for the third tax year is the 12 months leading up to the accounting date in the third tax year

The following diagram gives a comprehensive view of all possibilities for the **second tax year** in the form of a flowchart.

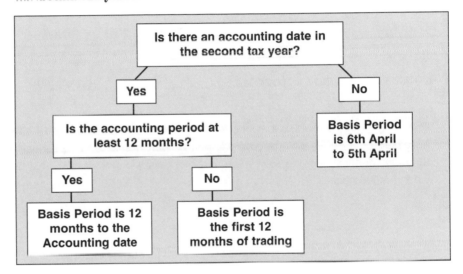

time-apportionment of trading profits

Each accounting period for the business will have adjusted trading profits. These profit figures will incorporate capital allowances that will have been worked out based on the same accounting period. The adjusted trading profits will then need to be matched to the basis periods that we have just examined, using time-apportionment where necessary. When carrying out time-apportionment, note that

■ we will use whole months – each one assumed to be 1/12 of a calendar year

■ the few days between 31 March and 5 April can be ignored – so for example the period 1 January to 5 April will be treated as exactly 3 months

We will follow both these practices in all examples. These calculation methods are acceptable by HM Revenue & Customs.

example: time-apportionment of profits

Using the data from the previous example we will now show how the time-apportionment of profits is carried out.

The adjusted trading profits for the business (after capital allowances) have been calculated as:

1 January 2013 - 31 December 2013   £24,000

1 January 2014 - 31 December 2014   £30,000

Using the basis periods calculated earlier, these profits are used to form trading income assessments for the first few tax years of the business as follows:

Tax Year	Basis Period	trading income assessment	
2012/13	1/1/2013 - 5/4/2013	£24,000 x 3/12	= £6,000
2013/14	1/1/2013 - 31/12/2013		= £24,000
2014/15	1/1/2014 - 31/12/2014		= £30,000

The overlap profits are those arising from the period 1/1/2013 - 5/4/2013, and are £6,000, which is assessed both on its own for 2012/13, and as part of the £24,000 assessment for 2013/14. This £6,000 is deductible in the calculation of the assessable profit for the final tax year of the business when trading ceases.

Different combinations of business start dates and accounting periods will produce various basis periods and amounts of overlap profits. If accounts are always produced up to 31 March, there will not be any overlap profits. The key to accurate calculations is to learn and follow the rules outlined earlier in this chapter, being especially careful to identify each tax year accurately. Mistakes can also easily be made by incorrectly counting months when carrying out time-apportionment. If you find it helpful to sketch a time-line diagram, then this can form part of your workings.

The following Case Study illustrates a variety of possible situations. Examine it carefully to make sure that you could arrive at the same results without assistance.

FRESHER AND CO:
ASSESSING NEW BUSINESSES

Fresher and Company is an accountancy practice that has several new clients who have recently commenced trading.

John Able started trading on 1 July 2012. He produced accounts with adjusted trading profits (after capital allowances) as follows:

1/7/2012 - 30/6/2013	£18,000
1/7/2013 - 30/6/2014	£30,000
1/7/2014 - 30/6/2015	£33,000

The partnership of Joe and Jo Barclay started trading on 1 December 2012. They produced accounts with adjusted trading profits (after capital allowances) as follows:

1/12/2012 - 31/3/2013 (4 months)	£20,000
1/4/2013 - 31/3/2014	£50,000
1/4/2014 - 31/3/2015	£60,000

Karen Cabot started trading on 1 October 2012. She produced accounts with adjusted trading profits (after capital allowances) as follows:

1/10/2012 - 30/6/2013 (9 months)	£27,000
1/7/2013 - 30/6/2014	£42,000
1/7/2014 - 30/6/2015	£47,000

David Daley started trading on 1 November 2012. He produced accounts with adjusted trading profits (after capital allowances) as follows:

1/11/2012 - 31/12/2013 (14 months)	£28,000
1/1/2014 - 31/12/2014	£26,000
1/1/2015 - 31/12/2015	£29,000

Edgar Evans started trading on 1 January 2013. He produced accounts with adjusted trading profits (after capital allowances) as follows:

1/1/2013 - 31/7/2014 (19 months)	£47,500
1/8/2014 - 31/7/2015	£36,000
1/8/2015 - 31/7/2016	£41,000

required

For each of the clients, calculate the assessable profits for each of their first three tax years, and show the amount of any overlap profits, and how it has arisen.

solution

John Able

Tax Year	Basis Period	trading income assessment	
2012/13	1/7/2012 - 5/4/2013	£18,000 x 9/12	= £13,500
2013/14	1/7/2012 - 30/6/2013		= £18,000
2014/15	1/7/2013 - 30/6/2014		= £30,000

The overlap profits are £13,500, and relate to the nine month period 1/7/2012 - 5/4/2013, which is assessed in both 2012/13 and 2013/14. The following diagram shows the periods.

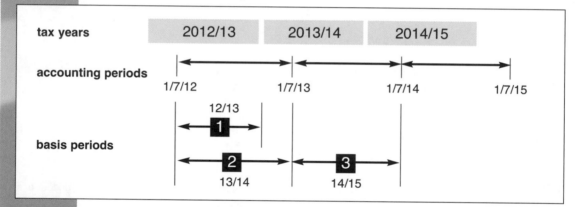

Joe and Jo Barclay

Tax Year	Basis Period	trading income assessment
2012/13	1/12/2012 - 5/4/2013	= £20,000
2013/14	1/4/2013 - 31/3/2014	= £50,000
2014/15	1/4/2014 - 31/3/2015	= £60,000

There are no overlap profits for this business, since the accounting date of 31 March has been chosen. The diagram on the next page shows the periods.

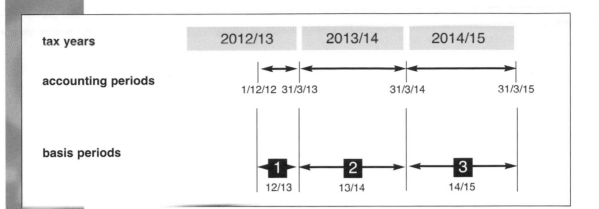

Karen Cabot

Tax Year	Basis Period	trading income assessment	
2012/13	1/10/2012 - 5/4/2013	£27,000 x 6/9	= £18,000
2013/14	1/10/2012 - 30/9/2013	£27,000 + (£42,000 x 3/12)	= £37,500
2014/15	1/7/2013 - 30/6/2014		= £42,000

This situation is a little more complicated than those seen so far.

- Note that the apportionment for the first tax year is 6/9 since the first accounting period is for only nine months.
- For the second tax year there is no 12-month accounting period ending in the tax year, because the accounting period is only 9 months. This means that the alternative of the first 12 months of the business must be used.
- The overlap profits are for nine months and total £28,500, and arise from two separate periods:

  1/10/2012 - 5/4/2013 (profits of £18,000), and

  1/7/2013 - 30/9/2013 (profits of £42,000 x 3/12 = £10,500)

The diagram on the next page shows the periods.

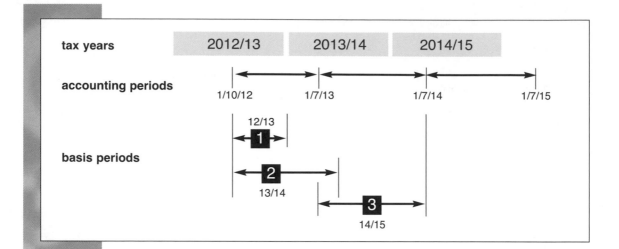

David Daley

Tax Year	Basis Period	trading income assessment	
2012/13	1/11/2012 - 5/4/2013	£28,000 x 5/14	= £10,000
2013/14	1/1/2013 - 31/12/2013	£28,000 x 12/14	= £24,000
2014/15	1/1/2014 - 31/12/2014		= £26,000

The overlap profits are 3/14 x £28,000 = £6,000, and relate to the period 1/1/2013 - 5/4/2013, which is assessed in both 2012/13 and 2013/14.

The fact that 5 + 12 = 17 months of the 14-month period profits have been assessed confirms the 3 months that have been assessed twice. The following diagram shows the periods.

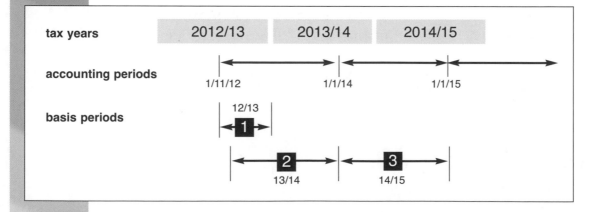

Edgar Evans

Note that we have a situation here where there is no accounting date in the second tax year, and we will therefore follow the special rules noted earlier that apply to the second and third tax years.

Tax Year	Basis Period	trading income assessment	
2012/13	1/1/2013 - 5/4/2013	£47,500 x 3/19	= £7,500
2013/14	6/4/2013 - 5/4/2014	£47,500 x 12/19	= £30,000
2014/15	1/8/2013 - 31/7/2014	£47,500 x 12/19	= £30,000

The overlap profits are 8/19 x £47,500 = £20,000, and relate to the period 1/8/2013 - 5/4/2014, which is assessed in both 2013/14 and 2014/15. The second and third years are therefore where the overlap occurs in this situation.

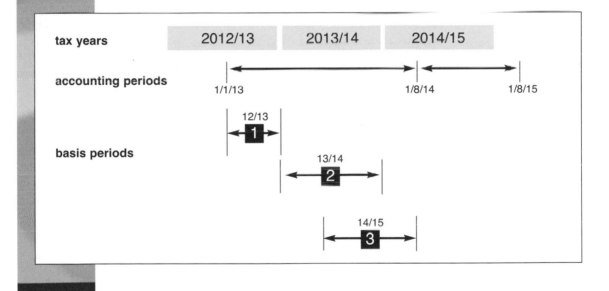

WHEN BUSINESSES STOP TRADING

basis periods

When a business closes down and stops trading, the last tax year in which the business is taxed is the tax year in which trading ceases. For this tax year only there is a special rule regarding the basis period, so that no period of time is missed out for assessment purposes.

The basis period for the final tax year is from the end of the basis period of the previous tax year to the date that the business ceases i.e. all profits that have not yet been assessed.

The previous year will have been assessed on the normal current year basis, so this means that the final basis period will run from the accounting date in that tax year to the date the business stops. The profits of this final period will be reduced by any overlap profits that are brought forward from the start of the business.

Take, for example, a sole trader who has been in business for several years, making accounts up to 31 December. He ceases trading on 30 June 2015, with the following adjusted profits (after capital allowances) for the final accounting periods:

1/1/2014 - 31/12/2014	£25,000
1/1/2015 - 30/6/2015 (6 months)	£15,000

There are overlap profits of £6,000 brought forward from when he started the business.

The assessable profits for the last two tax years of the business are:

Tax Year	Basis Period	trading income assessment	
2014/15	1/1/2014 - 31/12/2014		£25,000
2015/16	1/1/2015 - 30/6/2015		£15,000
		less overlap profits	(£6,000)
			£9,000

The mechanism for basis periods at the beginning and end of a business, and the way that overlap profits are deducted in the final tax year means that over the whole life of the business all profits are assessed. Therefore,

total adjusted profits over the life of the business

= total assessments over the life of the business

As well as showing that the system has some fairness, this also gives us a useful way to check total assessments if we are presented with data for a business from start to finish. The following Case Study will demonstrate this.

<table>
<tr><td>**Case Study**</td><td></td></tr>
</table>

HOLE TRADING:
ASSESSMENTS THROUGHOUT A BUSINESS

Hole Trading is a shop run by Roger Hole that specialises in caving equipment. The business started on 1/6/2011, and ceased trading on 31/12/2014. The accounts were produced annually up to 31 May, and the adjusted profits (after capital allowances) were as follows:

	£
1/6/2011 - 31/5/2012	18,000
1/6/2012 31/5/2013	36,000
1/6/2013 - 31/5/2014	24,000
1/6/2014 - 31/12/2014 (7 months)	21,000
Total	99,000

required

Calculate the trading income assessments for each tax year in which the business will be assessed.

solution

2011/12	1/6/2011 - 5/4/2012	£18,000 x 10/12	= £15,000
2012/13	1/6/2011 - 31/5/2012		= £18,000
	(overlap profits 1/6/2011 - 5/4/2012 £15,000)		
2013/14	1/6/2012 - 31/5/2013		= £36,000
2014/15	1/6/2013 - 31/12/2014	£24,000 + £21,000	= £45,000
		less overlap profits	(£15,000)
			£30,000

The trading income assessments for the four years that the business is taxed total (£15,000 + £18,000 + £36,000 + £30,000) = £99,000. This agrees with the total adjusted profits over the life of the business.

capital allowances when a business ceases

Capital allowances are calculated separately for each accounting period of a business, and the result forms part of the adjusted trading profits of each accounting period.

When a business ceases capital allowances will need to be calculated for the final accounting period, but special care must be taken since:

- there can be <u>no</u> WDA, FYA or AIA in this last period
- all remaining assets will have been disposed of by the business
- balancing allowances and / or balancing charges will occur for all pools (including the main pool) since there can be no written down values to carry forward

Where there is partial private use of assets any allowances or charges will need to reflect only the business proportion of the asset use. However, you may remember that balancing allowances and charges are not time-apportioned if we have long or short accounting periods, so at least that will not create a complication.

Any asset bought from the business by the owner of the business must be included as a disposal at open market value.

Case Study

S. TOPP TRADING:
CAPITAL ALLOWANCES AT END OF TRADE

Steve Topp has been running his business for many years, with an accounting date of 31 December.

The written down values carried forward at 31 December 2014 were:

Main Pool	£32,000
Car (80% business use)	£16,000

The business ceased trading on 30/6/2015. The adjusted trading profit for the period 1/1/2015 to 30/6/2015 was £40,000, before deducting capital allowances. There is also £10,000 overlap profit from the start of the business available for set-off.

Steve managed to sell all the remaining business assets (except the car) for £14,000. He bought the car from the business himself to use privately for a market value figure of £17,000.

required

- Calculate the plant & machinery capital allowances for the accounting period 1/1/2015 to 30/6/2015.
- Calculate the trading income assessment for the final tax year of the business.

solution

Plant & machinery capital allowances computation

	Main Pool	Single Asset Pool Car (20% Private Use)	Capital Allowances
	£	£	£
WDV bf	32,000	16,000	
Disposals	(14,000)	(17,000)	
	18,000	(1,000)	
Balancing allowances	(18,000)		18,000
Balancing charge		1,000 x 80%	(800)
WDV cf	0	0	
Total Capital Allowances			17,200

Trading Income assessment working:

	£
Accounting period 1/1/2015 - 30/6/2015:	
Adjusted trading profits (before capital allowances)	40,000
less capital allowances	(17,200)
	22,800

Tax Year 2015/16	Basis period 1/1/2015 - 30/6/2015:	
	Adjusted Profit (as above)	22,800
	Less overlap profits	(10,000)
	Trading Income assessment	12,800

DIVIDING TRADING PROFITS BETWEEN PARTNERS

We have seen throughout the last two chapters that a partnership is taxed in the same way as a sole trader. It uses the same adjustment mechanism for trading profits; capital allowances are calculated in exactly the same way, and basis periods throughout the business are also identical.

The way in which partners decide to divide their profits is entirely their choice, and is stated in their partnership agreement. The division agreed will not only apply to the actual profits that the partnership generates, but also to the amount that is assessable on each partner for Income Tax purposes.

simple profit splits

If a partnership is made up of two individuals who agree to share profits and losses equally, then the calculation of each partner's trading income assessment is straightforward. The adjusted trading profits for the partnership (after capital allowances) is simply halved, and each partner is assessed on this figure.

So, for example, suppose the ongoing partnership of Sue and Adam had adjusted profits for the accounting period of 12 months to 31/12/2015 of £40,000 (after capital allowances). If their agreement was to divide profits and losses equally then the trading income assessment for Sue for the tax year 2015/16 would be £20,000, and the assessment for Adam for the same tax year would also be £20,000. Note that the current year basis of assessment is used here, just as it is for sole traders.

The simplest split is to agree a percentage that each partner will be entitled to. This could be a straightforward 50%:50% as just mentioned, or could be any other figures that the partners feel is fair. A partnership of three individuals may, for example agree that a 60%:30%:10% split is fair in their particular circumstances. These divisions could also be expressed as ratios – 50%:50% would be shown as 1:1, while 60%:30%:10% could be expressed as 6:3:1.

more complex profit splits

Some partnerships may, however, agree a more complex division of profits and losses. They may for example agree that out of the profits,

- 'salaries' are to be provided for some or all partners, and/or
- 'interest on capital' should be paid to partners based on their investment in the partnership

Both these types of appropriation would be made out of the total profits that the partnership has made. The larger these payments are, the less profit will remain to be shared by the partners by using the agreed percentages or ratios.

For tax purposes the starting point would always be the adjusted profits of the accounting period (after capital allowances), and this is the amount that the combined trading income assessments of each partner must total. Any salaries or interest on capitals are allocated first, and then the remaining profit (or loss) is shared amongst the partners. Note that partners' salaries and interest on capitals are trading profits, and are taxed as part of trading income. Partners' salaries are not assessed as employment income, which only relates to employees.

If a profit sharing arrangement changes, the agreement that is in existence during the accounting period is the one that applies to dividing the tax-adjusted profits of that accounting period.

The Case Study that follows shows how individual partners' assessments are calculated for an ongoing partnership where the normal 'current year basis' is operating. We will then go on to look at some other situations.

PENN, QUILL AND WRIGHT: PARTNERS' ASSESSMENTS

John Penn, Daisy Quill and Sue Wright have been trading in partnership for several years. The partnership produces accounts each year up to the 30 June. Their partnership agreement states that the following salaries, rates of interest on capitals, and shares of remaining profits or losses should apply:

	Salary (pa)	Interest on Capital	Share of Profit/Loss
John Penn	£10,000	5%	30%
Daisy Quill	£15,000	5%	20%
Sue Wright	-	5%	50%

The partnership accounts for the twelve month accounting period to 30/6/2015 shows tax-adjusted profits of £95,000 (after deducting capital allowances):

The capital accounts balances for the partners are:

John Penn	£100,000
Daisy Quill	£50,000
Sue Wright	£250,000

required

Calculate the trading income assessments for each of the three partners that will be based on the adjusted profits for this period, and state the tax year that the assessments will be for.

solution

The following calculation shows how the adjusted profits are divided up:

	John Penn	Daisy Quill	Sue Wright	Total Remaining
	£	£	£	£
Adjusted Profits				95,000
Salaries	10,000	15,000	0	(25,000)
Balance Remaining				70,000
Interest on Capitals	5,000	2,500	12,500	(20,000)
Balance Remaining				50,000
Share of Balance	15,000	10,000	25,000	(50,000)
	30,000	27,500	37,500	

The calculation follows the same principles that are used for dividing profits for financial accounting purposes (with which you may be familiar) – the only difference is that here our starting point is the adjusted profits after capital allowances.

Notes:

- Salaries and interest on capitals are deducted from the original adjusted profit first, leaving a balance of £50,000 to be shared using the profit sharing percentages.

- Interest on capitals are calculated using the individual partners' balances on their capital accounts.

- The overall amounts allocated to each partner of £30,000, £27,500, and £37,500 total the original adjusted profit figure of £95,000.

The trading income assessments for each partner for 2015/16 (since the accounting period ends in that tax year) will be:

John Penn	£30,000
Daisy Quill	£27,500
Sue Wright	£37,500

partnership losses

If a partnership incurs a trading loss, each partner's share of the loss can be dealt with independently. This means that each partner has the same choices of how their own share of the trading loss should be relieved as a sole trader. The individual partners could all choose different ways to relieve their own loss, according to their personal circumstances.

when partnerships start or cease trading

When a partnership is first formed and starts trading, the basis periods that apply to each partners' share will be exactly the same as if they were sole traders. Therefore the rules that we saw earlier in the chapter for commencing or ceasing trading apply to both sole traders and partnerships.

CHANGES IN A PARTNERSHIP

when the profit sharing agreement changes

Depending on when the existing partners decide to alter their profit sharing agreement, there are two possible implications:

- if the change is made with effect from a normal accounting date (ie the start/end of an accounting period), then the new arrangement will simply apply to the new accounting period. This will mean that the new share of profits will apply entirely to the basis period of a new tax year

■ if the change is made during an accounting period, the adjusted profits (after capital allowances) will first have to be time-apportioned into the two parts of the period – before and after the change. Each part of the profits will then be divided amongst the partners according to the agreement in force at the time, and the two parts for each partner added together to form their assessment for the tax year

when a new partner joins a partnership

When a new partner joins an established partnership (or a partnership is formed by an individual joining an established sole trader) the new partner is treated as if they had started a new business on the date that they joined. There will need to be a new profit sharing agreement that incorporates the additional partner, and this will operate from the date the new partner started.

The new partner will be subject to the opening basis of assessment rules, but the established partners (or established sole trader) will carry on applying the normal 'current year' basis to their shares of the adjusted profits. The new partner may therefore have personal overlap profits that will be carried forward until they leave the partnership, or the partnership ceases trading.

If the new partner starts on a normal accounting date for the partnership the situation is not too complicated, as the following example shows.

example: introduction of a new partner at the start of an accounting period

Rose and Daisy have been in partnership for several years, sharing profits and losses equally. They have always made their accounts up to 31 December each year. On 1 January 2015 they are joined by Bud, and the partnership agreement is changed to Rose 40%, Daisy 40%, Bud 20% from that date. They have never used salaries or interest on capitals as part of their profit sharing arrangement.

The first accounting year of the revised partnership (the year ended 31 December 2015) produced adjusted profits (after capital allowances) of £120,000.

For both Rose and Daisy their share of the profits for the y/e 31/12/2015 will be £120,000 x 40% = £48,000 each. The figure will form their trading income assessments for 2015/16 under the normal 'current year basis' rules.

Bud will be treated as if he started a new business on 1 January 2015. His share of the profits for the accounting year ended 31/12/2015 of 20% x £120,000 = £24,000 will be used to calculate the assessments for his first two tax years:

Bud's assessment for the tax year 2014/15 will use the basis period 1/1/2015 - 5/4/2015. His assessment for 2014/15 will therefore be £24,000 x 3/12 = £6,000.

His assessment for the tax year 2015/16 will use the basis period 1/1/2015 - 31/12/2015. His assessment for 2015/16 will therefore be £24,000.

This means that Bud will have overlap profits of £6,000, (relating to the period 1/1/2015 - 5/4/2015) that he will carry forward until either he leaves the partnership or it ceases trading.

a partner joining partway through an accounting period

If the new partner joins partway through an accounting period, the adjusted profits of the period must first be time-apportioned into the parts either side of that date. Each existing partner's assessment will then be generated by adding together their shares from each part of the period, just as if they had simply changed their profit sharing arrangement. The new partner will be treated as if he had started a new business on the date he joined. The following example will illustrate the situation.

example: introduction of a new partner partway into an accounting period

Oak and Ash have been in partnership for several years, sharing profits and losses equally. They have always made their accounts up to 31 December each year. On 1 October 2014 they are joined by Elm, and the partnership agreement is changed to Oak 40%, Ash 40%, Elm 20% from that date. They have never used salaries or interest on capitals as part of their profit sharing arrangement.

The year ended 31 December 2014 produced adjusted profits (after capital allowances) of £120,000. The year ended 31 December 2015 produced adjusted profits (after capital allowances) of £180,000.

The first step is to time-apportion the adjusted profits into the periods before and after Elm joined:

    1/1/2014 - 30/9/2014   £120,000 x 9/12 = £90,000

    1/10/2014 - 31/12/2014   £120,000 x 3/12 = £30,000

Oak and Ash

For the existing partners, Oak and Ash, they will each have a share of the profits for the whole accounting year made up of:

    1/1/2014 - 30/9/2014   £90,000 x 50%   =   £45,000, plus

    1/10/2014 - 31/12/2014 £30,000 x 40%   =   £12,000

                                               £57,000

For both Oak and Ash this figure will form the assessment for 2014/15 under the normal rules.

For 2015/16 their assessments will each be based on £180,000 x 40% = £72,000.

Elm

The new partner, Elm will be treated as if he started a new business on 1 October 2014.

He has a share of the profits for the period 1/10/2014 - 31/12/2014 of

20% x £30,000 = £6,000.

He has a share of the profits for the period 1/1/2015 - 31/12/2015 of

20% x £180,000 = £36,000.

These amounts will be used to calculate the assessments for his first two tax years:

Elm's assessment for his first tax year - 2014/15 will use the basis period 1/10/2014 - 5/4/2015.

His trading income assessment for 2014/15 will therefore be made up of:

1/10/2014 - 31/12/2014		£6,000, plus
1/1/2015 - 5/4/2015 £36,000 x 3/12	=	£9,000
		£15,000

His assessment for the tax year 2015/16 will use the basis period 1/1/2015 - 31/12/2015. His assessment for 2015/16 will therefore be £36,000.

Elm will have overlap profits of £9,000, (relating to the period 1/1/2015 - 5/4/2015) that he will carry forward until either he leaves the partnership or it ceases trading.

when a partner leaves a partnership

If a partner leaves then the treatment follows the same logic as we have just seen. It is only the leaving partner that has the closing basis period rules applied to his/her share of the profits. The individual's own overlap profits (if any) would be deducted from their final share of profits. The existing partners carry on as normal.

The following example illustrates the situation.

example: partner leaving a partnership

Reddy, Eddy and Go have been in business for several years, sharing profits equally, and making accounts up to 31 December. Go decides to leave the partnership on 30 June 2015.

The partnership had the following adjusted profits (after capital allowances) for their accounting periods.

| 1/1/2014 - 31/12/2014 | £75,000 |
| 1/1/2015 - 31/12/2015 | £60,000 |

Go has personal overlap profits of £1,000 brought forward from when he started in partnership.

For **Go**, the assessable profits for his last two tax years of the business are:

Tax Year	Basis Period	trading income assessment	
2014/15	1/1/2014 - 31/12/2014	£75,000 x 1/3	= **£25,000**
2015/16	1/1/2015 - 30/6/2015	£60,000 x 6/12 x 1/3	= £10,000
		less overlap profits	(£1,000)
			£9,000

NATIONAL INSURANCE FOR THE SELF-EMPLOYED

As we saw in Chapter 1, sole traders and partners are liable to Class 2 and Class 4 National Insurance contributions.

■ Class 2 contributions are payable at a flat rate of £2.80 per week (unless the 'small profits threshold' applies), and in addition

■ Class 4 contributions are payable on the profits above £8,060 per year

The profits for self-employed NIC purposes are the same ones that are used for Income Tax purposes – the assessable trading profits. For partners this refers to their personal share of the assessable profits, not those relating to the whole partnership.

Where an individual's profits are less than £5,965 then Class 2 contributions need not be paid.

The rates for Class 4 contributions are:

9% of profits for the year between £8,060 and £42,385, plus
2% of profits above £42,385.

If profits are below £8,060 then there are no Class 4 contributions.

A REVIEW OF INCOME TAX PAYMENT DATES

In Chapter 1 we saw that the final date for payment of Income Tax is 31 January following the end of the tax year (eg 31/1/17 for 2015/16). We also discussed briefly the timing of payments on account that are sometimes due. We will now look a little more closely at these interim payments.

payments on account

The two payments on account are calculated as follows:

Each payment on account is based on **half** the Income Tax amount due for the **previous** year, (after deducting tax paid under PAYE and other Income Tax deducted at source).

Suppose, for example, that a partner only had trading income, and no other income. If his Income Tax for liability for 2014/15 was £7,000, none of this would have been paid by deduction at source.

This means that for 2015/16 he would need to make two payments on account. Each of the two payments on account would be:

1/2 x £7,000 = £3,500.

These payments on account for 2015/16 would be made on 31/1/16 and 31/7/16. If the Income Tax amount for each year is quite similar, there would not be much left to pay (or have refunded) on the final date of 31/1/17.

Payments on account do not have to be made if either

■ the amount of tax payable the previous year was less than £1,000 (excluding tax deducted at source), or

■ more than 80% of the tax due the previous year was collected at source

Payments on account can also be reduced or eliminated if the taxpayer makes a claim that his tax for the coming year will be less than for the previous year.

INTEREST AND PENALTIES

Interest on tax is payable on late payments, and also on any underpayment of the amount due on account. The rate is 3.0% at the time of going to press.

Penalties are also payable for:

1. Late submission of tax return:

■ a £100 penalty for missing the deadline – regardless of the amount of tax involved

■ for returns over 3 months late – an additional daily penalty of £10 per day up to a 90 day maximum of £900

- for returns over 6 months late – an additional £300 or 5% of the tax due if this is higher
- for returns over 12 months late – a further £300 or 5% of the tax due if this is higher

There are very limited 'reasonable excuses' for late returns; for example a fire or flood destroying paperwork or a serious illness.

The tax return submission deadlines are:

- 31 October following end of tax year for paper-based returns
- 31 January following end of tax year for online submission

2. Late payment of the balancing payment by more than 30 days:

- 5% of the tax due plus
- further 5% of the tax due if still unpaid by 31 July
- a third 5% of the tax due if payment has still not been made 12 months after it was due

Note that the penalties are in addition to the interest charges.

incorrect returns

If after submitting a tax return, the taxpayer discovers that he has made an error or omission, he should notify HM Revenue & Customs as soon as possible. If the alteration results in less tax being payable than was originally thought, the taxpayer will receive a refund. Where additional tax is due this will of course need to be paid, plus interest that will run from the normal payment date.

If a taxpayer (or his agent) finds that they have made a mistake on a tax return they have normally got 12 months from 31 January following the end of the tax year to correct it. For the tax year 2015/16 amendments can therefore be made by 31 January 2018.

HMRC can still be told about errors after the above date, but then they must be notified to HMRC in writing. Such notifications must be made within four years of the end of the tax year. This means the deadline relating to the tax year 2015/16 is 5 April 2020.

The following system for penalties applies for incorrect information stated in tax returns and documents. This is based on a percentage of the extra tax due, depending on the behaviour that gave rise to the error.

If the error is:

- due to **lack of reasonable care**, the penalty is between 0% and 30% of the extra tax due
- **deliberate**, the penalty is between 20% and 70% of the extra tax due, and if

■ **deliberate and concealed**, the penalty is between 30% and 100% of the extra tax due.

The penalty also depends on whether the disclosure was prompted or unprompted. This gives the following series of penalty rates:

Type of behaviour	Unprompted disclosure	Prompted disclosure
Reasonable care	No penalty	No penalty
Careless	0% to 30%	15% to 30%
Deliberate	20% to 70%	35% to 70%
Deliberate and concealed	30% to 100%	50% to 100%

The percentage can be reduced if the taxpayer tells HMRC about the error(s), helps them work out the extra tax, and gives HMRC access to check the figures. If the taxpayer took 'reasonable care' there is no penalty.

These penalties also apply if a taxpayer fails to notify HMRC that he has self employed income that is subject to tax.

This system also applies to Corporation Tax, as we saw earlier.

failure to keep records

There can be a penalty for not keeping the required records for the correct length of time of up to £3,000 per tax year for individuals.

COMPLETING THE TAX RETURN PAGES

The tax return for individuals has to be completed and submitted at the latest by 31 January that follows the end of the tax year – for example 31 January 2017 for the tax year 2015/16. This assumes online submission. The completed tax return contains information about the individual's income from all sources, and supplementary pages are used for those with specific types of income. In studying this learning area, we are concerned with the supplementary pages that relate to sole traders and partners, and you may be asked to complete these in your assessment.

We have illustrated all the return pages with the 2014/15 versions, since the 2015/16 versions were not available when this book was published.

self-employment pages

There are two alternative versions of the supplementary self-employment pages:

■ the 'full' version is 6 pages long and is suitable for dealing with situations with any level of turnover, and where there are complexities, for example businesses that are starting or ceasing

- the 'short' version is 2 pages long and can only be used for sole traders where (amongst other conditions):
  - Turnover is less than £81,000 p.a. (2014/15 limit)
  - The accounting period is the same as the basis period.
  - There is no claim to set off overlap profits.

Completion of either version of these supplementary pages could form an assessment task.

We will start by looking at the full version, and then see how the short version simplifies the reporting of some information.

self-employment (full)

The pages that you may be asked to complete are pages SEF 1 to SEF 3 and these (2014/15 versions) are reproduced on pages 7.27-7.29. We do not need to examine the other pages. The whole form is shown in the appendix to this book.

The following commentary gives an overview of the main issues. Later on, we will demonstrate how the pages are completed by using a Case Study.

Page SEF 1 commences with a section for **business details**. As well as the name, address and description of the business, the relevant accounting period dates are also required. For those starting or ceasing trading in the tax year the appropriate date is also required.

After a short section for other information (that will not concern us) the first page ends with boxes to insert the **business income**. Here the turnover is inserted into box 15.

Page SEF 2 contains boxes for a comprehensive analysis of the statement of profit or loss (income statement). It provides two columns for expenses,

- the one on the left (boxes 17 - 30) for total expenses (i.e. taken from the income statement, before adjusting for any disallowable amounts), and
- the one on the right (boxes 32 - 45) for any disallowable items.Both columns have total boxes (31 for total expenses and 46 for total disallowable amounts)

Page SEF 3 commences with the net profit (box 47) or loss (box 48). Note that these boxes are for figures straight from the income statement - i.e. before the adjustments noted in boxes 32-46.

There follows a section where capital allowances are inserted into boxes 49 to 59. At the bottom of the page is the start of a section headed 'Calculating your taxable profit or loss'. This is where the disallowable expenses and capital allowances that have been previously summarised are taken into account, along with any other adjustments to arrive at the net business profit for tax purposes (box 64). This figure (or the equivalent loss in box 65) relates to the accounting period. If further adjustments are required to bring the figures into line with the basis period they would be dealt with on the next page.

HM Revenue & Customs

Self-employment (full)

Tax year 6 April 2014 to 5 April 2015 (2014–15)

Please read the 'Self-employment (full) notes' to check if you should use this page or the 'Self-employment (short)' page.

ℹ To get notes and helpsheets that will help you fill in this form, go to **www.hmrc.gov.uk/selfassessmentforms**

Your name	Your Unique Taxpayer Reference (UTR)

Business details

1 Business name – unless it is in your own name

2 Description of business

3 First line of your business address – unless you work from home

4 Postcode of your business address

5 If the details in boxes 1, 2, 3 or 4 have changed in the last 12 months, put 'X' in the box and give details in the 'Any other information' box

6 If your business started after 5 April 2014, enter the start date DD MM YYYY

7 If your business ceased after 5 April 2014 but before 6 April 2015, enter the final date of trading

8 Date your books or accounts start – the beginning of your accounting period

9 Date your books or accounts are made up to or the end of your accounting period – read the notes if you have filled in box 6 or 7

10 If you used the cash basis, money actually received and paid out, to calculate your income and expenses, put 'X' in the box - read the notes

Other information

11 If your accounting date has changed permanently, put 'X' in the box

12 If your accounting date has changed more than once since 2009, put 'X' in the box

13 If special arrangements apply, put 'X' in the box - read the notes

14 If you provided the information about your 2014-15 profit on last year's tax return, put 'X' in the box - read the notes

Business income

15 Your turnover – the takings, fees, sales or money earned by your business

£ · 0 0

16 Any other business income not included in box 15

£ · 0 0

Business expenses

Please read the 'Self-employment (full) notes' before filling in this section.

Total expenses

If your annual turnover was below £81,000, you may just put your total expenses in box 31

Disallowable expenses

Use this column if the figures in boxes 17 to 30 include disallowable amounts

17 Cost of goods bought for resale or goods used

£ _____ · 0 0

32 £ _____ · 0 0

18 Construction industry – payments to subcontractors

£ _____ · 0 0

33 £ _____ · 0 0

19 Wages, salaries and other staff costs

£ _____ · 0 0

34 £ _____ · 0 0

20 Car, van and travel expenses

£ _____ · 0 0

35 £ _____ · 0 0

21 Rent, rates, power and insurance costs

£ _____ · 0 0

36 £ _____ · 0 0

22 Repairs and renewals of property and equipment

£ _____ · 0 0

37 £ _____ · 0 0

23 Phone, fax, stationery and other office costs

£ _____ · 0 0

38 £ _____ · 0 0

24 Advertising and business entertainment costs

£ _____ · 0 0

39 £ _____ · 0 0

25 Interest on bank and other loans

£ _____ · 0 0

40 £ _____ · 0 0

26 Bank, credit card and other financial charges

£ _____ · 0 0

41 £ _____ · 0 0

27 Irrecoverable debts written off

£ _____ · 0 0

42 £ _____ · 0 0

28 Accountancy, legal and other professional fees

£ _____ · 0 0

43 £ _____ · 0 0

29 Depreciation and loss/profit on sale of assets

£ _____ · 0 0

44 £ _____ · 0 0

30 Other business expenses

£ _____ · 0 0

45 £ _____ · 0 0

31 Total expenses (total of boxes 17 to 30)

£ _____ · 0 0

46 Total disallowable expenses (total of boxes 32 to 45)

£ _____ · 0 0

Net profit or loss

47 **Net profit** – if your business income is more than your expenses (if box 15 + box 16 minus box 31 is positive)

£ [   ] · 0 0

48 **Or, net loss** – if your expenses are more than your business income (if box 31 minus (box 15 + box 16) is positive)

£ [   ] · 0 0

Tax allowances for vehicles and equipment (capital allowances)

There are 'capital' tax allowances for vehicles, equipment and certain buildings used in your business (don't include the cost of these in your business expenses). Please read the 'Self-employment (full) notes' and use the examples to work out your capital allowances.

49 **Annual Investment Allowance**

£ [   ] · 0 0

50 **Capital allowances at 18% on equipment, including cars with lower CO$_2$ emissions**

£ [   ] · 0 0

51 **Capital allowances at 8% on equipment, including cars with higher CO$_2$ emissions**

£ [   ] · 0 0

52 **Restricted capital allowances for cars costing more than £12,000 – if bought before 6 April 2009**

£ [   ] · 0 0

53 **Agricultural or Industrial Buildings Allowance**

£ [   ] · 0 0

54 **Business Premises Renovation Allowance (Assisted Areas only)** – read the notes

£ [   ] · 0 0

55 **100% and other enhanced capital allowances** – read the notes

£ [   ] · 0 0

56 **Allowances on sale or cessation of business use (where you have disposed of assets for less than their tax value)**

£ [   ] · 0 0

57 **Total capital allowances (total of boxes 49 to 56)**

£ [   ] · 0 0

58 **Balancing charge on sale or cessation of business use (only where Business Premises Renovation Allowance has been claimed)** – read the notes

£ [   ] · 0 0

59 **Balancing charge on sales of other assets or on the cessation of business use (where you have disposed of assets for more than their tax value)**

£ [   ] · 0 0

Calculating your taxable profit or loss

You may have to adjust your net profit or loss for disallowable expenses or capital allowances to arrive at your taxable profit or your loss for tax purposes. Please read the 'Self-employment (full) notes' and fill in the boxes below that apply.

60 **Goods and services for your own use** – read the notes

£ [   ] · 0 0

61 **Total additions to net profit or deductions from net loss (box 46 + box 58 + box 59 + box 60)**

£ [   ] · 0 0

62 **Income, receipts and other profits included in business income or expenses but not taxable as business profits**

£ [   ] · 0 0

63 **Total deductions from net profit or additions to net loss (box 57 + box 62)**

£ [   ] · 0 0

64 **Net business profit for tax purposes (if box 47 + box 61 minus (box 48 + box 63) is positive)**

£ [   ] · 0 0

65 **Net business loss for tax purposes (if box 48 + box 63 minus (box 47 + box 61) is positive)**

£ [   ] · 0 0

self-employment (short)

This version of the self-employment pages can only be used for simple situations where the annual turnover is below £81,000. At only two pages, it is a lot shorter that the full version, and it achieves this by summarising much of the detail into only a few boxes.

The first page, **SES 1**, contains sections for **business details**, **business income**, and **allowable business expenses**. The expenses section is very different to that on the full form, since here the figures required in boxes 11 to 20 are those **after adjusting for disallowable amounts**. The disallowable amounts are not shown separately.

Page **SES 2** commences with a net profit (box 21) or net loss (box 22). This figure will be after deducting only allowable expenses from the turnover, but before capital allowances and any other adjustments. These are summarised in the next sections, to arrive at final figures for taxable profits for the business (i.e. the assessable trading income) in box 31, or an equivalent loss figure in box 32. The main options for offsetting a current year loss are dealt with in the final section.

The 2014/15 version is shown on the next two pages.

HM Revenue & Customs

Self-employment (short)
Tax year 6 April 2014 to 5 April 2015 (2014-15)

Please read the 'Self-employment (short) notes' to check if you should use this page or the 'Self-employment (full)' page.

ℹ To get notes and helpsheets that will help you fill in this form, go to www.hmrc.gov.uk/selfassessmentforms

Your name	Your Unique Taxpayer Reference (UTR)

Business details

1 Description of business

2 Postcode of your business address

3 If your business name, description, address or postcode have changed in the last 12 months, put 'X' in the box and give details in the 'Any other information' box of your tax return

4 If you are a foster carer or shared lives carer, put 'X' in the box – read the notes

5 If your business started after 5 April 2014, enter the start date DD MM YYYY

6 If your business ceased before 6 April 2015, enter the final date of trading DD MM YYYY

7 Date your books or accounts are made up to – read the notes

8 If you used the cash basis, money actually received and paid out, to calculate your income and expenses put 'X' in the box – read the notes

Business income – if your annual business turnover was below £81,000

9 Your turnover – the takings, fees, sales or money earned by your business
£ · 0 0

10 Any other business income not included in box 9
£ · 0 0

Allowable business expenses

If your annual turnover was below £81,000 you may just put your total expenses in box 20, rather than filling in the whole section.

11 Costs of goods bought for resale or goods used
£ · 0 0

12 Car, van and travel expenses – after private use proportion
£ · 0 0

13 Wages, salaries and other staff costs
£ · 0 0

14 Rent, rates, power and insurance costs
£ · 0 0

15 Repairs and renewals of property and equipment
£ · 0 0

16 Accountancy, legal and other professional fees
£ · 0 0

17 Interest and bank and credit card etc. financial charges
£ · 0 0

18 Phone, fax, stationery and other office costs
£ · 0 0

19 Other allowable business expenses – client entertaining costs are not an allowable expense
£ · 0 0

20 Total allowable expenses – total of boxes 11 to 19
£ · 0 0

Net profit or loss

21 Net profit – if your business income is more than your expenses (if box 9 + box 10 minus box 20 is positive)

£ [ ][ ][ ][ ][ ][ ] · [0][0]

22 Or, net loss – if your expenses exceed your business income (if box 20 minus (box 9 + box 10) is positive)

£ [ ][ ][ ][ ][ ][ ] · [0][0]

Tax allowances for vehicles and equipment (capital allowances)

There are 'capital' tax allowances available for vehicles and equipment used in your business. (Please don't include the cost of these in your business expenses)

23 Annual Investment Allowance

£ [ ][ ][ ][ ][ ][ ] · [0][0]

24 Allowance for small balance of unrelieved expenditure

£ [ ][ ][ ][ ][ ][ ] · [0][0]

25 Other capital allowances

£ [ ][ ][ ][ ][ ][ ] · [0][0]

26 Total balancing charges – where you have disposed of items for more than their value

£ [ ][ ][ ][ ][ ][ ] · [0][0]

Calculating your taxable profits

Your taxable profit may not be the same as your net profit. Please read the 'Self-employment (short) notes' to see if you need to make any adjustments and fill in the boxes which apply to arrive at your taxable profit for the year.

27 Goods and/or services for your own use – read the notes

£ [ ][ ][ ][ ][ ][ ] · [0][0]

28 Net business profit for tax purposes (if box 21 + box 26 + box 27 minus (boxes 22 to 25) is positive)

£ [ ][ ][ ][ ][ ][ ] · [0][0]

29 Loss brought forward from earlier years set off against this year's profits – up to the amount in box 28

£ [ ][ ][ ][ ][ ][ ] · [0][0]

30 Any other business income not included in box 9 or box 10 – for example, non arm's length reverse premiums

£ [ ][ ][ ][ ][ ][ ] · [0][0]

Total taxable profits or net business loss

31 Total taxable profits from this business (if box 28 + box 30 minus box 29 is positive)

£ [ ][ ][ ][ ][ ][ ] · [0][0]

32 Net business loss for tax purposes (if boxes 22 to 25 minus (box 21 + box 26 + box 27) is positive)

£ [ ][ ][ ][ ][ ][ ] · [0][0]

Losses, Class 4 National Insurance contributions (NICs) and CIS deductions

If you have made a loss for tax purposes (box 32), read the 'Self-employment (short) notes' and fill in boxes 33 to 35 as appropriate.

33 Loss from this tax year set off against other income for 2014–15

£ [ ][ ][ ][ ][ ][ ] · [0][0]

34 Loss to be carried back to previous year(s) and set off against income (or capital gains)

£ [ ][ ][ ][ ][ ][ ] · [0][0]

35 Total loss to carry forward after all other set-offs – including unused losses brought forward

£ [ ][ ][ ][ ][ ][ ] · [0][0]

36 If you are exempt from paying Class 4 NICs, put 'X' in the box – read the notes

[ ]

37 If you have been given a 2014–15 Class 4 NICs deferment certificate, put 'X' in the box – read the notes

[ ]

38 Deductions on payment and deduction statements from contractors – construction industry subcontractors only

£ [ ][ ][ ][ ][ ][ ] · [0][0]

The following Case Study will revise some of the main issues relating to a sole trader that we have examined, and show how in practice the full version supplementary pages are completed.

MARK UPP:
A COMPREHENSIVE PROBLEM

Mark Upp commenced in business as a market trader on 1 January 2016. He produced a set of accounts for the period 1/1/2016 - 31/12/2016 as follows:

	£	£
Sales		90,000
less cost of sales:		45,000
Gross profit		45,000
less expenses:		
Insurance	2,500	
Part Time Employees' Wages & NIC	6,500	
Depreciation	3,250	
Motor Expenses	1,000	
General Expenses	3,000	
Bank Interest	1,000	
		17,250
Net Profit		27,750

Notes:

1   Mark has agreed that his car is used 75% for business purposes and 25% privately. The motor expenses figure in the accounts relates to both business and private mileage. The car was bought for £13,000 on 1/1/2016. It has emissions of 125 g/km.

2   Mark took goods from his market stall shop throughout the year to use privately. The cost of sales figure in the accounts of £45,000 is after deducting the £2,000 cost price of these goods. Mark's normal mark-up is 100% on cost.

3   Mark bought his portable stall for £6,400 when he commenced business. It qualifies as plant & machinery.

required
• Calculate the capital allowances claimable by Mark for the accounting year ended 31/12/2016.
• Calculate the adjusted profits for the same period, after taking into account the capital allowances.
• Calculate the trading income assessment for Mark for 2015/16.

- Calculate the Class 4 National Insurance contributions payable by Mark for 2015/16.
- Complete the full version supplementary pages SEF1-3 of the tax return for Mark for 2015/16.

solution

Capital Allowances

AIA is claimable on the portable stall of £6,400.

	Main Pool	Single Asset Pool Car (25% private)	Capital Allowances
	£	£	£	£
WDV bf	-		-	
Additions				
without FYAs:				
Car			13,000	
WDA 18%			(2,340) x 75%	1,755
Acquisition - stall	6,400			
AIA claimed	(6,400)	0		6,400
WDV cf		-	10,660	
Total Capital Allowances				8,155

Adjustment of Profits

	£	£
Net Profit per accounts		27,750
Add Back:		
Expenditure that is shown in the accounts but is not allowable		
Depreciation		3,250
Private motor expenses (£1,000 x 25%)		250
Adjustment to reflect profit in goods taken for own use		2,000
		33,250
Deduct:		
Allowable expenditure not shown in accounts		
Capital Allowances	8,155	
		(8,155)
Adjusted Profits for y/e 31/12/2016		25,095

Trading Income assessment for 2015/16

This is Mark's first tax year for the business. The basis period is:
1/1/2016 - 5/4/2016

This is apportioned from the adjusted profits as:
£25,095 x 3/12 = £6,274

Class 4 National Insurance

This is calculated based on the trading income. As his income is below £8,060 there is no Class 4 NIC payable for 2015/16.

Supplementary tax return pages

These are shown on the next three pages.

Make sure that you can understand where the data has been obtained for each box that has been completed.

Note that we have used the 2014/15 version of the form here as the 2015/16 version was not available when this book was published.

HM Revenue & Customs

Self-employment (full)

Tax year 6 April 2014 to 5 April 2015 (2014-15)

Please read the 'Self-employment (full) notes' to check if you should use this page or the 'Self-employment (short)' page.

ℹ To get notes and helpsheets that will help you fill in this form, go to **www.hmrc.gov.uk/selfassessmentforms**

Your name

MARK UPP

Your Unique Taxpayer Reference (UTR)

Business details

1 Business name – unless it is in your own name

2 Description of business

MARKET TRADER

3 First line of your business address – unless you work from home

4 Postcode of your business address

5 If the details in boxes 1, 2, 3 or 4 have changed in the last 12 months, put 'X' in the box and give details in the 'Any other information' box

6 If your business started after 5 April 2014, enter the start date DD MM YYYY

01 01 2016

7 If your business ceased after 5 April 2014 but before 6 April 2015, enter the final date of trading

8 Date your books or accounts start – the beginning of your accounting period

01 01 2016

9 Date your books or accounts are made up to or the end of your accounting period – read the notes if you have filled in box 6 or 7

31 12 2016

10 If you used the cash basis, money actually received and paid out, to calculate your income and expenses, put 'X' in the box – read the notes

Other information

11 If your accounting date has changed permanently, put 'X' in the box

12 If your accounting date has changed more than once since 2009, put 'X' in the box

13 If special arrangements apply, put 'X' in the box – read the notes

14 If you provided the information about your 2014–15 profit on last year's tax return, put 'X' in the box – read the notes

Business income

15 Your turnover – the takings, fees, sales or money earned by your business

£ 90000 · 00

16 Any other business income not included in box 15

£ · 00

Business expenses

Please read the 'Self-employment (full) notes' before filling in this section.

Total expenses

If your annual turnover was below £81,000, you may just put your total expenses in box 31

17 Cost of goods bought for resale or goods used

£ 45 000 . 0 0

18 Construction industry – payments to subcontractors

£ . 0 0

19 Wages, salaries and other staff costs

£ 6 500 . 0 0

20 Car, van and travel expenses

£ 1 000 . 0 0

21 Rent, rates, power and insurance costs

£ 2 500 . 0 0

22 Repairs and renewals of property and equipment

£ . 0 0

23 Phone, fax, stationery and other office costs

£ . 0 0

24 Advertising and business entertainment costs

£ . 0 0

25 Interest on bank and other loans

£ 1 000 . 0 0

26 Bank, credit card and other financial charges

£ . 0 0

27 Irrecoverable debts written off

£ . 0 0

28 Accountancy, legal and other professional fees

£ . 0 0

29 Depreciation and loss/profit on sale of assets

£ 3 250 . 0 0

30 Other business expenses

£ 3 000 . 0 0

31 Total expenses (total of boxes 17 to 30)

£ 62 250 . 0 0

Disallowable expenses

Use this column if the figures in boxes 17 to 30 include disallowable amounts

32

£ . 0 0

33

£ . 0 0

34

£ . 0 0

35

£ 250 . 0 0

36

£ . 0 0

37

£ . 0 0

38

£ . 0 0

39

£ . 0 0

40

£ . 0 0

41

£ . 0 0

42

£ . 0 0

43

£ . 0 0

44

£ 3 250 . 0 0

45

£ . 0 0

46 Total disallowable expenses (total of boxes 32 to 45)

£ 3 500 . 0 0

Net profit or loss

47 **Net profit** – if your business income is more than your expenses (if box 15 + box 16 minus box 31 is positive)

£ 27750 . 0 0

48 **Or, net loss** – if your expenses are more than your business income (if box 31 minus (box 15 + box 16) is positive)

£ . 0 0

Tax allowances for vehicles and equipment (capital allowances)

There are 'capital' tax allowances for vehicles, equipment and certain buildings used in your business (don't include the cost of these in your business expenses). Please read the 'Self-employment (full) notes' and use the examples to work out your capital allowances.

49 Annual Investment Allowance

£ 6400 . 0 0

50 Capital allowances at 18% on equipment, including cars with lower CO_2 emissions

£ 1755 . 0 0

51 Capital allowances at 8% on equipment, including cars with higher CO_2 emissions

£ . 0 0

52 Restricted capital allowances for cars costing more than £12,000 – if bought before 6 April 2009

£ . 0 0

53 Agricultural or Industrial Buildings Allowance

£ . 0 0

54 Business Premises Renovation Allowance (Assisted Areas only) – read the notes

£ . 0 0

55 100% and other enhanced capital allowances – read the notes

£ . 0 0

56 Allowances on sale or cessation of business use (where you have disposed of assets for less than their tax value)

£ . 0 0

57 Total capital allowances (total of boxes 49 to 56)

£ 8155 . 0 0

58 Balancing charge on sale or cessation of business use (only where Business Premises Renovation Allowance has been claimed) – read the notes

£ . 0 0

59 Balancing charge on sales of other assets or on the cessation of business use (where you have disposed of assets for more than their tax value)

£ . 0 0

Calculating your taxable profit or loss

You may have to adjust your net profit or loss for disallowable expenses or capital allowances to arrive at your taxable profit or your loss for tax purposes. Please read the 'Self-employment (full) notes' and fill in the boxes below that apply.

60 Goods and services for your own use – read the notes

£ 2000 . 0 0

61 Total additions to net profit or deductions from net loss (box 46 + box 58 + box 59 + box 60)

£ 5500 . 0 0

62 Income, receipts and other profits included in business income or expenses but not taxable as business profits

£ . 0 0

63 Total deductions from net profit or additions to net loss (box 57 + box 62)

£ 8155 . 0 0

64 Net business profit for tax purposes (if box 47 + box 61 minus (box 48 + box 63) is positive)

£ 25095 . 0 0

65 Net business loss for tax purposes (if box 48 + box 63 minus (box 47 + box 61) is positive)

£ . 0 0

PARTNERSHIP TAX RETURN

Each partnership needs to complete a tax return (the SA800) which records the profits of the partnership as a whole, as well as the amount of profit allocated to each partner.

Each partner would also complete partnership supplementary pages on their own individual tax returns, but we do not need to consider those pages for our studies.

We need to be able to complete relevant parts of the short version of the partnership tax return, and the 2014/15 version is reproduced on the following 8 pages. We will first explain how the return works in outline, and then use a case study to show how to complete the pages that we need to concentrate on.

Page 1 of the partnership tax return is a narrative that explains how and when to submit the return. It also explains that the return should be completed on behalf of the whole partnership by the nominated partner.

Page 2 of the return has boxes to tick based on income sources of the partnership, and then starts requesting information (including relevant dates) about the trading and professional income.

Page 3 is for a summary of the capital allowances claimed by the partnership. There follow summary boxes for income expenses and profit. This 'three line summary' is only to be used if the partnership has turnover of less than £81,000. For partnerships with greater turnover, page 4 is used instead.

Page 4 requires completion if the partnership turnover is between £81,000 and £15 million. It uses two columns for expenses, the column on the right for total expenses, with the column on the left for disallowable expenses that are included in the column on the right. This is a similar format to the self-employment pages (full version) that we examined earlier.

Page 5 completes the calculation of trading profit, and is followed by a summary of the partnership statement of financial position (balance sheet).

Page 6 is where the allocation of the partnership profits commences. The left side of the page is for a summary of the partnership profits, and the right side is the allocation of those profits to the first partner.

Within the left column, the following boxes in particular may need to be completed in an examination:

> **Box 11**   Profit from a trade or profession – this is the profit of the partnership after adjustments for disallowable expenses and capital allowances etc.

Box 22 UK taxed interest etc – this is for the gross amount of interest received from banks etc. If you are provided with the net amount you will need to add back the tax deducted to arrive at the correct gross amount.

Box 24 CIS deductions – this is for tax deductions made from amounts received by the partnership. It relates to the construction industry where there is a scheme set up so that sub-contractors (eg the partnership) receive amounts after deduction of tax (in a similar way to PAYE).

Box 25 Income Tax taken off – this would apply where bank interest was received net of tax. The gross amount would go in box 22, and the tax deducted in box 25.

Box 29 Partnership charges – these are amounts paid out by the partnership that individual partners can claim relief for. These must be for wholly commercial reasons, but the detail of these is beyond the scope of your studies.

Page 7 is for the allocation to up to two further partners, and effectively duplicates the right side of page 6.

Page 8 is for mainly contact information, plus a declaration for signature if a paper version of the form is completed.

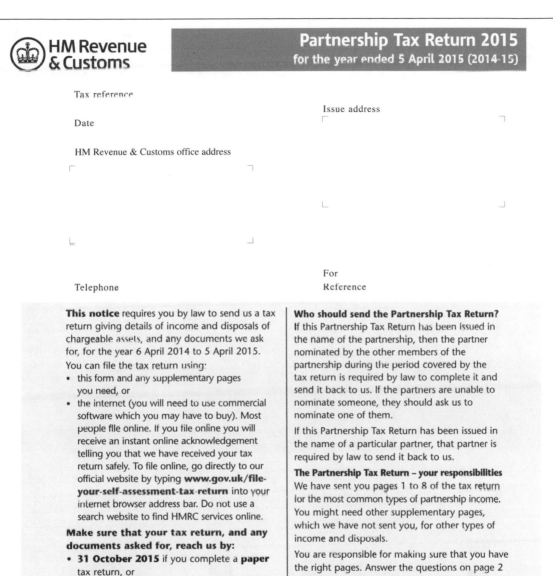

HM Revenue & Customs

Partnership Tax Return 2015
for the year ended 5 April 2015 (2014-15)

Tax reference

Date

HM Revenue & Customs office address

Issue address

For
Reference

Telephone

This notice requires you by law to send us a tax return giving details of income and disposals of chargeable assets, and any documents we ask for, for the year 6 April 2014 to 5 April 2015.

You can file the tax return using:

- this form and any supplementary pages you need, or
- the internet (you will need to use commercial software which you may have to buy). Most people file online. If you file online you will receive an instant online acknowledgement telling you that we have received your tax return safely. To file online, go directly to our official website by typing **www.gov.uk/file-your-self-assessment-tax-return** into your internet browser address bar. Do not use a search website to find HMRC services online.

Make sure that your tax return, and any documents asked for, reach us by:

- **31 October 2015** if you complete a **paper** tax return, or
- **31 January 2016** if you file online

Please see the Partnership Tax Return Guide for filing dates if this notice was given after 31 July 2015 or if the partnership includes a company as a partner.

Each partner who was a member of the partnership during the return period is liable to automatic penalties if the Partnership Tax Return does not reach us by the relevant filing date shown above. They will have to pay interest and may have to pay a late payment penalty on any tax they pay late.

We check all tax returns and there are penalties for supplying false or incomplete information.

Who should send the Partnership Tax Return?
If this Partnership Tax Return has been issued in the name of the partnership, then the partner nominated by the other members of the partnership during the period covered by the tax return is required by law to complete it and send it back to us. If the partners are unable to nominate someone, they should ask us to nominate one of them.

If this Partnership Tax Return has been issued in the name of a particular partner, that partner is required by law to send it back to us.

The Partnership Tax Return – your responsibilities
We have sent you pages 1 to 8 of the tax return for the most common types of partnership income. You might need other supplementary pages, which we have not sent you, for other types of income and disposals.

You are responsible for making sure that you have the right pages. Answer the questions on page 2 of this form to find out if you have the right ones.

You should make sure that the information needed by individual partners to complete their personal tax returns is given to them as quickly as possible (some partners may want to send their own returns by 31 October 2015).

If you need help:

- refer to the Partnership Tax Return Guide (included with this return, unless we know you have a tax adviser), or
- phone the number above – we can answer most questions by phone, or
- when the office is closed, phone our helpline on **0300 200 3310** for general advice, or
- go to **www.gov.uk/self-assessment-tax-returns**

PARTNERSHIP BUSINESS AND INVESTMENT INCOME for the year ended 5 April 2015

Answer Questions 1 to 6 on this page and Question 7 on page 8 to check that you have the pages you need to make a complete return of partnership income and related information for the year ended 5 April 2015. If you answer 'Yes', you must make sure that you have the right pages and then fill in the relevant boxes. If not, go to the next question.

To get the appropriate supplementary pages and notes that will help you fill in this form, go to www.hmrc.gov.uk/selfassessmentforms

Check to make sure that you have the right supplementary pages (including the Partnership Savings pages – see Question 7) and then tick the box below

Q1 Did the partnership receive any rent or other income from UK property (read the Partnership Tax Return Guide if you have furnished holiday lettings)?

YES [ ]   UK PROPERTY [ ]

Q2 Did the partnership have any foreign income?

YES [ ]   FOREIGN [ ]

Q3 Did the partnership business include a trade or profession at any time between 6 April 2014 and 5 April 2015?

YES [ ]   If yes, complete boxes 3.1 to 3.117 on pages 2 to 5 as appropriate.

Q4 Did the partnership dispose of any chargeable assets?

YES [ ]   CHARGEABLE ASSETS [ ]

Q5 During the return period has the partnership included any member who is:

- a company

YES [ ]

- not resident in the UK

YES [ ]   If yes, read the Partnership Tax Return Guide about filling in the Partnership Statement, go to hmrc.gov.uk/selfassessmentforms

- a partner in a business controlled and managed abroad and who is not domiciled in the UK or is not ordinarily resident in the UK?

YES [ ]   If yes, read the Partnership Tax Return Guide.

Q6 Are you completing this tax return on behalf of a European Economic Interest Grouping (EEIG)?

YES [ ]   If yes, read the Partnership Tax Return Guide.

TRADING AND PROFESSIONAL INCOME for the year ended 5 April 2015

You have to fill in a set of boxes for each trade carried on by the partnership and you may have to fill in a separate set if partnership accounts were made up to more than one date in the year ended 5 April 2015. Check the rules in the Partnership Tax Return Guide.

Box numbers 3.3, 3.6, 3.74 to 3.81, 3.85 to 3.92 and 3.94 to 3.96 are not used.

■ **Partnership details**

Name of business

3.1 [ ]

Description of partnership trade or profession

3.2 [ ]

Accounting period – read the Partnership Tax Return Guide, go to www.hmrc.gov.uk/selfassessmentforms

Start

3.4 [/ /]

End

3.5 [/ /]

- Date of commencement (if after 5 April 2012)

3.7 [/ /]

- Date of cessation (if before 6 April 2015)

3.8 [/ /]

- Tick box 3.9 if you used the 'cash basis', money actually received and paid out, to calculate your income and expenses – read the guide

3.9 [ ]

- Tick box 3.10 if you do not need to complete boxes 3.14 to 3.93 and boxes 3.99 to 3.115

3.10 [ ]

- Tick box 3.11 if the partnership's accounts do not cover the period from the last accounting date (explain why in the 'Additional information' box, box 3.116 on page 3)

3.11 [ ]

- Tick box 3.12 if your accounting date has changed (only if this is a permanent change and you want it to count for tax)

3.12 [ ]

- Tick box 3.13 if this is the second or further change (explain why you have not used the same date as last year in the 'Additional information' box, box 3.116 on page 3).

3.13 [ ]

TRADING AND PROFESSIONAL INCOME for the year ended 5 April 2015 – continued

■ Capital allowances – summary

	Capital allowances	Balancing charges
● Annual Investment Allowance (include any balancing charges in box 3.17 below)	**3.13A** £	
● Cars costing more than £12,000 – if bought before 6 April 2009. (You should make a separate calculation for each car.)	**3.14** £	**3.15** £
● Capital allowances at 18% on equipment, including cars with lower CO_2 emissions	**3.14A** £	**3.15A** £
● Capital allowances at 8% on equipment, including cars with higher CO_2 emissions	**3.16** £	**3.17** £
● Agricultural or Industrial Buildings Allowance. (You must make a separate calculation for each block of expenditure.)	**3.18** £	**3.19** £
● 100% and other enhanced capital allowances claimed (you must make separate calculations). (Claims to and balancing charges arising on Business Premises Renovation Allowance must also be included in boxes 10.4 and 10.5 respectively.)	**3.20** £	**3.21** £
	total of column above	total of column above
Total capital allowances/balancing charges	**3.22** £	**3.23** £

■ Income and expenses for this accounting period

Read the **Partnership Tax Return Guide** before completing this section.

If your annual turnover was below £81,000 (or would have been if you had traded for the whole year) **fill in boxes 3.24 to 3.26 instead of page 4**.

If your annual turnover was between £81,000 and £15m (or would have been if you had traded for a whole year) **ignore boxes 3.24 to 3.26. Now fill in page 4**.

If the combined annualised turnover from all of your activities was **more than £15m fill in boxes 3.24 to 3.26 and send in partnership accounts and computations as well.**

In all cases, complete box 3.83 or box 3.84 on page 5, and the other boxes on page 5 if applicable.

● Turnover including other business receipts, and goods etc taken for personal use (and balancing charges from box 3.23)	**3.24** £
● Expenses allowable for tax (including capital allowances from box 3.22)	**3.25** £
	box 3.24 minus box 3.25
Net profit for this accounting period (put figure in brackets if a loss)	**3.26** £

3.116 Additional information

TRADING AND PROFESSIONAL INCOME for the year ended 5 April 2015 – continued

■ **Income and expenses for this accounting period**

You must fill in this page if your annual turnover was between £81,000 and £15m. If the combined annualised turnover from all your activities was more than £15m, fill in boxes 3.24 to 3.26 on page 3 and send in the partnership accounts and computations as well. In all cases, complete box 3.83 or box 3.84 on page 5, and the other boxes on page 5 if applicable. Read the Partnership Tax Return Guide, go to **www.hmrc.gov.uk/selfassessmentforms**

If you were registered for VAT, do the figures in boxes 3.29 to 3.64 include VAT? **3.27** [ ] or exclude VAT? **3.28** [ ]

	Disallowable expenses included in boxes 3.46 to 3.63	Total expenses	Sales/business income (turnover)
			3.29 £
• Cost of sales	**3.30** £	**3.46** £	
• Construction industry subcontractor costs	**3.31** £	**3.47** £	
• Other direct costs	**3.32** £	**3.48** £	
		Gross profit/(loss)	box 3.29 minus (boxes 3.46 + 3.47 + 3.48) **3.49** £
		Other income/profits	**3.50** £
• Employee costs	**3.33** £	**3.51** £	
• Premises costs	**3.34** £	**3.52** £	
• Repairs	**3.35** £	**3.53** £	
• General administrative expenses	**3.36** £	**3.54** £	
• Motor expenses	**3.37** £	**3.55** £	
• Travel and subsistence	**3.38** £	**3.56** £	
• Advertising, promotion and entertainment	**3.39** £	**3.57** £	
• Legal and professional costs	**3.40** £	**3.58** £	
• Bad debts	**3.41** £	**3.59** £	
• Interest and alternative finance payments	**3.42** £	**3.60** £	
• Other finance charges	**3.43** £	**3.61** £	
• Depreciation and loss/(profit) on sale	**3.44** £	**3.62** £	
• Other expenses including partnership charges	**3.45** £	**3.63** £	
	Put the total of boxes 3.30 to 3.45 in box 3.66 below	Total expenses	boxes 3.51 to 3.63 **3.64** £
		Net profit/(loss)	boxes 3.49 + 3.50 minus 3.64 **3.65** £

■ **Tax adjustments to net profit or loss for this accounting period**

• Disallowable expenses	boxes 3.30 to 3.45 **3.66** £	
• Goods, etc taken for personal use and other adjustments (apart from disallowable expenses) that increase profits	**3.67** £	
• Balancing charges (from box 3.23)	**3.68** £	
Total additions to net profit (deduct from net loss)		boxes 3.66 + 3.67 + 3.68 **3.69** £
• Capital allowances (from box 3.22)	**3.70** £	
• Deductions from net profit (add to net loss)	**3.71** £	boxes 3.70 + 3.71 **3.72** £
Net business profit for tax purposes for this accounting period (put figure in brackets if a loss)		boxes 3.65 + 3.69 minus box 3.72 **3.73** £

TRADING AND PROFESSIONAL INCOME for the year ended 5 April 2015 – continued

■ **Taxable profit or loss for this accounting period**

● Adjustment on change of basis   **3.82** £ _____

Copy this figure to box 11A in the Partnership Statement

Net profit for this accounting period (if loss, enter '0' here) from box 3.26 or box 3.73   **3.83** £ _____

Copy this figure to box 11 in the Partnership Statement

Allowable loss for this accounting period (if profit, enter '0' here) from box 3.26 or box 3.73   **3.84** £ _____

Copy this figure to box 12 in the Partnership Statement

Tick box 3.93 if the figure in box 3.83 or box 3.84 is provisional   **3.93** _____

■ **Subcontractors in the construction industry**

● Deductions on payment and deduction statements from contractors – construction industry subcontractors only   **3.97** £ _____

Copy this figure to box 24 in the Partnership Statement

■ **Tax taken off trading income**

● Tax taken off trading income (excluding deductions made by contractors on account of tax)   **3.98** £ _____

Read the Partnership Tax Return Guide if you are a 'CT Partnership', go to **hmrc.gov.uk/selfassessmentforms**

Copy this figure to box 24A in the Partnership Statement

■ **Summary of balance sheet for this accounting period**

Leave these boxes blank if you do not have a balance sheet or your annual turnover was more than £15m.

Assets

● Plant, machinery and motor vehicles   **3.99** £ _____

● Other fixed assets (premises, goodwill, investments, etc)   **3.100** £ _____

● Stock and work in progress   **3.101** £ _____

● Debtors/prepayments/other current assets   **3.102** £ _____

● Bank/building society balances   **3.103** £ _____

● Cash in hand   **3.104** £ _____

boxes 3.99 to 3.104   **3.105** £ _____

Liabilities

● Trade creditors/accruals   **3.106** £ _____

● Loans and overdrawn bank accounts   **3.107** £ _____

● Other liabilities   **3.108** £ _____

boxes 3.106 to 3.108   **3.109** £ _____

box 3.105 minus box 3.109

Net business assets (put the figure in brackets if you had net business liabilities)   **3.110** £ _____

Represented by partners' current and capital accounts

● Balance at start of period*   **3.111** £ _____

● Net profit/(loss)*   **3.112** £ _____

● Capital introduced   **3.113** £ _____

● Drawings   **3.114** £ _____

boxes 3.111 to 3.113 minus box 3.114

● Balance at end of period*   **3.115** £ _____

* If the capital account is overdrawn, or the business made a net loss, show the figure in brackets.

Box 3.116 'Additional information' is on page 3.

■ **Partnership trade charges**

● Net partnership charges paid in the period 6 April 2014 to 5 April 2015 (**not** the accounting period)   **3.117** £ _____

SA800 2015   PARTNERSHIP TAX RETURN: PAGE 5

PARTNERSHIP STATEMENT (SHORT) for the year ended 5 April 2015

Please read these instructions before completing the Statement

Use these pages to allocate partnership income if the only income for the relevant return period was trading and professional income or taxed interest and alternative finance receipts from banks and building societies. Otherwise you must download or ask the SA Orderline for the 'Partnership Statement (Full)' pages to record details of the allocation of all the partnership income. Go to **www.hmrc.gov.uk/selfassessmentforms**

Step 1   Fill in boxes 1 to 29 and boxes A and B as appropriate. Get the figures you need from the relevant boxes in the Partnership Tax Return. Complete a separate Statement for each accounting period covered by this Partnership Tax Return and for each trade or profession carried on by the partnership.

Step 2   Then allocate the amounts in boxes 11 to 29 attributable to each partner using the allocation columns on this page and page 7, read the Partnership Tax Return Guide, go to **hmrc.gov.uk/selfassessmentforms** If the partnership has more than 3 partners, please photocopy page 7.

Step 3   Each partner will need a copy of their allocation of income to fill in their personal tax return.

PARTNERSHIP INFORMATION

If the partnership business includes a trade or profession, enter here the accounting period for which appropriate items in this statement are returned.

Start   **1**   /   /

End   **2**   /   /

Nature of trade   **3**

MIXED PARTNERSHIPS

Tick here if this Statement is drawn up using Corporation Tax rules   **4**

Tick here if this Statement is drawn up using tax rules for non-residents   **5**

Individual partner details

6   Name of partner

Address

Postcode

Date appointed as a partner (if during 2013–14 or 2014–15)

7   /   /

Date ceased to be a partner (if during 2013–14 or 2014–15)

9   /   /

Partner's Unique Taxpayer Reference (UTR)

8

Partner's National Insurance number

10

Partnership's profits, losses, income, tax credits, etc

Tick this box if the items entered in the box had foreign tax taken off

Partner's share of profits, losses, income, tax credits, etc

Copy figures in boxes 11 to 29 to boxes in the individual's **Partnership (short)** pages as shown below

● **for an accounting period ended in 2014–15** ▼

from box 3.83 Profit from a trade or profession **A**	**11** £	Profit **11** £	Copy this figure to box 8
from box 3.82 Adjustment on change of basis	**11A** £	**11A** £	Copy this figure to box 10
from box 3.84 Loss from a trade or profession **B**	**12** £	Loss **12** £	Copy this figure to box 8
from box 10.4 Business Premises Renovation Allowance	**12A** £	**12A** £	Copy this figure to box 15

● **for the period 6 April 2014 to 5 April 2015***

from box 7.9A UK taxed interest and taxed alternative finance receipts	**22** £	**22** £	Copy this figure to box 28
from box 3.97 CIS deductions made by contractors on account of tax	**24** £	**24** £	Copy this figure to box 30
from box 3.98 Other tax taken off trading income	**24A** £	**24A** £	Copy this figure to box 31
from box 7.8A Income Tax taken off	**25** £	**25** £	Copy this figure to box 29
from box 3.117 Partnership charges	**29** £	**29** £	Copy this figure to box 4, 'Other tax reliefs' section on page Ai 2 in your personal tax return

* if you are a 'CT Partnership' see the Partnership Tax Return Guide

PARTNERSHIP STATEMENT (SHORT) for the year ended 5 April 2015 - continued

Individual partner details

6 Name of partner

Address

Postcode

Date appointed as a partner
(if during 2013–14 or 2014–15)

7 / /

Partner's Unique Taxpayer Reference (UTR)

8

Date ceased to be a partner
(if during 2013–14 or 2014–15)

9 / /

Partner's National Insurance number

10

Partner's share of profits, losses, income, tax credits, etc

Copy figures in boxes 11 to 29 to
boxes in the individual's Partnership
(short) pages as shown below

Profit **11** £	Copy this figure to box 8
11A £	Copy this figure to box 10
Loss **12** £	Copy this figure to box 8
12A £	Copy this figure to box 15
22 £	Copy this figure to box 28
24 £	Copy this figure to box 30
24A £	Copy this figure to box 31
25 £	Copy this figure to box 29
29 £	Copy this figure to box 4, 'Other tax reliefs' section on page Ai 2 in your personal tax return

Individual partner details

6 Name of partner

Address

Postcode

Date appointed as a partner
(if during 2013–14 or 2014–15)

7 / /

Partner's Unique Taxpayer Reference (UTR)

8

Date ceased to be a partner
(if during 2013–14 or 2014–15)

9 / /

Partner's National Insurance number

10

Partner's share of profits, losses, income, tax credits, etc

Copy figures in boxes 11 to 29 to
boxes in the individual's Partnership
(short) pages as shown below

Profit **11** £	Copy this figure to box 8
11A £	Copy this figure to box 10
Loss **12** £	Copy this figure to box 8
12A £	Copy this figure to box 15
22 £	Copy this figure to box 28
24 £	Copy this figure to box 30
24A £	Copy this figure to box 31
25 £	Copy this figure to box 29
29 £	Copy this figure to box 4, 'Other tax reliefs' section on page Ai 2 in your personal tax return

OTHER INFORMATION for the year ended 5 April 2015

Q7 **Did the partnership receive any other income which you have not already included elsewhere in the Partnership Tax Return?** Make sure that you fill in the pages for Questions 1 to 4 before answering Question 7

YES ☐ If Yes, read the guidance below

If you ticked the 'Yes' box and the only income was interest, or alternative finance receipts with tax taken off, from banks and building societies, fill in boxes 7.7A to 7.9A below. Otherwise download the Partnership Savings pages, go to www.hmrc.gov.uk/selfassessmentforms and leave boxes 7.7A to 7.9A blank. If you have more than one account, enter **totals** in the boxes.

Interest and alternative finance receipts from UK banks and building societies, paid **with** tax taken off for the period 6 April 2014 to 5 April 2015 (**not** the accounting period)	Amount after tax taken off **7.7A** £	Tax taken off **7.8A** £ Copy this figure to box 25 in the Partnership Statement	Gross amount before tax **7.9A** £ Copy this figure to box 22 in the Partnership Statement

Q8 **Are the details on the front of the Partnership Tax Return wrong?**

YES ☐ If yes, make any corrections on the front of the form

Q9 **Please give a daytime phone number (including the area code) in boxes 9.1 and 9.2** It is often simpler to phone if we need to ask you about your tax return.

Your phone number **9.1** ☐

or, if you prefer, your adviser's phone number **9.2** ☐

Your adviser's name and address **9.3** ☐

Postcode

Q10 **Other information**

Please tick box 10.1 if this Partnership Tax Return contains figures that are provisional because you do not yet have final figures. The Partnership Tax Return Guide explains the circumstances in which provisional figures may be used and asks you to provide some additional information in box 3.116 on page 3. **10.1** ☐

Disclosure of tax avoidance schemes – If the partnership is a party to one or more disclosable tax avoidance schemes, you must complete boxes 10.2 and 10.3. Give details of each scheme (up to 3) on a separate line. If the partnership is party to more than 3 schemes, details of the additional schemes must be reported on form AAG4, 'Disclosure of avoidance scheme'.

Scheme reference number or promoter reference number	**10.2** ☐	Tax year in which the expected advantage to the partners arises – year ended 5 April	**10.3** ☐

Business Premises Renovation Allowance (BPRA) – read the Partnership Tax Return Guide before you fill in these boxes. Extract from boxes 3.20 and 3.21 (and boxes 1.36 and 1.34 from the Partnership UK Property pages) the amounts that relate to any BPRA claims or charges. Enter claims to BPRA in box 10.4 and charges in box 10.5

Capital allowance **10.4** £ Copy this figure to box 12A in the Partnership Statement

Balancing charge **10.5** £

Q11 **Declaration** – I have filled in and am sending back to you the following:

1 TO 5 OF THIS FORM ☐	PARTNERSHIP FOREIGN ☐
6 & 7 PARTNERSHIP STATEMENT (SHORT) ☐	PARTNERSHIP TRADING ☐
6 & 7 PARTNERSHIP STATEMENT (FULL) ☐	PARTNERSHIP DISPOSAL OF CHARGEABLE ASSETS ☐
PARTNERSHIP UK PROPERTY ☐	PARTNERSHIP SAVINGS ☐

I attach **11.1** ☐ additional copies of page 7. There were **11.2** ☐ partners in this partnership for that period.

Before you send the completed tax return back to your current HM Revenue & Customs office, you must sign the statement below.

If you give false information or conceal any part of the partnership's income or details of the disposal of chargeable assets, you may be liable to financial penalties and/or we may prosecute you.

11.3 **I the nominated partner,** declare that the information I have given on this Partnership Tax Return is correct and complete to the best of my knowledge and belief.

Nominated Partner Signature

Date

Print name in full here

If you have signed for someone else, please also:
- state the capacity in which you are signing (for example, as executor or receiver)

11.4 ☐

- give the name of the person you are signing for and **your** name and address in the 'Additional information' box, box 3.116, on page 3.

PENN, QUILL AND WRIGHT: PARTNERSHIP TAX RETURN

John Penn, Daisy Quill and Sue Wright have been trading in partnership for several years. They produce accounts each year up to 30 June. Their individual trading income assessments have already been calculated for 2015/16 as follows (see Case Study on pages 7.17 – 7.18):

John Penn	£30,000
Daisy Quill	£27,500
Sue Wright	£37,500

These profit figures are based on the accounting year ended 30 June 2015, which recorded an adjusted profit for tax purposes (after capital allowances) of £95,000.

In addition to the above trading income, the partnership also receives non-trading interest, which is split equally amongst the partners. This totalled £3,000 (gross) for the tax year 2015/16. Tax of £600 had been deducted.

required

Complete (as far as information permits) pages 6 and 7 of the partnership tax return for 2015/16.

solution

See next two pages.

Note that we have used the 2014/15 version of the form here as the 2015/16 version was not available.

PARTNERSHIP STATEMENT (SHORT) for the year ended 5 April 2015

Please read these instructions before completing the Statement

Use these pages to allocate partnership income if the only income for the relevant return period was trading and professional income or taxed interest and alternative finance receipts from banks and building societies. Otherwise you must download or ask the SA Orderline for the 'Partnership Statement (Full)' pages to record details of the allocation of all the partnership income. Go to www.hmrc.gov.uk/selfassessmentforms

Step 1 Fill in boxes 1 to 29 and boxes A and B as appropriate. Get the figures you need from the relevant boxes in the Partnership Tax Return. Complete a separate Statement for each accounting period covered by this Partnership Tax Return and for each trade or profession carried on by the partnership.

Step 2 Then allocate the amounts in boxes 11 to 29 attributable to each partner using the allocation columns on this page and page 7, read the Partnership Tax Return Guide, go to **hmrc.gov.uk/selfassessmentforms** If the partnership has more than 3 partners, please photocopy page 7.

Step 3 Each partner will need a copy of their allocation of income to fill in their personal tax return.

PARTNERSHIP INFORMATION

If the partnership business includes a trade or profession, enter here the accounting period for which appropriate items in this statement are returned.

Start **1** 1 / 7 / 14

End **2** 30 / 6 / 15

Nature of trade **3**

MIXED PARTNERSHIPS

Tick here if this Statement is drawn up using Corporation Tax rules **4**

Tick here if this Statement is drawn up using tax rules for non-residents **5**

Individual partner details

6 Name of partner

Address   JOHN PENN

Postcode

Date appointed as a partner (if during 2013–14 or 2014–15) **7**   /   /

Partner's Unique Taxpayer Reference (UTR) **8**

Date ceased to be a partner (if during 2013–14 or 2014–15) **9**   /   /

Partner's National Insurance number **10**

Partnership's profits, losses, income, tax credits, etc

Tick this box if the items entered in the box had foreign tax taken off

Partner's share of profits, losses, income, tax credits, etc

Copy figures in boxes 11 to 29 to boxes in the individual's **Partnership (short)** pages as shown below

● **for an accounting period ended in 2014–15** ▼

		Partnership	Partner's share	
from box 3.83 Profit from a trade or profession **A**	**11** £ 95000	Profit **11** £ 30000	Copy this figure to box 8
from box 3.82 Adjustment on change of basis	**11A** £	**11A** £	Copy this figure to box 10
from box 3.84 Loss from a trade or profession **B**	**12** £	Loss **12** £	Copy this figure to box 8
from box 10.4 Business Premises Renovation Allowance	**12A** £	**12A** £	Copy this figure to box 15

● **for the period 6 April 2014 to 5 April 2015***

from box 7.9A UK taxed interest and taxed alternative finance receipts	**22** £ 3000	**22** £ 1000	Copy this figure to box 28
from box 3.97 CIS deductions made by contractors on account of tax	**24** £	**24** £	Copy this figure to box 30
from box 3.98 Other tax taken off trading income	**24A** £	**24A** £	Copy this figure to box 31
from box 7.8A Income Tax taken off	**25** £ 600	**25** £ 200	Copy this figure to box 29
from box 3.117 Partnership charges	**29** £	**29** £	Copy this figure to box 4, 'Other tax reliefs' section on page Ai 2 in your personal tax return

* if you are a 'CT Partnership' see the Partnership Tax Return Guide

PARTNERSHIP STATEMENT (SHORT) for the year ended 5 April 2015 – continued

Individual partner details

6 Name of partner DAISY QUILL

Address

Postcode

Date appointed as a partner
(if during 2013–14 or 2014–15)

7 / /

8 Partner's Unique Taxpayer Reference (UTR)

Date ceased to be a partner
(if during 2013–14 or 2014–15)

9 / /

10 Partner's National Insurance number

Partner's share of profits, losses, income, tax credits, etc

Copy figures in boxes 11 to 29 to
boxes in the individual's Partnership
(short) pages as shown below

Profit	**11**	£ 2 7 5 0 0	Copy this figure to box 8
	11A	£	Copy this figure to box 10
Loss	**12**	£	Copy this figure to box 8
	12A	£	Copy this figure to box 15
	22	£ 1 0 0 0	Copy this figure to box 28
	24	£	Copy this figure to box 30
	24A	£	Copy this figure to box 31
	25	£ 2 0 0	Copy this figure to box 29
	29	£	Copy this figure to box 4, 'Other tax reliefs' section on page Ai 2 in your personal tax return

Individual partner details

6 Name of partner SUE WRIGHT

Address

Postcode

Date appointed as a partner
(if during 2013–14 or 2014–15)

7 / /

8 Partner's Unique Taxpayer Reference (UTR)

Date ceased to be a partner
(if during 2013–14 or 2014–15)

9 / /

10 Partner's National Insurance number

Partner's share of profits, losses, income, tax credits, etc

Copy figures in boxes 11 to 29 to
boxes in the individual's Partnership
(short) pages as shown below

Profit	**11**	£ 3 7 5 0 0	Copy this figure to box 8
	11A	£	Copy this figure to box 10
Loss	**12**	£	Copy this figure to box 8
	12A	£	Copy this figure to box 15
	22	£ 1 0 0 0	Copy this figure to box 28
	24	£	Copy this figure to box 30
	24A	£	Copy this figure to box 31
	25	£ 2 0 0	Copy this figure to box 29
	29	£	Copy this figure to box 4, 'Other tax reliefs' section on page Ai 2 in your personal tax return

KEEPING RECORDS

Sole traders and partnerships need to keep records relating to their trading for five years after the online tax return is due to be submitted. For the tax year 2015/16 the return is due on 31 January 2017, and so the records must be kept until 31 January 2022. This date would be extended if HM Revenue & Customs were holding an enquiry into the taxpayer.

The records kept would be very similar to those retained by a limited company, as explained earlier. The records should be able to back up the information on the tax return, and would include:

- statement of profit or loss (income statement) and statements of financial position (balance sheets)
- cash books and bank statements
- account ledgers or working papers
- invoices relating to allowable expenses and the acquisition of non-current (fixed) assets
- non-current asset schedules
- taxation working papers, including capital allowance computations
- copies of tax returns

Chapter Summary

- When sole traders or partnerships commence trading they are subject to special basis period rules. The first tax year in which they are assessed is the year into which the start date falls. The basis period for this tax year is from the date of commencement until the following 5 April. The following tax year will usually have as its basis period as either the 12 months ending on the accounting date in that tax year, or if that is impossible, the first 12 months of the business. Overlap profits may arise that have been assessed twice, and these can be relieved on cessation.

- When sole traders or partnerships cease trading the final tax year will be the one in which the final date of trading falls. The basis period for this tax year will be from the last day of the basis period of the previous tax year to the date of cessation.

- Trading profits and losses for a partnership are divided amongst the partners according to the profit sharing agreement that is in force during the accounting period. This could include the allocation of salaries and/or interest on capitals, as well as a share of remaining profits or losses. These amounts all form part of the individual partners' trading income assessment.

- When an individual partner joins or leaves a partnership they are subject to the opening or closing basis of assessment rules, just like a sole trader. The basis periods for the other partners are not affected.

- Both sole traders and partners are subject to Class 2 and Class 4 National Insurance contributions. Class 2 is a flat rate, whereas Class 4 is based on profits.

- Income tax is payable by the 31 January following the end of the tax year. Payments on account are often also required. These are payable on the previous 31 January, and 31 July, and are based on the last year's Income Tax.

- There are separate supplementary pages in the Income Tax return for sole traders and there is a separate partnership tax return. These must be completed for each tax year and submitted with the rest of the tax return by the 31 October or 31 January following the end of the tax year, the later date relating to online returns.

Accounting Date

the date to which the accounts are made up. Sole traders and partnerships can choose their regular accounting dates without restriction

Accounting Period

the period for which the business produces its accounts

Basis Period

the link between accounting periods and tax years. For a continuing business, the basis period for a particular tax year is the twelve month accounting period that ends in that tax year. There are special basis period rules when businesses start and cease trading, which may require time-apportionment of adjusted trading profits after capital allowances

Adjusted Trading Profits

the trading profits that have been adjusted for tax purposes by excluding income not taxable as trading income, and non-allowable expenditure

Trading Income Assessment

the taxable trading profit for the tax year. It is made up – after deducting any capital allowances – of adjusted trading profits for the basis period

Activities

7.1   Rashid started in business as a sole trader on 1 December 2014. He made his accounts up to 30 November each year from then on. His adjusted profits (after capital allowances) for his first two years trading were as follows:

1/12/2014 - 30/11/2015   £48,000

1/12/2015 - 30/11/2016   £30,000

Required:

State what the first three tax years will be for the business, and calculate the trading income assessments for each of these tax years.

State the amount of any overlap profits, and the period in which they arose.

7.2   Zorah started in business as a sole trader on 1 February 2013. She made her accounts up to 31 December each year, with the first set of accounts relating to 11 months. Her adjusted profits (after capital allowances) for the first two accounting periods were as follows:

1/2/2013 - 31/12/2013   £33,000

1/1/2014 - 31/12/2014   £48,000

Required:

State what the first three tax years will be for the business, and calculate the trading income assessments for each of these tax years.

State the amount of any overlap profits, and the period in which they arose.

7.3   Adam has been in business as a sole trader for many years, with an accounting date of 30 June. On 31 May 2014 he ceased trading. He had overlap profits brought forward from the start of his business of £5,000. His adjusted profits (after deducting capital allowances) for the last three accounting periods of the business were as follows:

1/7/2011 - 30/6/2012   £40,000

1/7/2012 - 30/6/2013   £36,000

1/7/2013 - 31/5/2014   £20,000

Required:

Calculate the trading income assessment for each of the tax years 2013/14 and 2014/15.

7.4 Alice and Bob have been in partnership for several years, sharing profits and losses equally. They have always made their accounts up to 31 December each year. On 1 October 2013 Colin joined the partnership, and the partnership agreement was changed to Alice 45%, Bob 40%, Colin 15% from that date.

The year ended 31 December 2013 produced adjusted profits (after capital allowances) of £96,000. The year ended 31 December 2014 produced adjusted profits (after capital allowances) of £108,000.

Required:

Calculate separately the trading income assessments for the tax years 2013/14 and 2014/15 for each of the partners, and note any overlap profits for Colin.

7.5 Mark, Norma and Olga had been trading in partnership for many years, sharing profits and losses equally. They had always used 31 March as their accounting date. On 31 March 2016 Olga left the partnership. She had overlap profits brought forward from when she joined the partnership of £4,000.

The partnership accounts for the year ended 31/3/2016 were as follows:

	£	£
Sales		180,000
less cost of sales:		55,000
Gross profit		125,000
less expenses:		
Rent	12,500	
Employees' Wages & NIC	16,500	
Depreciation	12,250	
Motor Expenses	8,000	
General Expenses	3,000	
Bank Interest	1,750	
		54,000
Net Profit		71,000

Notes:

1 There were the following written down values for plant & machinery capital allowances purposes as at 31/3/2015:

General Pool	£35,000
Car (30% private use by Olga)	£16,000

Olga bought the car from the partnership on 31/3/2016 for the market value of £10,000. There were no other transactions in non-current assets during the period.

2   The motor expenses shown in the accounts include £500 relating to private mileage by Olga.

3   General Expenses includes:

Increase in General Provision for Bad Debts   £200

Gift Vouchers as presents for customers   £400

Required:

•   Calculate the capital allowances claimable by the partnership for the accounting year ended 31/3/2016 (Plant & Machinery).

•   Calculate the adjusted profits for the same period, after taking into account the capital allowances.

•   Calculate the trading income assessment for Olga for 2015/16.

•   Calculate the Class 4 National Insurance contributions payable by Olga for 2015/16.

•   Complete pages 3, 4 and 6 of the partnership tax return for the partnership, with the profit appropriated to Olga shown on page 6. Note that adjustment for overlap profits are not taken into account on this form.

        (Blank pages of the 2014/15 version are reproduced in the Appendix of this book or may be downloaded from the Resource pages of www.osbornebooks.co.uk or from www.gov.uk)

7.6   John was an employee for many years, paying Income Tax through PAYE. During the tax year 2013/2014 he left his job and became self-employed. The Income Tax liability and Class 4 NIC has been accurately calculated for each of the tax years 2013/14 and 2014/15 as follows:

2013/14   £8,500 (including £2,300 paid via PAYE)

2014/15   £11,000 (none paid via PAYE)

Based on the above figures, complete the following table by inserting the amounts that John was due to pay relating to the tax years 2013/14 to 2015/16 on the dates shown. Insert zeros in any cells that do not apply.

Payment date	31 Jan 2014 £	31 July 2014 £	31 Jan 2015 £	31 July 2015 £	31 Jan 2016 £	31 July 2016 £
Tax year 2013/14						
Tax year 2014/15						
Tax year 2015/16						
Totals due						

7.7   Shaun Slapp has been in business for many years as a self-employed plasterer, running his business from home. He produces accounts each year to 30 November. His accounts for the year ended 30/11/2015 are as follows:

	£	£
Sales		55,000
less cost of materials		11,000
Gross profit		44,000
less expenses:		
Van running costs	6,300	
Depreciation	2,800	
Wages of part time employee	9,800	
Insurance	1,200	
Accountancy costs	600	
Entertaining	1,000	
Telephone and Postage	800	
		22,500
Net Profit		21,500

The van is used 20% privately, and the van expenses include this element. The telephone and postage costs are 75% business and 25% private. Capital allowances have already been calculated at £4,200 after taking account of private use of the van. It has been agreed that the amount of costs not shown in the above accounts that relate to heating and lighting the room in his house that is used as his business office is £150 per year.

Shaun has an unrelieved trading loss of £6,000 brought forward from 2014/15.

Required:

- Calculate the trading income assessment for Shaun for 2015/16 after taking account of the brought forward loss.

- Record the relevant information on the self-employment (short) supplementary pages SES1 and SES 2 (shown on the next pages).

HM Revenue & Customs

Self-employment (short)

Tax year 6 April 2014 to 5 April 2015 (2014-15)

Please read the 'Self-employment (short) notes' to check if you should use this page or the 'Self-employment (full)' page.

ⓘ To get notes and helpsheets that will help you fill in this form, go to **www.hmrc.gov.uk/selfassessmentforms**

Your name	Your Unique Taxpayer Reference (UTR)

Business details

1 Description of business

2 Postcode of your business address

3 If your business name, description, address or postcode have changed in the last 12 months, put 'X' in the box and give details in the 'Any other information' box of your tax return

4 If you are a foster carer or shared lives carer, put 'X' in the box – read the notes

5 If your business started after 5 April 2014, enter the start date DD MM YYYY

6 If your business ceased before 6 April 2015, enter the final date of trading DD MM YYYY

7 Date your books or accounts are made up to – read the notes

8 If you used the cash basis, money actually received and paid out, to calculate your income and expenses put 'X' in the box – read the notes

Business income – if your annual business turnover was below £81,000

9 Your turnover – the takings, fees, sales or money earned by your business

£ · 0 0

10 Any other business income not included in box 9

£ · 0 0

Allowable business expenses

If your annual turnover was below £81,000 you may just put your total expenses in box 20, rather than filling in the whole section.

11 Costs of goods bought for resale or goods used

£ · 0 0

12 Car, van and travel expenses – after private use proportion

£ · 0 0

13 Wages, salaries and other staff costs

£ · 0 0

14 Rent, rates, power and insurance costs

£ · 0 0

15 Repairs and renewals of property and equipment

£ · 0 0

16 Accountancy, legal and other professional fees

£ · 0 0

17 Interest and bank and credit card etc. financial charges

£ · 0 0

18 Phone, fax, stationery and other office costs

£ · 0 0

19 Other allowable business expenses – client entertaining costs are not an allowable expense

£ · 0 0

20 Total allowable expenses – total of boxes 11 to 19

£ · 0 0

Net profit or loss

21	**Net profit** – if your business income is more than your expenses (if box 9 + box 10 minus box 20 is positive)	22	**Or, net loss** – if your expenses exceed your business income (if box 20 minus (box 9 + box 10) is positive)
	£ · 0 0		£ · 0 0

Tax allowances for vehicles and equipment (capital allowances)

There are 'capital' tax allowances available for vehicles and equipment used in your business. (Please don't include the cost of these in your business expenses)

23	**Annual Investment Allowance**	25	**Other capital allowances**
	£ · 0 0		£ · 0 0
24	**Allowance for small balance of unrelieved expenditure**	26	**Total balancing charges** – where you have disposed of items for more than their value
	£ · 0 0		£ · 0 0

Calculating your taxable profits

Your taxable profit may not be the same as your net profit. Please read the 'Self-employment (short) notes' to see if you need to make any adjustments and fill in the boxes which apply to arrive at your taxable profit for the year.

27	**Goods and/or services for your own use** – read the notes	29	**Loss brought forward from earlier years set off against this year's profits** – up to the amount in box 28
	£ · 0 0		£ · 0 0
28	**Net business profit for tax purposes** (if box 21 + box 26 + box 27 minus (boxes 22 to 25) is positive)	30	**Any other business income not included in box 9 or box 10** – for example, non arm's length reverse premiums
	£ · 0 0		£ · 0 0

Total taxable profits or net business loss

31	**Total taxable profits from this business** (if box 28 + box 30 minus box 29 is positive)	32	**Net business loss for tax purposes** (if boxes 22 to 25 minus (box 21 + box 26 + box 27) is positive)
	£ · 0 0		£ · 0 0

Losses, Class 4 National Insurance contributions (NICs) and CIS deductions

If you have made a loss for tax purposes (box 32), read the 'Self-employment (short) notes' and fill in boxes 33 to 35 as appropriate.

33	**Loss from this tax year set off against other income for 2014–15**	36	**If you are exempt from paying Class 4 NICs, put 'X' in the box** – read the notes
	£ · 0 0		☐
34	**Loss to be carried back to previous year(s) and set off against income (or capital gains)**	37	**If you have been given a 2014–15 Class 4 NICs deferment certificate, put 'X' in the box** – read the notes
	£ · 0 0		☐
35	**Total loss to carry forward after all other set-offs** – including unused losses brought forward	38	**Deductions on payment and deduction statements from contractors** – construction industry subcontractors only
	£ · 0 0		£ · 0 0

7.8 Adrian started trading on 1 February 2014. He makes up his accounts to 31 December each year. The profits were calculated at:

	£
Period to 31 December 2014	66,000
Year to 31 December 2015	81,000
Year to 31 December 2016	90,000

(a) The tax year in which he started trading was (select one):

2012/13   2013/14   2014/15   2015/16

(b) His taxable profits in his first tax year of trading were (select one):

£5,500   £6,000   £11,000   £12,000

(c) His taxable profits in his second tax year of trading were (select one):

£66,000   £72,750   £81,000   £90,000

(d) His taxable profits in his third tax year of trading were (select one):

£66,000   £72,750   £81,000   £90,000

(e) His overlap profits were   £ ☐

(f) His overlap profits are deducted (select one):

- from his first year profits.

- from the profits in the third year of trading.

- from the profits in the final year of trading.

- from any profits chosen by Adrian.

7.9 State whether each of the following statements is true or false.

(a) A loss made by a sole trader can only be relieved against trading profits made in the same tax year.

(b) For a loss made by a sole trader to be relieved in the preceding tax year, it must first have been relieved in the current tax year.

(c) To be relieved in future years, a loss made by a sole trader must be relieved against the profits arising from the same trade.

(d) A loss made by a sole trader can be relieved against total income arising in future years.

(e) A sole trader can restrict the amount of loss carried back to any year so the personal allowances are not lost.

(f) A sole trader can only offet a trading loss against capital gains of the same year if the loss is first set against total income of that year.

8 Capital gains tax for individuals

this chapter covers...

In this final chapter we examine the impact of Capital Gains Tax on disposals of business assets made by individuals. We start by reviewing the basis of assessment and how the gains are calculated and the tax liability worked out.

We then go on to compare this system of tax for individuals to the one that applies to companies under Corporation Tax. Here we need to be especially careful as some rules are the same, but some are quite different.

We then see how to deal with shares and share pools, and the disposal of a business including goodwill. We learn about the reliefs that are specific to the business assets of individuals – entrepreneurs' relief, and gift relief.

Finally we briefly discuss record keeping in connection with Capital Gains Tax.

CAPITAL GAINS TAX – A PERSONAL AND BUSINESS TAX

We saw in Chapter 4 that any chargeable gains that a limited company generates are assessable to Corporation Tax.

Any chargeable gains that an individual makes are instead taxable under Capital Gains Tax (CGT). This tax can apply to the disposal of both **personal** and **business** assets. The disposal of personal assets under CGT is dealt with in the learning area 'Personal Tax' (covered in Osborne Books' *Personal Tax*). In this book we need to see its impact on business assets.

Some of the issues that were covered when we examined chargeable gains for limited companies also apply to sole traders. We will begin by examining the differences between disposals under Capital Gains Tax for sole traders and Corporation Tax for limited companies, and note any common ground. It is very important to distinguish clearly between these taxes, and be careful always to apply the correct rules.

basis of assessment

Capital Gains Tax is applied to individuals by using the same tax years as those used for Income Tax. The basis of assessment for Capital Gains Tax is the chargeable gains less capital losses arising from **disposals** that occur during the **tax year** (not in the basis period of the business). Both the definition of a disposal, and the types of asset that are exempt or chargeable are identical to those applicable under Corporation Tax. Most of the situations that we will come across will be based on the sale or gift of an asset. The interaction of capital allowances with chargeable gains is the same as was described for limited companies.

Two situations where disposals do not give rise to Capital Gains Tax are:

- disposals arising because the owner has died
- any disposal between spouses (husband and wife) or civil partners

HOW IS CAPITAL GAINS TAX CALCULATED?

annual exempt amount

Unlike limited companies, all individuals are entitled to an **annual exempt amount** (or annual exemption) for each tax year. This works in a similar way to a personal allowance under Income Tax. The exempt amount is deducted from the total net gains that have been calculated on the individual assets that have been disposed of during the year. Capital Gains Tax is then worked out on the balance.

The exempt amount is £11,100 in 2015/16. The exempt amount can only be used against capital gains, and is not set against income. It cannot be carried back or forward and used in another tax year.

Once the exempt amount has been deducted from the total net gains, the balance is subject to Capital Gains Tax at 18%, or 28% or a combination of these two rates.

Although Capital Gains Tax is a separate tax from Income Tax, it uses the same band structure. Gains are treated as if they were added on top of taxable income, and the 18% rate is applied to gains falling within the basic rate band and the 28% rate applies to gains within the higher or additional rate bands.

If an individual is already a higher rate or additional rate taxpayer then any gains will always be taxed at 28%. Where the taxpayer pays income tax only at the basic rate (or the starting rate) then any gains will be taxed at 18% provided they do not exceed the basic rate band of £31,785 when added to taxable income. Where they do exceed this amount the excess will be taxed at 28%.

The following example will illustrate the situation.

example

Raymond has total taxable income in 2015/16 of £30,000 after deducting his personal allowance. He made capital gains of £25,000 before deducting his exempt amount.

Raymond has taxable gains of £25,000 – £11,100 (exempt amount) = £13,900.

He has £31,785 – £30,000 = £1,785 remaining in his basic rate band after accounting for his taxable income. Therefore £1,785 of his gains will be taxed at 18%, and the remainder taxed at 28%, as follows:

£1,785 x 18%	£321.30
£12,115 (the remainder of the £13,900) x 28%	£3,392.20
Total Capital Gains tax	£3,713.50

THE COMPUTATION OF EACH GAIN

The standard format that we saw in Chapter 4 in the treatment of Corporation Tax is largely applicable to disposals by individuals chargeable to Capital Gains Tax.

However, Capital Gains Tax computations for individuals are much simpler than the equivalent computations for companies, since for individuals there is no indexation allowance whatsoever.

The basic computation format is as follows:

		£
	Proceeds on disposal	X
	less	
	Incidental costs of disposal	(x)
=	Net proceeds	X
	less	
	Original cost	(x)
	Incidental costs of acquisition	(x)
=	Gain	X

transfer to spouse or civil partner

When an asset is transferred to a spouse or civil partner no capital gain arises, as mentioned earlier. This is achieved by treating the disposal proceeds as the amount needed to generate exactly zero gain or loss.

For example if a wife had bought an asset some time ago for £10,000, (with no other costs) and gave it to her husband, the disposal proceeds would be treated as £10,000 so that no gain would arise. This would also mean that if the husband later sold the asset, his cost would also be considered to be £10,000, and any gain calculated on that basis.

A transfer between spouses or civil partners is often known as being made on a 'no gain, no loss' basis.

transfer to a 'connected person'

When an asset is sold to a connected person at less than market value, the market value is used in the computation of gains. This also applies to **all gifts** (whether to a connected person or not).

The following relatives of the person disposing of the asset are 'connected persons', and so are the relatives' spouses or civil partners:

■ ancestors and spouse's ancestors (parent, grandparent, etc)

■ siblings and spouse's siblings (brother, sister)

■ lineal descendants and spouse's lineal descendants (child, grandchild etc)

In addition, any business partners of the person disposing of the asset are also connected persons, plus their spouses, civil partners and relatives (as defined above).

If a loss is incurred on a disposal to a connected person, the loss cannot be set against general gains, but can only be set against gains made on other disposals to the same person.

exempt assets

The following are the main examples of assets that are exempt from Capital Gains Tax:

- trading inventory (stock)
- cars
- chattels bought and sold for £6,000 or less
- government securities (gilts)
- animals
- gifts to charities
- disposals made on the death of a taxpayer

You will notice that most of the items on this list are the same as those that were exempt under Corporation Tax.

dealing with capital losses

Capital losses arise from disposals in the same way as gains.

Once losses have been calculated they are dealt with as follows:

- firstly they are set against gains arising in the same tax year, until these are reduced to zero, then
- any unused loss is carried forward to set against the next gains that arise in future tax years

The key to offsetting losses is to remember that the order of calculation is:

1   firstly offset losses in the year
2   then deduct annual exempt amount

to arrive at the amount subject to Capital Gains Tax.

We will now look in more detail at how this process works.

offsetting against gains arising in the same tax year

Any losses that arise during a tax year are offset against capital gains arising from disposals in the same tax year. When dealing with losses arising in the same tax year there can be no safeguarding of the annual exempt amount. If there are sufficient losses the gains will be reduced to zero, wasting the exempt amount, before carrying forward any balance of loss.

offsetting against gains in a later tax year

This will only occur when there are insufficient gains in the same tax year to offset the loss (or no gains at all). The loss must be offset as soon as possible, by using any gains that occur in the next tax year. The system is very similar to the one just described, except that in these circumstances an amount of gain equal to the annual exempt amount is not offset, and any loss balance carried on forward again. This provides protection against wasting the exempt amount.

The Case Study that follows demonstrates the main issues that we have examined so far.

JOHN GAIN TRADING: CAPITAL GAINS TAX

John Gain has been in business as a sole trader for several years. During the tax year 2015/16 he disposed of the following business assets:

He sold a piece of land for £20,000. He had bought the land in June 2000 for £30,000 and was originally going to extend his factory onto it. However he was refused planning permission, and decided to sell it.

He sold a shop for £100,000. He had bought it for £72,000 in September 2005.

He sold a factory building for £300,000. He had bought it new in December 1990 for £120,000. John is a higher rate income tax payer.

required

Calculate the gain or loss on each disposal, and John's total Capital Gains Tax liability for 2015/16.

solution

Disposal of Land	£
Proceeds	20,000
Less Cost	(30,000)
Loss	(10,000)

Disposal of Shop	£
Proceeds	100,000
Less Cost	(72,000)
Gain	28,000

Disposal of Factory	£
Proceeds	300,000
Less Cost	(120,000)
Gain	180,000

Summary

	£
Gain on shop	28,000
Gain on factory	180,000
Less loss on land	(10,000)
Net gains	198,000
Less annual exempt amount	(11,100)
Amount subject to CGT	186,900

Capital Gains Tax   £186,900 x 28% = £52,332

ISSUES THAT ARE COMMON TO COMPANIES AND INDIVIDUALS

The following techniques and rules that we examined in Chapter 4 in respect of limited companies and Corporation Tax are also applicable to individuals under Capital Gains Tax. We will note them here in outline only – if you need further explanation you should refer back to the earlier chapter.

■ **links with capital allowances**

The issues outlined for companies are valid here. They are:

- Where losses occur on items where capital allowances have been claimed, no capital loss arises.

- Gains on chattels can only arise if the proceeds exceed £6,000, and this is subject to the chattels rules (dealt with below).

■ **part disposals**

These are dealt with in exactly the same way as for limited companies. The original cost of the whole asset is apportioned based on the proceeds of the part disposed of and the market value of the remainder at the time of the part disposal.

■ **improvement expenditure**

This follows the same logic under CGT rules as it does for chargeable gains under Corporation Tax. However, since there is no indexation allowance, the calculation is much simpler.

■ **chattels**

The special rules for chattels are identical to those for companies:

- The gain on chattels sold for over £6,000 cannot exceed 5/3 of (Gross proceeds minus £6,000).

- The capital loss on chattels sold for under £6,000 is limited by substituting £6,000 for the actual proceeds in the computation.

■ **rollover relief**

This is applicable to the same classes of business assets owned by individuals as owned by companies and in addition it is available for **goodwill** acquisitions and disposals by individuals. The rules work in exactly the same way, and defer the gain when the proceeds of one disposal are reinvested in another qualifying asset.

MATCHING RULES FOR SHARES

We saw earlier on that shares are chargeable assets, and that the computation for the acquisition and subsequent disposal of a block of shares is the same as for other assets.

The complication that can arise is when various quantities of the same type of share in the same company are bought and sold. The problem faced is similar to that in any inventory valuation situation – how to determine which of the shares that were bought are deemed to be the same ones that were sold. The dilemma is solved in this situation by the application of strict **matching rules**.

When some shares are sold the matching process is carried out by working down the following categories of acquisition, skipping any that do not apply, until all the shares sold have been matched. A separate CGT computation is then used for each separate match.

Note that these rules that apply to individuals are **not** the same as those that apply to companies under Corporation Tax.

1 Firstly, any shares bought on the **same day** that the disposal occurs are matched with that disposal.

2 Secondly, any shares bought in the **30 days after** the disposal are matched with those disposed of, (matching the earliest first if more than one acquisition). This probably seems illogical – selling something before it is bought!

3 Thirdly, any remaining shares not yet matched are deemed to have come from the 'FA 1985 pool' of shares. This is a device for merging shares.

The above order of matching is illustrated in the diagram below. The numbers in the diagram relate to the numbered stages described above.

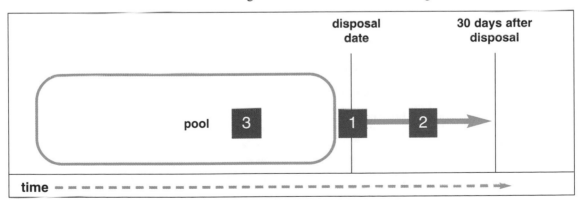

Remember that this matching process only applies where there have been several purchases of the same type of shares in the same company. It does not apply to a mixture of different company's shares, nor is it needed where a shareholding is bought and sold intact.

USING THE 'FA 1985 POOL'

This device was introduced in the 1985 Finance Act, and merges (or 'pools') shares in the same company and of the same type together. As we just saw, it occurs as the last of the matching rules, and is used to calculate the cost of shares acquired before the disposal date.

This is the same principle as the pool used for Corporation Tax gains, but is simpler here because there is no indexation allowance.

The pool needs to keep data relating to:

■ numbers of shares and

■ actual costs

These form the two main columns of the pool working.

The pool commences with the first shares bought. It then moves forward in time, adding each subsequent purchase of shares to provide cumulative numbers and costs of shares in the pool.

When any shares from the pool are disposed of, a proportion of the cumulative cost at the time of disposal is deducted from the pool, based on the numbers of shares. This cost amount that is deducted from the pool is then used in the gains calculation and compared with the proceeds in the normal way.

We will now demonstrate how the process works using a numerical example.

Although shares could be eligible for entrepreneurs' relief (see later) we will assume that it does not apply in this example.

example

On 1/1/2016 Julie sold 10,000 ordinary shares in WyeCo Ltd for £10 each, from her shareholding of 25,000. Her shareholding had been built up as follows:

1/1/1988 bought 17,000 shares for £5.00 each

1/1/1993 bought 8,000 shares for £7.00 each.

Since there are no acquisitions on or after 1/1/2016, the whole of the disposal of 10,000 shares will be matched with the pool. The pool will be built up as follows, with the disposal deducted as the latest transaction:

	Number	Cost
		£
1/1/1988 Purchase	17,000	85,000
1/1/1993 Purchase	8,000	56,000
Pool Totals	25,000	141,000
Less Disposal	(10,000)	(56,400)
Pool Balance after disposal	15,000	84,600

You should note the following:

- the cost figure for the disposal is a proportional amount of the pool costs before disposal, based on the number of shares (e.g. £141,000 x 10,000 / 25,000 = £56,400)

The computation for the disposal will now appear as follows:

	£
Proceeds (10,000 x £10)	100,000
Less cost	(56,400)
Gain	43,600

If at some future date there was another disposal of shares from the pool then the pool balance remaining would be used to determine the cost of the shares in the further disposal.

BONUS AND RIGHTS ISSUES

Bonus and rights issues were examined under Corporation Tax in Chapter 4. Here the princples are the same, but we will again explain the methods fully.

dealing with bonus shares

Bonus shares are additional shares given free to shareholders based on their current shareholding. This is sometimes called a 'scrip issue' and may be carried out as part of a capital restructuring of the company.

For CGT purposes the bonus shares are treated as if they were acquired at the same time as the original shares that generated the issue. For example a shareholder who owned 1,000 shares that were bought in January 2001 would be entitled to a further 200 shares if there were a bonus issue of 'one for five' shares. The total of 1,200 shares would be treated as bought in January 2001 for the amount paid for the 1,000 shares.

In virtually all situations, bonus shares are added to the pool when they are received. Since no payment is made, there is no adjustment to the cost figure.

If the bonus shares are received based on several acquisitions of original shares, the bonus shares will still be added into the pool, since the original shares will also be in the pool.

dealing with rights issues

A **rights issue** is the situation where additional shares are sold to existing shareholders, usually at a special price. For matching purposes, the shares that are bought in this way are treated as if they were bought with the original shares.

Rights issue shares will join the pool and be treated like any other share purchase. Their cost will be added into the pool.

We will now use a case study to make sure the principles relating to various matters studied are clear.

Case Study

CHER BYERS:
GAINS INCLUDING SHARES AND POOLING

Cher had acquired the following quoted ordinary shares in AbCo Limited (an unquoted company). We will assume that entrepreneurs' relief doesn't apply.

1/5/1985	1,000 shares at £4.00 each	£4,000
1/1/1990	Bonus issue of 1 for 4	
1/1/1992	1,750 shares at £4.20 each	£7,350
1/1/1995	1,500 shares at £4.10 each	£6,150 (Rights issue)
1/12/2001	1,800 shares at £5.10 each	£9,180

On 15/11/2001 she had sold 1,000 of her shareholding.

On 15/5/2015 she sold a further 2,500 ordinary shares in AbCo Limited for £10.00 each.

required

1   Identify which shares would have already been matched against the disposal that took place on 15/11/2001.

2   Show how the disposal of shares on 15/5/2015 will be matched against the acquisitions, and

3   Calculate the total gain arising from the sale of shares that took place on 15/5/2015.

solution

TASK 1

The disposal of 1,000 shares on 15/11/2001 would have been matched with 1,000 of the 1,800 shares that were bought on 1/12/2001 for £5.10 each (shares bought in the 30 days after disposal). This leaves 800 of that purchase to join the pool.

TASK 2

Matching of the 15/5/2015 disposal of 2,500 shares will be entirely against the pool, since there were no shares of that type bought on 15/5/2015 or the following 30 days.

TASK 3

We will first need to build up the pool to May 2015, so that we can calculate the balances.

		Number	Cost
			£
1/5/1985	Purchase	1,000	4,000
1/1/1990	Bonus Issue	250	-
1/1/1992	Purchase	1,750	7,350
1/1/1995	Rights Issue	1,500	6,150
1/12/2001	Balance of Purchase (1,800 less 1,000 already matched)	800	4,080
		5,300	21,580
15/5/2015	Disposal	(2,500)	(10,179)*
	Pool balance after disposal	2,800	11,401

* The cost of the shares disposed of is calculated as:
(2,500 / 5,300) x £21,580 = £10,179

We can now calculate the gain on the disposal of shares, using the cost figure calculated in the pool.

	£
Proceeds	25,000
less cost	(10,179)
Gain	14,821

DEALING WITH THE DISPOSAL OF A BUSINESS

We have already seen how trading profits are calculated when a business ceases trading, and how the capital allowances for the last accounting period are calculated.

In addition to these implications, if a sole trader sells his or her business, then Capital Gains Tax will apply **individually** to **each chargeable asset** that is included in the business. The sale of the business can therefore result in a number of separate capital gains computations.

The current assets and current liabilities of a business are not chargeable assets, which leaves **non-current (fixed) assets** and **goodwill** as items on which CGT may be assessable.

non-current assets

As we have already seen, land and buildings are chargeable assets, and could easily form part of a business that is being disposed of. Chattels bought and sold for under £6,000 are exempt, and so are cars. Other plant and machinery could theoretically give rise to a capital gain, but since it is rarely sold for more than it cost is unlikely to do so. Any plant and machinery disposed of for less than original cost would simply be dealt with through the capital allowances computation as we have seen previously.

goodwill

Goodwill is an intangible asset that may exist if the business is sold as a going concern. It arises when the buyer is prepared to pay more for the business as a whole than the market value of the net assets of the business. This could be, for example, because of the businesses' customer base that the new owner wishes to continue selling to. Where a sole trader has built up the business himself the goodwill is unlikely to be shown in the business statement of financial position (balance sheet), and will often have an original cost of zero for CGT purposes. If you are faced with a situation where the proceeds relating to the goodwill is not stated, you will need to calculate it as the balance of the proceeds that do not relate to any other assets.

ENTREPRENEURS' RELIEF

Entrepreneurs' Relief applies to individuals who dispose of

- all or part of a trading business
- shares in a 'personal trading company'

The relief is available for qualifying gains up to a 'lifetime limit' and applies a tax rate of 10% to these gains (instead of 18% or 28%). The lifetime limit is £10,000,000 of gains.

Where qualifying gains occur (and are therefore taxed at 10% if within the lifetime limit) they are treated as using up the basic rate band. Therefore any other gains that do not qualify for entrepreneurs' relief will be more likely to be taxed at 28%. However, where there are both qualifying and non-qualifying gains, the taxpayer can set the annual exempt amount as far as possible against the non-qualifying gains. This will be most tax-efficient.

conditions for entrepreneurs' relief

The qualifying conditions have to have been met for at least a **one year** period that ends on the **earlier** of:

- the date of disposal of the asset(s)
- the date of cessation of the business

The conditions (which are summarised below) depend on the type of disposal:

- disposal of whole or part of a business

  The business must have been owned by the sole trader who is making the claim, or by a partnership of which the claimant was a member. The disposal must be of either the whole business or a distinct part of a business.

- disposal of assets following cessation of a business

  The business that has ceased must have been owned by the sole trader who is making the claim, or by a partnership of which the claimant was a member. The cessation of the business cannot be more that three years before the disposal of the assets.

- disposal of shares in a personal limited company

  The claimant must have held at least 5% of the ordinary shares (that provide at least 5% of the voting rights) in the company. The company must normally be a trading company. The claimant must have been an officer or employee of the company.

Case Study

DUNN TRADING: DISPOSAL OF A BUSINESS

Jo Dunn had been in business as a sole trader since January 1995. She ceased trading on 31/1/2016, and on that date sold her business as a going concern for a total of £500,000.

The summarised statement of financial position of the business on 31/1/2016 was as follows:

	£
Premises	200,000
Plant & Machinery	20,000
Net Current Assets	80,000
Total Net Assets	300,000

The premises were bought in January 1995. No depreciation had been charged on the premises in the accounts. The plant and machinery value is based on amounts after depreciation has been charged. Capital allowances had been claimed on all plant and machinery.

It was agreed with the purchaser of the business that the premises were to be valued at £350,000 in the sale, and that the plant and machinery and the net current assets were valued at the amounts shown in the statement of financial position.

Jo has never made a claim for Entrepreneurs' Relief before this disposal.

required

Calculate the CGT arising on the sale of the business, assuming that the disposals qualify for Entrepreneurs' Relief.

solution

The first step is to allocate the sale proceeds to the individual assets, including any balance of proceeds to goodwill, and determine which assets are chargeable.

	£	
Premises	350,000	Chargeable
Plant & Machinery	20,000	Proceeds < Cost. Dealt with through capital allowance computation
Net Current Assets	80,000	Exempt
Goodwill	50,000	Chargeable
Total Proceeds	500,000	

The goodwill is calculated as the balancing figure, after accounting for the other assets. The computations are then carried out individually on the chargeable assets.

	£
Premises	
Proceeds	350,000
Less Cost	(200,000)
Gain	150,000
Goodwill	
Proceeds	50,000
Less Cost	0
Gain	50,000

Summary

Gain on premises	150,000
Gain on goodwill	50,000
Total Gains	200,000
Less Annual Exempt Amount	(11,100)
Amount subject to CGT	188,900
CGT £188,900 x 10%	18,890

Since the total of qualifying gains is £200,000, this is below the lifetime limit of £10,000,000 and the gains are taxed at 10%.

GIFT RELIEF

We saw earlier in our studies that the gift of an asset is a disposal for Capital Gains Tax purposes. This means that even though the donor (the person giving the item) has received nothing for the item he/she may still have to pay CGT. The disposal will be treated as if the donor had received the market value for the item, and the recipient will be treated as if he/she had acquired the asset at the same market value.

If an individual gives away a 'business asset', the transaction can qualify for 'gift relief'. This has the effect of delaying the onset of the tax, and transferring the liability to the recipient of the gift.

The relief can only be claimed if both parties agree. It means that the donor has no CGT liability, but that the CGT liability of the recipient in the future could be greater - if the item is disposed of.

Gift relief works by reducing the base cost of the asset for the recipient by the amount of the deferred gain. This means that the base cost would now be the market value less the deferred gain, and any eventual gain would therefore be greater than if gift relief had not been claimed.

Gift relief applies to business assets, including:

- assets used in the donor's business or in his/her personal trading company
- shares in the donor's personal trading company
- unquoted shares in other trading companies

Gift relief applies to some of the same business assets as entrepreneurs' relief. It is therefore possible that where an asset incorporating a gain deferred by gift relief is disposed of again, the gain could be subject to entrepreneurs' relief.

Case Study

JAN NICE: GIFT RELIEF

Jan Nice bought a shop in October 1998 for £100,000, and used it in her business until June 2007, when she gave it to her niece, Norah. The market value of the shop at that time was £180,000.

Norah ran the shop as a sole trader for a while, but decided to sell the shop in October 2015. She received £220,000 for the shop.

Jan and Norah claimed gift relief on the shop. Norah had no other disposals in 2015/16.

Norah is a higher rate income tax payer.

required

Calculate the Capital Gains Tax payable by Norah on her disposal of the shop:

(a) ignoring any entrepreneurs' relief

(b) assuming that Norah is entitled to entrepreneurs' relief

solution

(a) The gain deferred by Jan is (£180,000 – £100,000) = £80,000.

The disposal by Norah will have the following gain.

		£	£
Proceeds			220,000
Less Market value at acquisition		180,000	
less deferred gain		(80,000)	
			100,000
Gain			120,000
less annual exempt amount			(£11,100)
Amount subject to CGT			£108,900
Capital Gains Tax	£108,900 x 28% =		£30,492

(b) If entrepreneurs' relief is available the calculation would be identical up to the point where the amount subject to CGT is calculated. It will then be as follows:

		£
Amount subject to CGT		108,900
Capital Gains Tax	£108,900 x 10% =	£10,890

SUMMARY OF RULES AND RELIEFS

In this book we have looked at both chargeable gains for companies (taxed through Corporation Tax) and individuals (taxed through Capital Gains Tax). This is an area of study where it is easy to get confused, so the following table is produced to summarise the various rules and reliefs that we have looked at and to whom they apply.

	Individuals (Capital Gains Tax)	Companies (Corporation Tax)
Annual Exempt Amount	✔	Not applicable
Indexation	Not applicable	✔ (To date of disposal)
Links with capital allowances	✔	✔
Part Disposal Rules	✔	✔
Chattel Rules	✔	✔
Improvement Expenditure	✔	✔
Shares: matching rules/bonus/rights issues (but note rules are different)	✔ (Rules for individuals)	✔ (Rules for companies)
Gift Relief	✔	Not Applicable
Rollover Relief	✔	✔
Entrepreneurs' Relief	✔	Not applicable

PAYMENT OF CAPITAL GAINS TAX

Capital Gains Tax is payable as one amount on the 31 January following the end of the tax year. This is the same date as the final submission date of the online tax return (the paper-based tax return would be due by the preceding 31 October). There is no requirement for payments on account of CGT.

KEEPING RECORDS

Since capital gains can arise when assets that have been held for a considerable time are disposed of, this has implications for record keeping. Taxpayers need to plan ahead, and retain records relating to the acquisition of assets that will be chargeable if disposed of.

Typical records that should be kept include:
- contracts, invoices or other purchase documentation relating to the acquisition of assets
- details of any valuations (eg valuations relating to part disposals)
- documentation relating to the sale of assets

Records for CGT purposes should be retained for the same period of time as those relating to Income Tax. For those in business this is five years after the date that the online return must be submitted (eg for 2015/16, records should be kept until 31/01/22). Where records will also relate to later disposals, for example gift relief claims, rollover relief claims, entrepreneurs' relief claims, and information relating to part disposals, they will need to be retained until all the relevant assets have been disposed of.

Chapter Summary

- Capital Gains Tax applies to individuals (including sole traders and partners) who dispose of chargeable assets. In this unit we are concerned with the disposal of business assets. Although there is some common ground with the way that chargeable gains for companies are taxed under Corporation Tax, the computations for individuals exclude indexation allowances and include annual exempt amounts.

- The treatment of gains for individuals and companies include common areas such as capital allowances, part disposals, improvement expenditure, chattel rules and rollover relief.

- Where a whole business is disposed of, a separate computation is carried out for each chargeable asset that is included in the business. This includes goodwill, which is an intangible asset that may arise when the business is sold as a going concern. These gains may have entrepreneurs' relief available.

- Gift relief is available on the gift of business assets where both parties agree. It has the effect of deferring the gain, so that the donor is not subject to CGT, but the recipient may pay more tax if the asset is subsequently disposed of.

- CGT is payable on the 31 January following the tax year. Records must be kept for five years after that date, or longer if they relate to assets that are still owned or subject to deferral reliefs.

Key Terms

Capital Gains Tax (CGT) the tax that applies to individuals who dispose of chargeable personal or business assets

Disposal a disposal for CGT purposes is the sale, gift, loss or destruction of an asset

Chargeable Asset assets whose disposal can result in a CGT liability. All assets are chargeable unless they are exempt

Exempt Asset an asset that is not chargeable to CGT. Exempt assets include the current assets of a business

Chattel a tangible, movable asset

Annual Exempt Amount (or Annual Exemption)
the amount that is deductible from an individual's net gains in a tax year before CGT is payable

Capital Loss a capital loss results when the allowable costs of an asset exceed the sale proceeds (or market value). A loss is used by setting it against a gain in the same year, or if this is not possible, by carrying the loss forward to set against gains in the next available tax year

Part Disposal this occurs when part of an asset is disposed of, but the remainder is retained

Improvement Expenditure capital expenditure that enhances an asset. If the enhancement is still evident at disposal then the improvement expenditure is an allowable cost

Rollover Relief a deferral relief available to businesses (including sole traders). It has the effect of postponing a chargeable gain when the proceeds of disposal have been reinvested

Goodwill goodwill is a chargeable asset. It is the amount of the proceeds on disposal of a business that does not relate to any individual assets, but is instead due to the intangible value of the business as a going concern

Gift Relief a relief claimable jointly by the donor and the recipient of certain assets, including business assets. It allows the original gain by the donor to be deferred by increasing the possible future gain of the recipient

Entrepreneurs' Relief this relief applies to individuals who dispose of all or part of a trading business and / or shares in a 'personal trading company'. The relief works by charging CGT at 10%. It is subject to a lifetime limit of £10m gains

Activities

8.1 Analyse the following list of business assets into those that are chargeable to CGT and those that are exempt.

(a) Moveable plant, sold at a gain for £5,000

(b) Trading inventory (stock)

(c) Shares in CIC plc

(d) An office block

(e) Goodwill

(f) Land

(g) A car

(h) Government securities

8.2 Vikram is a sole trader. In January 1995 he bought a small shop for £40,000. In April 1998 he extended the shop at a cost of £20,000. He sold the shop for £140,000 in July 2015. This was his only disposal in the tax year. Vikram is a higher rate income tax payer.

Required:

Calculate the amount of Capital Gains Tax payable by Vikram for 2015/16, assuming that:

(a) Entrepreneurs' Relief does not apply.

(b) Vikram is entitled to Entrepreneurs' Relief.

8.3   Jane is a sole trader. In January 1999 she bought 1,000 unquoted shares at £10 each in a similar business to help her increase her market share. She sold 600 of the shares in July 2015 for a total of £23,000. This was her only disposal in the tax year. The company is not a 'Personal Trading Company'. Jane's taxable income in 2015/16 is £20,000.

Required:

Calculate the amount of Capital Gains Tax payable by Jane for 2015/16.

8.4   In January 1995 George bought an office building to use in his business. In December 2000 he gave the office building to his son, William, who used it in his business. The building was valued at £100,000 at that time, and they claimed gift relief on the transaction, deferring a gain of £33,160. William sold the building for £200,000 in July 2015. This was his only disposal in 2015/16. William is a higher rate income tax payer.

Required:

Calculate the amount of Capital Gains Tax payable by William for 2015/16, assuming that:

(a)   Entrepreneurs' Relief does not apply.

(b)   William is entitled to Entrepreneurs' Relief.

8.5   Josie started a business as a sole trader in January 1990. She ceased trading on 31/1/2016, and on that date sold her business as a going concern for a total of £900,000.

The summarised statement of financial position of the business on 31/1/2016 is as follows:

	£
Premises	400,000
Plant & Machinery	30,000
Net Current Assets	50,000
Total Net Assets	480,000

The premises were bought in January 1999. A gain of £60,000 on the previous premises was rolled over into these premises when the whole proceeds of the first premises were reinvested. The amount shown represents the actual cost in 1999 of the current premises.

The plant and machinery is shown at cost minus depreciation to date. Capital allowances had been claimed on all plant and machinery.

It was agreed with the purchaser of the business that the premises were to be valued at £700,000 in the sale. The plant and machinery is valued at £20,000 in the sale, and the net current assets are valued at the amounts shown in the statement of financial position.

Required:

Calculate the Capital Gains Tax liability arising on the sale of the business, assuming that Entrepreneurs' Relief **is available**.

8.6   Which of the following statements is correct?

(a) A capital loss made by an individual can be carried back against capital gains made in the preceding tax year.	
(b) A capital loss made by an individual can be carried forward to the following tax year without offsetting it against the current year gains.	
(c) When a capital loss made by an individual is offset against gains in the following tax year, it is only to the extent that it reduces those gains to the amount of the annual exemption.	
(d) A capital loss made by an individual can only be carried forward for one tax year.	

8.7   John made a disposal in August 2014 that qualified for entrepreneurs' relief. The proceeds were £6,000,000 and the gain was calculated as £3,000,000.

John is a higher rate income tax payer. This was John's only disposal in the tax year. He had claimed entrepreneurs' relief in the previous tax year on gains of £5,000,000.

How much Capital Gains Tax will John need to pay in 2015/16?

(a) none	
(b) £298,890	
(c) £300,000	
(d) £480,000	
(e) £836,892	
(f) £840,000	

8.8   Which of the following statements is correct? (select one)

(a) Entrepreneurial relief is restricted to £10,000,000 for the lifetime of the taxpayer.	
(b) Entrepreneurial relief is restricted to £10,000,000 for each capital disposal.	
(c) Entrepreneurial relief has no restrictions.	
(d) Entrepreneurial relief is restricted to £1,000,000 for the lifetime of the taxpayer.	

Answers to activities

CHAPTER 1: INTRODUCTION TO BUSINESS TAXATION

1.1   The following statements are true: (a), (d), (e).

The other statements are false as follows: (b) the Finance Act is not the only relevant law. (c) the return is completed for each CAP, not each financial year. (f) It is unethical to bend rules or omit items. (g) The self-employed do not pay income tax under PAYE.

1.2   **(a)**   Corporation Tax Computation for DonCom plc for year ended 31/3/2016

	£
Trading Profits	1,300,000
Income from Property	100,000
Chargeable Gains	500,000
Taxable Total Profits (TTP)	1,900,000
Corporation Tax on TTP (£1,900,000 x 20%)	380,000

Note: Taxable Total Profits is also known as PCTCT.

(b)   Filing date for CT600 return   31/3/2017
Final Payment date for Corporation Tax   1/1/2017

1.3   **(a)**   Income Tax Computation for 2015/16

	£
Trading Income (Share of Partnership Profits)	16,000
Other Taxable Income	2,000
	18,000
Less personal allowance	10,600
Taxable Income	7,400
Tax payable at 20%	1,480

(b)   A paper-based return must be submitted by 31/10/2016 whether or not HM Revenue & Customs are to calculate the tax.

Final payment date is 31/1/2017.

1.4   **John**

		£
Class 2	£2.80 x 52 weeks	145.60
Class 4	(£25,000 – £8,060) x 9%	1,524.60
		1,670.20

Class 2 and Class 4 is paid with the Income Tax liability.

1.5   The Walvern Water Company Limited will require a company tax return (form CT600). This will relate to the chargeable accounting period (CAP) 1/8/2014 to 31/7/2015. The form must be submitted online by 12 months after the end of the accounting period, ie 31/7/2016. The final Corporation Tax payment must be made by 1/5/2016 (nine months and one day after the end of the CAP).

Wally Weaver will need a tax return for the tax year 2015/16. The accounting period of 1/8/2014 to 31/7/2015 will form the basis period for this tax year. The main part of the form will need to be completed, along with the supplementary pages relating to self-employment. The online tax return must be submitted by 31/1/2017. The final income tax payment relating to 2015/16 will also need to be made by 31/1/2017.

1.6   **(1)**   The following statement is correct: (d)

The others are incorrect.

(2)   £70,000 – £42,385   = £27,615

(3)   (£35,000 – £8,060) x 9%   = £2,424.60

CHAPTER 2: CORPORATION TAX – TRADING PROFITS

2.1   1   no action (allowable)

2   add back (disallowable expense)

3   deduct (not trading income)

4   deduct (not taxable income)

5   no action (allowable)

6   deduct (not trading income – possible chargeable gain)

7   no action (taxable trading income)

8   add back (disallowable expense since tobacco)

9   add back (disallowable expense – not specific)

10   add back (disallowable expense – not trading)

11   no action (allowable)

12   add back (charge against whole TTP)

2.2

	£	£
Net Profit per accounts		130,300
Add Back:		
Expenditure that is shown in the accounts but is not allowable		
Depreciation		42,000
Loss on Sale of Non-current Assets		5,000
Gifts of Chocolates		4,900
Entertaining Customers		6,000
		188,200
Deduct:		
Income that is not taxable as Trading Income		
Interest Received	20,000	
Dividends Received	70,000	
Decrease in General Bad Debt Provision	5,000	
Capital Allowances	23,000	
		(118,000)
Trading Income Assessment		70,200

2.3

	£	£
Net Profit per accounts		276,600
Add Back:		
Expenditure that is shown in the accounts but is not allowable		
Depreciation		51,000
Directors' Speeding Fines		2,000
Gift Vouchers		5,000
Entertaining Customers		4,000
		338,600
Deduct:		
Income that is not taxable as Trading Income		
Interest Received	40,000	
Gains on Disposal of Non-current Assets	50,000	
Rental Income Received	60,000	
Capital Allowances	31,500	
		(181,500)
Trading Income Assessment		157,100

2.4

		£
Net Profit for 16-month period per accounts		4,070
Add back non-allowable expenditure:		
Depreciation etc		10,000
Entertaining customers		1,930
Adjusted profit before capital allowances		16,000

Time apportionment of adjusted profit:

CAP 1/12/2014 to 30/11/2015	£16,000 x 12/16	= £12,000
CAP 1/12/2015 to 31/3/2016	£16,000 x 4/16	= £4,000

Deduction of Capital Allowances:	1/12/14 - 30/11/15	1/12/15 - 31/3/16
	£	£
Adjusted profit	12,000	4,000
Capital allowances	(8,000)	(2,500)
Trading Income assessment	4,000	1,500

2.5

	£	£
Profit before Tax		294,000
Add Back:		
Expenditure that is shown in the accounts but is not allowable		
Depreciation		20,000
Employee Loan Written Off		8,000
Increase in General Bad Debt Provision		7,700
Entertaining Customers		9,100
		338,800
Deduct:		
Income that is not taxable as Trading Income		
Rental Income	200,000	
Interest Received from Investments	30,000	
Profit on Sale of Non-current Assets	33,000	
Dividends Received	15,000	
Capital Allowances	153,000	
		(431,000)
Adjusted Trading Loss		(92,200)
Trading Income assessment = zero		

The trading loss of £92,200 could be relieved without carrying it forward (provided the profits are large enough) as follows:

- by offsetting against the taxable total profits (TTP) before deduction of Gift Aid payments in the CAP y/e 31/3/2016, and then if any loss remains
- by offsetting against the taxable total profits (TTP) before deduction of Gift Aid payments arising in the 12 months to 31/3/2015

2.6   The following statements are true: (b), (c).

The other statements are false.

CHAPTER 3: CORPORATION TAX – CAPITAL ALLOWANCES

3.1

	Main Pool	Capital Allowances
	£	£
WDV bf	21,000	
add		
Acquisitions		
without FYA or AIA:		
Car (125 g/km)	16,000	
Acquisitions qualifying for AIA:		
Plant 493,000		
Van 10,000		
503,000		
AIA claimed (500,000)		500,000
	3,000	
less		
Proceeds of Disposals	(2,000)	
	38,000	
18% WDA	(6,840)	6,840
WDV cf	31,160	
Total Capital Allowances		506,840

3.2

	Main Pool	S/L Asset	Capital Allowances
	£	£	£
WDV bf	60,000	10,000	
add			
Acquisitions			
without FYA or AIA:			
Car (115 g/km)	24,000		
Acquisitions qualifying for AIA:			
FL Truck 30,000			
Computer 5,000			
35,000			
AIA claimed (35,000)*			35,000
	0		
less			
Proceeds of Disposals:	(3,000)	(4,000)	
	81,000	6,000	
WDA 18%	(14,580)		14,580
Balancing Allowance		(6,000)	6,000
WDV cf	66,420	0	
Total Capital Allowances			55,580

* The maximum AIA limit for the CAP is: (£500,000 x 9/12) + (£25,000 x 3/12) = £381,250

Trading Income for CAP year ended 31/3/2016:

	£
Adjusted trading profits	154,000
Plant & Machinery Capital Allowances	(55,580)
Trading Income	98,420

3.3

	Main Pool	Special Rate Pool	Capital Allowances
	£	£	£
WDV bf	10,000	2,800	
Acquisitions qualifying for AIA:			
Plant 253,000			
Machinery 12,000			
265,000			
AIA claimed (6,250)			6,250
	258,750		
less			
Proceeds of			
Disposals	(3,500)		
	265,250	2,800	
WDA at 18%	(47,745)		47,745
WDA at 8%		(224)	224
WDV cf	217,505	2,576	
Total Capital Allowances			54,219

Note – the AIA maximum for the CAP is (£500,000 x 9/12) + (£25,000 x 3/12) = £381,250. However, the limit of AIA on acquisitions after 31/12/2015 is £6,250 (ie £25,000 x 3/12).

3.4   The CAPs will be:

1/4/2014 - 31/3/2015   (12 months)
1/4/2015 - 30/6/2015   (3 months)

CAP YEAR ENDED 31/3/2015

	Main Pool	Special Rate Pool	Capital Allowances
	£	£	£
WDV bf	60,000	14,000	
add			
Acquisitions			
without FYA or AIA:			
Car (123 g/km)	16,000		
less			
Proceeds of			
Disposals:	(4,000)		
	72,000	14,000	
WDA 18% / 8%	(12,960)	(1,120)	14,080
WDV cf	59,040	12,880	
Total Capital Allowances			14,080

CAP 3 MONTHS ENDED 30/6/2015			
	Main Pool	Special Rate Pool	Capital Allowances
	£	£	£
WDV bf	59,040	12,880	
Acquisitions qualifying for AIA:			
Plant 45,000			
AIA claimed* (45,000)			45,000
	0		
	59,040	12,880	
WDA 18% x 3/12	(2,657)		2,657
WDA 8% x 3/12		(258)	258
WDV cf	56,383	12,622	
Total Capital Allowances			47,915

* AIA limit £500,000 x 3/12 = £125,000

Calculation of trading income assessments

Time apportionment of adjusted trade profits:
CAP 1/4/2014 to 31/3/2015   £480,000 x 12/15 = £384,000
CAP 1/4/2015 to 30/6/2015   £480,000 x 3/15 = £96,000

Capital allowances are then deducted from the adjusted profit for each CAP

	1/4/14 – 31/3/15	1/4/15 – 30/6/15
	£	£
Adjusted profit	384,000	96,000
Capital allowances:	(14,080)	(47,915)
Trading Income	369,920	48,085

3.5

PLANT & MACHINERY CAPITAL ALLOWANCES COMPUTATION:

	Main Pool	Special Rate Pool	Capital Allowances
	£	£	£
WDV bf	90,000	13,000	
Additions			
without FYA or AIA:			
BMW Car		27,000	
Low Emission Car 20,000			
100% FYA (20,000)	0		20,000
Additions qualifying for AIA:			
Plant 440,834			
AIA (416,667)			416,667
[limit of	24,167		
10/12 x £500,000			
= £416,667]			
Disposals			
Plant	(1,000)		
	113,167	40,000	
WDA 18% x 10/12	(16,975)		16,975
WDA 8% x 10/12		(2,667)	2,667
WDV cf	96,192	37,333	
Total Capital Allowances			456,309

	£
Adjusted trading profit for 10 month CAP to 31/3/2015	510,000
less capital allowances	(456,309)
Trading Income assessment	53,691

CHAPTER 4: CORPORATION TAX – CHARGEABLE GAINS

4.1   Chargeable Assets: (a), (b), (c), (d), (f).

Exempt Assets: (e – chattel sold for a gain for under £6,000), (g), (h), (i).

4.2

	£
Proceeds	1,300,000
less Cost	(600,000)
Unindexed gain	700,000
less Indexation allowance £600,000 x 0.707	(424,200)
Chargeable Gain	275,800
less capital loss brought forward	(15,000)
Chargeable Gain to be brought into the taxable total profits	260,800

4.3

	£
Proceeds	145,000
less Cost	(50,000)
less Indexation £50,000 x 0.571	(28,550)
Chargeable Gain	66,450
less capital loss brought forward	(25,000)
Chargeable Gain to be brought into the taxable total profits	41,450

4.4   Chargeable Gains

Factory   £

Proceeds   500,000

less Cost   (300,000)

less Indexation £300,000 x 1.615 (restricted)   (200,000)

Chargeable Gain   nil

The indexation is restricted to avoid turning an unindexed gain into a loss.

Land   £

Proceeds   30,000

less apportioned cost:

£50,000 x £30,000 / £150,000   (10,000)

less indexation allowance

£10,000 x 0.896   (8,960)

Chargeable Gain   11,040

Total Chargeable Gain from two disposals   =   £11,040

4.5   Chargeable Gain on Shares

The disposal in January 2000 will be matched with the pool, and deducted from it before the current disposal is dealt with.

FA 1985 Pool Workings

	Number	Cost	Indexed Cost
		£	£
1/1/1992 Purchase	3,000	9,000	9,000
Indexation to Jan 1995:			
£9,000 x 0.077			693
1/1/1995 Purchase	12,000	42,000	42,000
	15,000	51,000	51,693
Bonus Shares	3,000		
Indexation to January 2000:			
£51,693 x 0.141			7,289
Balance	18,000	51,000	58,982

1/1/2000 Disposal	(5,000)	(14,167)	(16,384)
Balance	13,000	36,833	42,598
Indexation to March 2015:			
£42,598 x 0.543			23,131
Balance	13,000	36,833	65,729
30/3/2015 Disposal	(10,000)	(28,333)	(50,561)
Balance	3,000	8,500	15,168

Share disposal March 2015:	£
Proceeds	60,000
less cost	(28,333)
less indexation (£50,561 – £28,333)	(22,228)
Chargeable Gain	9,439

Chargeable gain on machine

	£
Proceeds	6,900
less cost	(3,000)
less indexation allowance £3,000 x 0.543	(1,629)
Gain	2,271
But gain limited to 5/3 (£6,900 – £6,000) = £1,500.	1,500

The total Chargeable Gain from two disposals	=	£10,939

Capital allowances procedure regarding disposal of machine.

Since the machine is sold for more than the original cost, the original cost is deducted in the capital allowance computation instead of the disposal proceeds. There will be no balancing charge since the machine is in the main pool.

4.6   Vintage car   =   Exempt asset

Antique vase   =   Chargeable asset

Greyhound   =   Exempt asset

4.7

£

	£
Proceeds	12,000
Cost	4,000
Indexation allowance	2,052
Gain	5,948
Chattel restriction on gain	10,000

The chattel restriction will have no effect on the original gain.

4.8

	No. Shares	Cost £	Indexed Cost £
Purchase October 2001	5,000	15,500	15,500
Indexation 0.114			1,767
Rights Issue	100	200	200
Subtotal	5,100	15,700	17,467
Indexation 0.423			7,389
Total	5,100	15,700	24,856
Disposal	(5,100)	(15,700)	(24,856)
Pool balance	0	0	0

Proceeds	£45,900
Indexed Cost	£24,856
Gain	£21,044

CHAPTER 5: CORPORATION TAX – CALCULATING THE TAX

5.1   Corporation Tax Computation

	£	£
Adjusted Trading Profits	1,120,000	
less capital allowances - P & M	(63,000)	
Trading Income		1,057,000
Property Income		23,000
Interest Receivable		60,000
Chargeable Gains		48,000
less Gift-Aid payment		(15,000)
Taxable total profits		1,143,000

The CAP falls entirely into FY2015.

	£
Taxable total profits at main rate: £1,143,000 x 20%	228,600

5.2   Corporation Tax Computation

	£	£
Adjusted Trading Profits	1,420,000	
less capital allowances - P & M	(205,000)	
Trading Income		1,215,000
Property Income		92,000
Interest Receivable		12,000
Chargeable Gains	88,000	
less capital loss bf	(18,000)	
Net Chargeable Gains		70,000
less Gift-Aid payment		(8,000)
Taxable total profits		1,381,000

The CAP falls entirely into FY2014.
'Augmented Profits' = £1,381,000 + (£27,000 x 100/90)= £1,411,000

The company will therefore pay Corporation Tax at main rate minus marginal relief:

	£
Taxable total profits at main rate: £1,381,000 x 21%	290,010
less marginal relief:	
1/400 x (£1,500,000 − £1,411,000) x (£1,381,000 / £1,411,000)	(218)
Corporation Tax Liability	289,792

5.3   Corporation Tax Computation

	£	£
Trading Income		0
Property Income		35,000
Interest Receivable		40,000
Chargeable Gains	90,000	
less capital loss bf	(8,000)	
Net Chargeable Gains		82,000
		157,000
less trading loss		(120,000)
less rental loss bf		(13,000)
less Gift-Aid payment		(10,000)
Taxable total profits		14,000

'Augmented Profits' = £14,000

The company will therefore pay Corporation Tax at the small profits rate in FY2014.

Since the CAP falls into two financial years with the same tax rates applicable the taxable total profits need not be time-apportioned.

Corporation Tax is £14,000 x 20% = £2,800

An alternative option would be to carry the loss forward against future trading profits.

5.4

	£	£
Net Profit per accounts		251,000
Add Back:		
Expenditure that is shown in the accounts but is not allowable		
Depreciation		41,000
Directors' Speeding Fines		1,000
Gifts of Food (Hampers)		10,000
Entertaining Customers		6,000
		309,000
Deduct:		
Income that is not taxable as trading income:		
Interest Receivable	50,000	
Profit on Disposal of Non-current Assets	50,000	
Rental Income Receivable	40,000	
Capital Allowances	11,000	
		(151,000)
Trading Income Assessment		158,000

Corporation Tax Computation

	£
Trading Income	158,000
Property Income	40,000
Interest Receivable	50,000
Chargeable Gains	41,000
Taxable total profits	289,000

'Augmented Profits' = £289,000

FY2014:

Taxable total profits at small profit rate: £144,500 x 20%	28,900
FY2015:	
Taxable total profits at main rate: £144,500 x 20%	28,900
Total Corporation Tax	57,800

The CT600 extract is shown on the next page.

Page 2
Company tax calculation

Turnover

1	Total turnover from trade or profession	**1** £ 720,000

Income

3	Trading and professional profits	**3** £ 158,000
4	Trading losses brought forward claimed against profits	**4** £ -
5	Net trading and professional profits	box 3 minus box 4 **5** £ 158,000
6	Bank, building society or other interest, and profits and gains from non-trading loan relationships	**6** £ 50,000
11	Income from UK land and buildings	**11** £ 40,000
14	Annual profits and gains not falling under any other heading	**14** £

Chargeable gains

16	Gross chargeable gains	**16** £ 41,000
17	Allowable losses including losses brought forward	**17** £
18	Net chargeable gains	box 16 minus box 17 **18** £ 41,000

21	**Profits before other deductions and reliefs**	sum of boxes 5, 6, 11, 14 & 18 **21** £ 289,000

Deductions and Reliefs

24	Management expenses under S75 ICTA 1988	**24** £
30	Trading losses of this or a later accounting period under S393A ICTA 1988	**30** £
31	Put an 'X' in box 31 if amounts carried back from later accounting periods are included in box 30	**31**
32	Non-trade capital allowances	**32** £
35	Charges paid	**35** £

37	**Profits chargeable to corporation tax**	box 21 minus boxes 24, 30, 32 and 35 **37** £ 289,000

Tax calculation

38	Franked investment income	**38** £
39	Number of associated companies in this period or	**39** 0
40	Associated companies in the first financial year	**40**
41	Associated companies in the second financial year	**41**
42	Put an 'X' in box 42 if the company claims to be charged at the starting rate or the small companies' rate on any part of its profits, or is claiming marginal rate relief	**42** X

Enter how much profit has to be charged and at what rate of tax

Financial year (yyyy)	Amount of profit	Rate of tax	Tax	
43 2 0 1 4	**44** £ 144,500	**45** 20%	**46** £ 28,900	p
53 2 0 1 5	**54** £ 144,500	**55** 20%	**56** £ 28,900	p
			total of boxes 46 and 56 **63** £ 57,800	p

63	Corporation tax	
64	Marginal rate relief	**64** £ _ p
65	Corporation tax net of marginal rate relief	**65** £ 57,800 p
66	Underlying rate of corporation tax	**66** 20•00 %
67	Profits matched with non-corporate distributions	**67**
68	Tax at non-corporate distributions rate	**68** £ p
69	Tax at underlying rate on remaining profits	**69** £ p
70	**Corporation tax chargeable**	See note for box 70 in CT600 Guide **70** £ 57,800 p

5.5

	£
Net Profit for 16-month period per accounts	4,070
Add back non-allowable expenditure:	
Depreciation etc.	10,000
Entertaining customers	1,930
Adjusted profit before capital allowances	16,000

Time apportionment of adjusted profit:

CAP 1/4/2014 to 31/3/2015 £16,000 x 12/16 = £12,000

CAP 1/4/2015 to 31/7/2015 £16,000 x 4/16 = £ 4,000

Deduction of Capital Allowances:

	1/4/2014 to 31/3/2015	1/4/2015 to 31/7/2015
	£	£
Adjusted profit	12,000	4,000
Capital allowances	(8,000)	(2,500)
Trading Income	4,000	1,500

Corporation Tax Computation – CAP 1/4/2014 to 31/3/2015

	£
Trading Income	4,000
Taxable total profits	4,000

'Augmented Profits' = £4,000

Corporation Tax (FY 2014) £4,000 x 20%	£800

Corporation Tax Computation – CAP 1/4/2015 to 31/7/2015

	£
Trading Income	1,500
Chargeable Gains	45,000
Taxable total profits	46,500

Corporation Tax (FY 2015) at main rate:

£46,500 x 20%	£9,300

5.6   The following statements are true: (a), (c), (d).

5.7

	Financial Year 2014	Financial Year 2015
	£	£
Taxable total profits	156,250	468,750
Augmented profits	170,000	
Max of band	187,500	
Tax at main rate	32,812	93,750
Marginal Relief	40	
Tax re Financial Year	32,772	93,750
Total Corporation Tax for CAP		126,522

Workings:

Taxable total profits: £625,000 split 3/12 and 9/12

Augmented profits re FY2014: £625,000 + (£49,500 x 100/90) x 3/12 = £170,000

Max of band re FY2014: (£1,500,000 / 2) x 3/12 = £187,500

Tax at main rate: FY2014: £156,250 x 21% = £32,812

FY2015: £468,750 x 20% = £93,750

Marginal relief re FY2014:

1/400 x (£187,500 – £170,000) x (£156,250 / £170,000) = £40

CHAPTER 6: INCOME TAX – TRADING PROFITS

6.1   **Profit motive**. Michelle seems to deliberately buy and sell at a profit. She buys property in need of renovation, and times the sale to obtain most profit. This indicates trading.

Subject matter. Michelle gets personal use from the properties that she buys, and this could indicate that she is not trading. She could argue that she is simply changing homes like most people.

Length of ownership. After renovating the buildings, Michelle only keeps them for a few months. Such a short time indicates trading.

Frequency of transactions. The buying and selling of property seems to be quite a regular activity, although with each transaction spaced nearly a year apart it could be argued that it is not particularly frequent.

Supplementary work. Renovating the properties counts as supplementary work, and this is clearly carried out with a view to a future sale.

Reason for acquisition and sale. Although the first property was bequeathed to her, she seems to have subsequently bought with the ultimate sale in mind. This indicates trading.

6.2
1   add back (disallowable expense)
2   add back (disallowable expense)
3   deduct (not trading income)
4   deduct (not trading income)
5   add back (disallowable expense)
6   deduct (not taxable income)
7   add back (disallowable expense)
8   add back (disallowable expense since food)
9   no action (taxable trading income)
10 add back (disallowable expense – part of drawings)
11 no action (allowable)
12 add back (disallowable expense)

6.3

	£	£
Net Profit per accounts		144,000
Add Back:		
Expenditure that is shown in the accounts but is not allowable		
Drawings		18,000
Depreciation		22,000
Loss on Sale of Non-current Assets		4,000
Gift Vouchers		3,000
Entertaining Customers		4,500
Owner's Pension Contribution		2,400
		197,900
Deduct:	£	£
Income that is not taxable as trading income		
Interest Received	12,000	
Rental Income	10,000	
Capital Allowances	23,000	
		(45,000)
Trading Income Assessment		152,900

6.4   **The capital allowance computation is as follows:**

The following acquisitions qualify for AIA:

Computer System	£2,000
Shop Counter	£3,000
Total	£5,000 (below AIA limit)

		Main Pool	Single Asset Pool Car (40% private)	Capital Allowances
	£	£	£	£
WDV bf		25,000	10,000	
Additions with FYAs:				
Low emission car	26,000			
FYA (100%)	(26,000) x 60%			15,600
Acquisitions qualifying for AIA:				
Computer	2,000			
Shop Counter	3,000			
AIA claimed	(5,000)	0		5,000
Disposals:				
Private use car			(4,000)	
Food Processor		(200)		
Sub totals		24,800	6,000	
WDA 18%		(4,464)		4,464
Balancing Allowance			(6,000) x 60%	3,600
WDV cf		20,336	-	
Total Capital Allowances				28,664

Calculation of Adjusted Profit (Loss):

	£
Adjusted trading profits (before capital allowances)	12,000
Capital allowances (as above)	(28,664)
Loss	(16,664)

The trading income assessment for 2015/16 is nil.

The loss of £16,664 could be:

- carried forward against future trading profits
- set against the total income of John for 2015/16 and / or 2014/15
- total income claims could be extended to capital gains

6.5   There is no AIA claimable.

Plant & Machinery Capital Allowances Computation

	Main Pool	Car 20% private BMW	S/L Asset	Single Asset Pools Special Rate 20% private Range Rover	Capital Allowances
	£	£	£	£	£
WDV bf	66,300	16,000	2,000	-	
Additions without FYA or AIA:					
Range Rover (200 g/km)				28,000	
Ford Focus (125g/km)	19,000				
Disposals:					
BMW		(12,000)			
Vauxhall	(4,000)				
	81,300	4,000	2,000	28,000	
WDA 18%	(14,634)		(360)		14,994
WDA 8%				(2,240) x 80%	1,792
Balancing Allowance		(4,000) x 80%			3,200
WDV cf	66,666	-	1,640	25,760	
Total Capital Allowances					19,986

Adjustment of Trading Profits:

	£	£
Net Profit per accounts		110,000

Add Back:
Expenditure that is shown in the accounts but is not allowable

Drawings		45,000
Depreciation		38,000
Loss on Sale of BMW		3,000
Entertaining Customers		2,000
		198,000

Deduct:

Income that is not taxable as trading income

Reduction in general bad debt provision	4,000	
Gain on Sale of Vauxhall	1,000	
Capital Allowances – Plant & Machinery	19,986	
		(24,986)
Trading Income Assessment		173,014

6.6

Net loss		(3,785)
Add		
Depreciation	28,019	
Mr Chang's salary	30,000	
Gifts to customers	2,250	
Subscription to golf club	220	
Motor expenses for Mr Chang's car	5,700	
		66,189
		62,404
Less		
Capital allowances		9,878
Adjusted trading profits		52,526

CHAPTER 7: INCOME TAX – FURTHER ISSUES

7.1   The first three tax years for the business will be 2014/15, 2015/16 and 2016/17.
The assessments for these years are calculated as follows:

Tax Year	Basis Period	trading income assessment	
2014/15	1/12/2014 - 5/4/2015	£48,000 x 4/12 =	£16,000
2015/16	1/12/2014 - 30/11/2015		£48,000
2016/17	1/12/2015 - 30/11/2016		£30,000

Overlap profits are £16,000, relating to the period 1/12/2014 – 5/4/2015.

7.2 The first three tax years for the business will be 2012/13, 2013/14 and 2014/15.

The assessments for these years are calculated as follows:

Tax Year	Basis Period		trading income assessment
2012/13	1/2/2013 - 5/4/2013	£33,000 x 2/11 =	£6,000
2013/14	1/2/2013 - 31/1/2014 (First 12 months)	£33,000 + (£48,000 x 1/12)	£37,000
2014/15	1/1/2014 - 31/12/2014		£48,000

Overlap profits total £10,000, relating to the periods 1/2/2013 - 5/4/2013 (£6,000) and 1/1/2014 - 31/1/2014 (£4,000).

7.3

Tax Year	Basis Period		trading income assessment
2013/14	1/7/2012 - 30/6/2013		£36,000
2014/15	1/7/2013 - 31/5/2014	£20,000	
	less overlap profits bf	(£5,000)	
			£15,000

7.4 The accounting year to 31/12/2013 profits of £96,000 will need to be time-apportioned before dividing them amongst the partners:

1/1/2013 - 30/9/2013	9/12 x £96,000 = £72,000
Alice (50%)	£36,000
Bob (50%)	£36,000
1/10/2013 - 31/12/2013	3/12 x £96,000 = £24,000
Alice (45%)	£10,800
Bob (40%)	£9,600
Colin (15%)	£3,600

The accounting year to 31/12/2014 profits of £108,000 are divided as follows:

Alice (45%)	£48,600
Bob (40%)	£43,200
Colin (15%)	£16,200

The basis periods for the partners and assessments are as follows:

Tax Year	Basis Period	Trading Income Assessments	
Alice			
2013/14	y/e 31/12/2013	£36,000+ £10,800	£46,800
2014/15	y/e 31/12/2014		£48,600
Bob			
2013/14	y/e 31/12/2013	£36,000+ £9,600	£45,600
2014/15	y/e 31/12/2014		£43,200
Colin			
2013/14	1/10/2013 - 5/4/2014	£3,600 + (3/12 x £16,200)	£7,650
2014/15	y/e 31/12/2014		£16,200

(Colin's overlap profits are £4,050)

7.5   Capital Allowances:

Plant & Machinery

	Main Pool	Single Asset Pool Car (30% private)	Capital Allowances
	£	£	£
WDV bf	35,000	16,000	
Disposal:			
Car		(10,000)	
WDA 18%	(6,300)		6,300
Balancing Allowance		(6,000) x 70%	4,200
WDV cf	28,700	0	-
Total Capital Allowances			10,500

Adjustment of Profits

	£	£
Net Profit per accounts		71,000
Add Back:		
Expenditure that is shown in the accounts but is not allowable		
Depreciation		12,250
Private motor expenses		500
Increase in General Provision for Bad Debts		200
Gift Vouchers for customers		400
		84,350
Deduct:		
Allowable expenditure not shown in accounts		
Plant & Machinery Capital Allowances	10,500	
		(10,500)
Adjusted Profits for y/e 31/3/2016		73,850

Trading Income assessment for Olga for 2015/16

This is her last tax year for the business. The basis period is 1/4/2015 - 31/3/2016.

Her share of the adjusted profits is: £73,850 x 1/3 = £24,617

Less her overlap profits brought forward   (£4,000)

Trading Income assessment   £20,617

Class 4 National Insurance

This is calculated based on the trading income figure.

9% of (£20,617 – £8,060) = £1,130.13

Supplementary tax return pages

These are shown on the next three pages. The 2014/15 version is used to illustrate the form.

TRADING AND PROFESSIONAL INCOME for the year ended 5 April 2015 – continued

■ **Capital allowances – summary**

	Capital allowances	Balancing charges
● Annual Investment Allowance (include any balancing charges in box 3.17 below)	**3.13A** £	
● Cars costing more than £12,000 – if bought before 6 April 2009. (You should make a separate calculation for each car.)	**3.14** £	**3.15** £
● Capital allowances at 18% on equipment, including cars with lower CO_2 emissions	**3.14A** £ 10500	**3.15A** £
● Capital allowances at 8% on equipment, including cars with higher CO_2 emissions	**3.16** £	**3.17** £
● Agricultural or Industrial Buildings Allowance. (You must make a separate calculation for each block of expenditure.)	**3.18** £	**3.19** £
● 100% and other enhanced capital allowances claimed (you must make separate calculations). (Claims to and balancing charges arising on Business Premises Renovation Allowance must also be included in boxes 10.4 and 10.5 respectively.)	**3.20** £	**3.21** £
	total of column above	total of column above
Total capital allowances/balancing charges	**3.22** £ 10500	**3.23** £

■ **Income and expenses for this accounting period**

Read the **Partnership Tax Return Guide** before completing this section.

If your annual turnover was below £81,000 (or would have been if you had traded for the whole year) **fill in boxes 3.24 to 3.26 instead of page 4.**

If your annual turnover was between £81,000 and £15m (or would have been if you had traded for a whole year) **ignore boxes 3.24 to 3.26. Now fill in page 4.**

If the combined annualised turnover from all of your activities was **more than £15m fill in boxes 3.24 to 3.26 and send in partnership accounts and computations as well.**

In all cases, complete box 3.83 or box 3.84 on page 5, and the other boxes on page 5 if applicable.

● Turnover including other business receipts, and goods etc taken for personal use (and balancing charges from box 3.23)	**3.24** £
● Expenses allowable for tax (including capital allowances from box 3.22)	**3.25** £
Net profit for this accounting period (put figure in brackets if a loss)	box 3.24 minus box 3.25 **3.26** £

3.116 Additional information

TRADING AND PROFESSIONAL INCOME for the year ended 5 April 2015 – continued

■ **Income and expenses for this accounting period**

You must fill in this page if your annual turnover was between £81,000 and £15m. If the combined annualised turnover from all your activities was more than £15m, fill in boxes 3.24 to 3.26 on page 3 and send in the partnership accounts and computations as well. In all cases, complete box 3.83 or box 3.84 on page 5, and the other boxes on page 5 if applicable. Read the Partnership Tax Return Guide, go to **www.hmrc.gov.uk/selfassessmentforms**

If you were registered for VAT, do the figures in boxes 3.29 to 3.64 include VAT?   **3.27** [ ]   or exclude VAT?   **3.28** [ ]

Sales/business income (turnover)

3.29 £ 1 8 0 0 0 0

	Disallowable expenses included in boxes 3.46 to 3.63	Total expenses	
● Cost of sales	**3.30** £	**3.46** £ 5 5 0 0 0	
● Construction industry subcontractor costs	**3.31** £	**3.47** £	
● Other direct costs	**3.32** £	**3.48** £	

box 3.29 minus (boxes 3.46 + 3.47 + 3.48)

Gross profit/(loss)   **3.49** £ 1 2 5 0 0 0

Other income/profits   **3.50** £

● Employee costs	**3.33** £	**3.51** £ 1 6 5 0 0
● Premises costs	**3.34** £	**3.52** £ 1 2 5 0 0
● Repairs	**3.35** £	**3.53** £
● General administrative expenses	**3.36** £	**3.54** £
● Motor expenses	**3.37** £ 5 0 0	**3.55** £ 8 0 0 0
● Travel and subsistence	**3.38** £	**3.56** £
● Advertising, promotion and entertainment	**3.39** £	**3.57** £
● Legal and professional costs	**3.40** £	**3.58** £
● Bad debts	**3.41** £	**3.59** £
● Interest and alternative finance payments	**3.42** £	**3.60** £ 1 7 5 0
● Other finance charges	**3.43** £	**3.61** £
● Depreciation and loss/(profit) on sale	**3.44** £ 1 2 2 5 0	**3.62** £ 1 2 2 5 0
● Other expenses including partnership charges	**3.45** £ 6 0 0	**3.63** £ 3 0 0 0

Put the total of boxes 3.30 to 3.45 in box 3.66 below

boxes 3.51 to 3.63

Total expenses   **3.64** £ 5 4 0 0 0

boxes 3.49 + 3.50 minus 3.64

Net profit/(loss)   **3.65** £ 7 1 0 0 0

■ **Tax adjustments to net profit or loss for this accounting period**

boxes 3.30 to 3.45

● Disallowable expenses	**3.66** £ 1 3 3 5 0
● Goods, etc taken for personal use and other adjustments (apart from disallowable expenses) that increase profits	**3.67** £
● Balancing charges (from box 3.23)	**3.68** £

boxes 3.66 + 3.67 + 3.68

Total additions to net profit (deduct from net loss)   **3.69** £ 1 3 3 5 0

● Capital allowances (from box 3.22)	**3.70** £ 1 0 5 0 0
● Deductions from net profit (add to net loss)	**3.71** £

boxes 3.70 + 3.71

3.72 £ 1 0 5 0 0

boxes 3.65 + 3.69 minus box 3.72

Net business profit for tax purposes for this accounting period (put figure in brackets if a loss)   **3.73** £ 7 3 8 5 0

PARTNERSHIP STATEMENT (SHORT) for the year ended 5 April 2015

Please read these instructions before completing the Statement

Use these pages to allocate partnership income if the only income for the relevant return period was trading and professional income or taxed interest and alternative finance receipts from banks and building societies. Otherwise you must download or ask the SA Orderline for the 'Partnership Statement (Full)' pages to record details of the allocation of all the partnership income. Go to www.hmrc.gov.uk/selfassessmentforms

Step 1 Fill in boxes 1 to 29 and boxes A and B as appropriate. Get the figures you need from the relevant boxes in the Partnership Tax Return. Complete a separate Statement for each accounting period covered by this Partnership Tax Return and for each trade or profession carried on by the partnership.

Step 2 Then allocate the amounts in boxes 11 to 29 attributable to each partner using the allocation columns on this page and page 7, read the Partnership Tax Return Guide, go to hmrc.gov.uk/selfassessmentforms If the partnership has more than 3 partners, please photocopy page 7.

Step 3 Each partner will need a copy of their allocation of income to fill in their personal tax return.

PARTNERSHIP INFORMATION

If the partnership business includes a trade or profession, enter here the accounting period for which appropriate items in this statement are returned.

Start **1** 1 , 4 , 15

End **2** 31 , 3 , 16

Nature of trade **3**

MIXED PARTNERSHIPS

Tick here if this Statement is drawn up using Corporation Tax rules **4**

Tick here if this Statement is drawn up using tax rules for non-residents **5**

Individual partner details

6 Name of partner   O L G A

Address

Postcode

Date appointed as a partner (if during 2013–14 or 2014–15)
7 / /

Partner's Unique Taxpayer Reference (UTR)
8

Date ceased to be a partner (if during 2013–14 or 2014–15)
9 31 , 3 , 16

Partner's National Insurance number
10

Partnership's profits, losses, income, tax credits, etc

Tick this box if the items entered in the box had foreign tax taken off

Partner's share of profits, losses, income, tax credits, etc

Copy figures in boxes 11 to 29 to boxes in the individual's **Partnership (short)** pages as shown below

- **for an accounting period ended in 2014–15** ▼

		Partnership		Partner's share	
from box 3.83 Profit from a trade or profession **A**	**11** £ 7 3 8 5 0	Profit **11** £ 2 4 6 1 7	Copy this figure to box 8
from box 3.82 Adjustment on change of basis	**11A** £	**11A** £	Copy this figure to box 10
from box 3.84 Loss from a trade or profession **B**	**12** £	Loss **12** £	Copy this figure to box 8
from box 10.4 Business Premises Renovation Allowance	**12A** £	**12A** £	Copy this figure to box 15

- **for the period 6 April 2014 to 5 April 2015***

from box 7.9A UK taxed interest and taxed alternative finance receipts	**22** £	**22** £	Copy this figure to box 28
from box 3.97 CIS deductions made by contractors on account of tax	**24** £	**24** £	Copy this figure to box 30
from box 3.98 Other tax taken off trading income	**24A** £	**24A** £	Copy this figure to box 31
from box 7.8A Income Tax taken off	**25** £	**25** £	Copy this figure to box 29
from box 3.117 Partnership charges	**29** £	**29** £	Copy this figure to box 4, 'Other tax reliefs' section on page Ai 2 in your personal tax return

* if you are a 'CT Partnership' see the Partnership Tax Return Guide

7.6

Payment date	31 Jan 2014 £	31 July 2014 £	31 Jan 2015 £	31 July 2015 £	31 Jan 2016 £	31 July 2016 £
Tax year 2013/14	0	0	6,200	0	0	0
Tax year 2014/15	0	0	3,100	3,100	4,800	0
Tax year 2015/16	0	0	0	0	5,500	5,500
Totals due	0	0	9,300	3,100	10,300	5,500

7.7

	£	£
Net profit per accounts		21,500
add disallowable expenditure		
Private van running costs		1,260
Depreciation		2,800
Entertaining		1,000
Private telephone and postage		200
		26,760
less allowable expenditure		
Heating and lighting office	150	
Capital allowances	4,200	
		(4,350)
Adjusted profit		22,410
Less Trading Loss brought forward		(6,000)
Trading Income Assessment 2015/16		16,410

Self Employment pages (short) are shown on the next two pages. The 2014/15 version has been used here.

HM Revenue & Customs

Self-employment (short)

Tax year 6 April 2014 to 5 April 2015 (2014-15)

Please read the 'Self-employment (short) notes' to check if you should use this page or the 'Self-employment (full)' page.

To get notes and helpsheets that will help you fill in this form, go to www.hmrc.gov.uk/selfassessmentforms

Your name

SHAUN SLAPP

Your Unique Taxpayer Reference (UTR)

Business details

1 Description of business

PLASTERER

2 Postcode of your business address

3 If your business name, description, address or postcode have changed in the last 12 months, put 'X' in the box and give details in the 'Any other information' box of your tax return

4 If you are a foster carer or shared lives carer, put 'X' in the box – read the notes

5 If your business started after 5 April 2014, enter the start date DD MM YYYY

6 If your business ceased before 6 April 2015, enter the final date of trading DD MM YYYY

7 Date your books or accounts are made up to – read the notes

30 11 2015

8 If you used the cash basis, money actually received and paid out, to calculate your income and expenses put 'X' in the box – read the notes

Business income – if your annual business turnover was below £81,000

9 Your turnover – the takings, fees, sales or money earned by your business

£ 55000 . 00

10 Any other business income not included in box 9

£ . 0 0

Allowable business expenses

If your annual turnover was below £81,000 you may just put your total expenses in box 20, rather than filling in the whole section.

11 Costs of goods bought for resale or goods used

£ 11000 . 0 0

12 Car, van and travel expenses – after private use proportion

£ 5040 . 0 0

13 Wages, salaries and other staff costs

£ 9800 . 0 0

14 Rent, rates, power and insurance costs

£ 1350 . 0 0

15 Repairs and renewals of property and equipment

£ . 0 0

16 Accountancy, legal and other professional fees

£ 600 . 0 0

17 Interest and bank and credit card etc. financial charges

£ . 0 0

18 Phone, fax, stationery and other office costs

£ 600 . 0 0

19 Other allowable business expenses – client entertaining costs are not an allowable expense

£ . 0 0

20 Total allowable expenses – total of boxes 11 to 19

£ 28390 . 0 0

Net profit or loss

| 21 | **Net profit** – if your business income is more than your expenses (if box 9 + box 10 minus box 20 is positive)
£ 2 6 6 1 0 · 0 0 | 22 | **Or, net loss** – if your expenses exceed your business income (if box 20 minus (box 9 + box 10) is positive)
£ · 0 0 |

Tax allowances for vehicles and equipment (capital allowances)

There are 'capital' tax allowances available for vehicles and equipment used in your business. (Please don't include the cost of these in your business expenses)

| 23 | **Annual Investment Allowance**
£ · 0 0 | 25 | **Other capital allowances**
£ 4 2 0 0 · 0 0 |
| 24 | **Allowance for small balance of unrelieved expenditure**
£ · 0 0 | 26 | **Total balancing charges** – where you have disposed of items for more than their value
£ · 0 0 |

Calculating your taxable profits

Your taxable profit may not be the same as your net profit. Please read the 'Self-employment (short) notes' to see if you need to make any adjustments and fill in the boxes which apply to arrive at your taxable profit for the year.

| 27 | **Goods and/or services for your own use** – read the notes
£ · 0 0 | 29 | **Loss brought forward from earlier years set off against this year's profits** – up to the amount in box 28
£ 6 0 0 0 · 0 0 |
| 28 | **Net business profit for tax purposes** (if box 21 + box 26 + box 27 minus (boxes 22 to 25) is positive)
£ 2 2 4 1 0 · 0 0 | 30 | **Any other business income not included in box 9 or box 10** – for example, non arm's length reverse premiums
£ · 0 0 |

Total taxable profits or net business loss

| 31 | **Total taxable profits from this business** (if box 28 + box 30 minus box 29 is positive)
£ 1 6 4 1 0 · 0 0 | 32 | **Net business loss for tax purposes** (if boxes 22 to 25 minus (box 21 + box 26 + box 27) is positive)
£ · 0 0 |

Losses, Class 4 National Insurance contributions (NICs) and CIS deductions

If you have made a loss for tax purposes (box 32), read the 'Self-employment (short) notes' and fill in boxes 33 to 35 as appropriate.

33	**Loss from this tax year set off against other income for 2014–15** £ · 0 0	36	**If you are exempt from paying Class 4 NICs, put 'X' in the box** – read the notes ☐
34	**Loss to be carried back to previous year(s) and set off against income (or capital gains)** £ · 0 0	37	**If you have been given a 2014–15 Class 4 NICs deferment certificate, put 'X' in the box** – read the notes ☐
35	**Total loss to carry forward after all other set-offs** – including unused losses brought forward £ · 0 0	38	**Deductions on payment and deduction statements from contractors** – construction industry subcontractors only £ · 0 0

7.8   (a)   2013/14

(b)   £12,000

(c)   £72,750

(d)   £81,000

(e)   £18,750

(f)   from the profits in the final year of trading

7.9   Only (c) and (f) are true, the rest are false

CHAPTER 8: CAPITAL GAINS TAX FOR INDIVIDUALS

8.1   (a)   Exempt, as a chattel

(b)   Exempt

(c)   Chargeable

(d)   Chargeable

(e)   Chargeable

(f)   Chargeable

(g)   Exempt

(h)   Exempt

8.2

		£
(a)	Proceeds	140,000
	less cost	(40,000)
	extension	(20,000)
	Gain	80,000
	less annual exempt amount	(11,100)
	Amount subject to CGT	68,900
	Capital Gains Tax £68,900 x 28% =	19,292

		£
(b)	Gain	80,000
	less annual exempt amount	(11,100)
	Amount subject to CGT	68,900
	Capital Gains Tax £68,900 x 10% =	6,890

8.3

	£
Proceeds	23,000
less cost (600 x £10)	(6,000)
Gain	17,000
less annual exempt amount	(11,100)
Amount subject to CGT	5,900
Capital Gains Tax £5,900 x 18% =	1,062

All the gain is within the basic rate band limit of £31,785 when added to the taxable income.

8.4   (a) Amount of William's gain:

	£	£
Proceeds		200,000
less market value when received	100,000	
minus deferred gain	(33,160)	
		(66,840)
Gain		133,160
less annual exempt amount		(11,100)
Amount subject to CGT		122,060
Capital Gains Tax £122,060 x 28% =		34,176

(b)

	£
Gain	133,160
less annual exempt amount	(11,100)
Amount subject to CGT	122,060
Capital Gains Tax £122,060 x 10% =	12,206

8.5   The first step is to allocate the sale proceeds to the individual assets, and determine which assets are chargeable.

	£	
Premises	700,000	Chargeable
Plant & Machinery	20,000	Proceeds < Cost. Dealt with through capital allowance computation
Net Current Assets	50,000	Exempt
Goodwill	130,000	Chargeable
Total Proceeds	900,000	

The goodwill is calculated as the balancing figure, after accounting for the other assets.
The computations are then carried out individually on the chargeable assets.

	£	£
Premises		
Proceeds		700,000
less Cost	400,000	
minus deferred gain	(60,000)	
		(340,000)
Gain		360,000
Goodwill		
Proceeds		130,000
Less Cost		0
Gain		130,000

Summary	£
Gain on premises	360,000
Gain on goodwill	130,000
Total Gains	490,000
Less Annual Exempt Amount	(11,100)
Amount subject to CGT	478,900
CGT £478,900 x 10%	47,890

8.6 Only (c) is correct, the rest are not.

8.7 (b) Gain = £3,000,000
Less annual exempt amount £11,100 = £2,988,900
Taxed at 10% = £298,890.

8.8 Only (a) is correct, the rest are not.

Appendix

These pages may be photocopied for student use.

It is recommended that they are enlarged to A4 size.

These pages are also available for download from the Resources Section of www.osbornebooks.co.uk or from www.hmrc.gov.uk

All these forms illustrated are those in use for 2014/15. The forms for 2015/16 were not available when this book was published.

10.0

HM Revenue & Customs

Company - Short Tax Return form
CT600 (Short) (2008) Version 2
for accounting periods ending on or after 1 July 1999

Your company tax return

If we send the company a *Notice* to deliver a company tax return (form *CT603*) it has to comply by the filing date, or we charge a penalty, even if there is no tax to pay. A return includes a company tax return form, any Supplementary Pages, accounts, computations and any relevant information.

Is this the right form for the company? Read the advice on pages 3 to 6 of the Company tax return guide (the *Guide*) before you start.

The forms in the CT600 series set out the information we need and provide a standard format for calculations. Use the *Guide* to help you complete the return form. It contains general information you may need and box by box advice.

Company information

Company name

Company registration number

Tax Reference as shown on the CT603

Type of company

Registered office address

Postcode

About this return

This is the above company's return for the period

from (dd/mm/yyyy)

to (dd/mm/yyyy)

Put an 'X' in the appropriate box(es) below

A repayment is due for this return period

A repayment is due for an earlier period

Making more than one return for this company now

This return contains estimated figures

Company part of a group that is not small

Disclosure of tax avoidance schemes

Notice of disclosable avoidance schemes

Transfer pricing

Compensating adjustment claimed

Company qualifies for SME exemption

Accounts

I attach accounts and computations

- for the period to which this return relates

- for a different period

If you are not attaching accounts and computations, say why not

Supplementary Pages

If you are enclosing any Supplementary Pages put an 'X' in the appropriate box(es)

Loans to participators by close companies, form *CT600A*

Charities and Community Amateur Sports Clubs (CASCs), form *CT600E*

Disclosure of tax avoidance schemes, form *CT600J*

Page 2

Company tax calculation

Turnover

1	Total turnover from trade or profession	**1**	£

Income

3	Trading and professional profits	**3** £	
4	Trading losses brought forward claimed against profits	**4** £	
5	Net trading and professional profits	box 3 minus box 4 **5** £	
6	Bank, building society or other interest, and profits and gains from non-trading loan relationships	**6** £	
11	Income from UK land and buildings	**11** £	
14	Annual profits and gains not falling under any other heading	**14** £	

Chargeable gains

16	Gross chargeable gains	**16** £	
17	Allowable losses including losses brought forward	**17** £	
18	Net chargeable gains	box 16 minus box 17 **18** £	

21 Profits before other deductions and reliefs

sum of boxes 5, 6, 11, 14 & 18
21 £

Deductions and Reliefs

24	Management expenses under S75 ICTA 1988	**24** £	
30	Trading losses of this or a later accounting period under S393A ICTA 1988	**30** £	
31	Put an 'X' in box 31 if amounts carried back from later accounting periods are included in box 30	**31**	
32	Non-trade capital allowances	**32** £	
35	Charges paid	**35** £	

37 Profits chargeable to corporation tax

box 21 minus boxes 24, 30, 32 and 35
37 £

Tax calculation

38	Franked investment income	**38** £	
39	Number of associated companies in this period or	**39**	
40	Associated companies in the first financial year	**40**	
41	Associated companies in the second financial year	**41**	
42	Put an 'X' in box 42 if the company claims to be charged at the starting rate or the small companies' rate on any part of its profits, or is claiming marginal rate relief	**42**	

Enter how much profit has to be charged and at what rate of tax

Financial year (yyyy)	Amount of profit	Rate of tax	Tax	
43	**44** £	**45**	**46** £	p
53	**54** £	**55**	**56** £	p

		total of boxes 46 and 56	
63	Corporation tax	**63** £	p
64	Marginal rate relief	**64** £	p
65	Corporation tax net of marginal rate relief	**65** £	p
66	Underlying rate of corporation tax	**66** • %	
67	Profits matched with non-corporate distributions	**67**	
68	Tax at non-corporate distributions rate	**68** £	p
69	Tax at underlying rate on remaining profits	**69** £	p
70	**Corporation tax chargeable**	See note for box 70 in CT600 Guide **70** £	p

CT600 (Short) (2008) Version 2

| 79 | Tax payable under S419 ICTA 1988 | 79 £ | p |

80 *Put an 'X' in box 80 if you completed box A11 in the Supplementary Pages CT600A*   80 [ ]

| 84 | Income tax deducted from gross income included in profits | 84 £ | p |

| 85 | Income tax repayable to the company | 85 £ | p |

86 Tax payable - this is your self-assessment of tax payable

total of boxes 70 and 79 minus box 84

86 £   p

Tax reconciliation

| 91 | Tax already paid (and not already repaid) | 91 £ | p |

92 Tax outstanding

box 86 minus box 91

92 £   p

93 Tax overpaid

box 91 minus box 86

93 £   p

Information about capital allowances and balancing charges

Charges and allowances included in calculation of trading profits or losses

		Capital allowances	Balancing charges
172	Annual investment allowance	172 £	
105 - 106	Machinery and plant - special rate pool	105 £	106 £
107 - 108	Machinery and plant - main pool	107 £	108 £
109 - 110	Cars	109 £	110 £
111 - 112	Industrial buildings and structures	111 £	112 £
113 - 114	Other charges and allowances	113 £	114 £

Charges and allowances not included in calculation of trading profits or losses

		Capital allowances	Balancing charges
173	Annual investment allowance	173 £	
115 - 116	Other non-trading charges and allowances	115 £	116 £
117	*Put an 'X' in box 117 if box 115 includes flat conversion allowances*	117 [ ]	

Qualifying expenditure

118	Expenditure on machinery and plant on which first year allowance is claimed	118 £
174	Designated environmentally friendly machinery and plant	174 £
120	Machinery and plant on long-life assets and integral features	120 £
121	Other machinery and plant	121 £

Losses, deficits and excess amounts

122 Trading losses Case I	*calculated under S393 ICTA 1988* 122 £	124 Trading losses Case V	*calculated under S393 ICTA 1988* 124 £
125 Non-trade deficits on loan relationships and derivative contracts	*calculated under S82 FA 1996* 125 £	127 Schedule A losses	*calculated under S392A ICTA 1988* 127 £
129 Overseas property business losses Case V	*calculated under S392B ICTA 1988* 129 £	130 Losses Case VI	*calculated under S396 ICTA 1988* 130 £
131 Capital losses	*calculated under S16 TCGA 1992* 131 £	136 Excess management expenses	*calculated under S75 ICTA 1988* 136 £

Page 4
Overpayments and repayments

Small repayments

If you do not want us to make small repayments please either put an 'X' in box 139 or complete box 140 below. 'Repayments' here include tax, interest, and late-filing penalties or any combination of them.

Do not repay £20 or less **139** [ ]   Do not repay sums of **140** £ [ ] or less. *Enter whole figure only*

Bank details (for person to whom the repayment is to be made)

Repayment is made quickly and safely by direct credit to a bank or building society account.
Please complete the following details:

Name of bank or building society
149 [ ]

Branch sort code
150 [ ][ ][ ]

Account number
151 [ ]

Name of account
152 [ ]

Building society reference
153 [ ]

Payments to a person other than the company

Complete the authority below if you want the repayment to be made to a person other than the company.
I, as *(enter status - company secretary, treasurer, liquidator or authorised agent, etc.)*
154 [ ]

of *(enter name of company)*
155 [ ]

authorise *(enter name)*
156 [ ]

(enter address)
157 [ ]
                                        Postcode

Nominee reference
158 [ ]

to receive payment on the company's behalf.

Signature
159 [ ]

Name *(in capitals)*
160 [ ]

Declaration

Warning - Giving false information in the return, or concealing any part of the company's profits or tax payable, can lead to both the company and yourself being prosecuted.

Declaration
The information I have given in this company tax return is correct and complete to the best of my knowledge and belief.

Signature
[ ]

Name *(in capitals)*
[ ]

Date *(dd/mm/yyyy)*
[ ]

Status
[ ]

CT600 (Short) (2008) Version 2

HM Revenue & Customs

Self-employment (short)
Tax year 6 April 2014 to 5 April 2015 (2014-15)

Please read the 'Self-employment (short) notes' to check if you should use this page or the 'Self-employment (full)' page.

To get notes and helpsheets that will help you fill in this form, go to www.hmrc.gov.uk/selfassessmentforms

Your name	Your Unique Taxpayer Reference (UTR)

Business details

1 Description of business

2 Postcode of your business address

3 If your business name, description, address or postcode have changed in the last 12 months, put 'X' in the box and give details in the 'Any other information' box of your tax return

4 If you are a foster carer or shared lives carer, put 'X' in the box – read the notes

5 If your business started after 5 April 2014, enter the start date DD MM YYYY

6 If your business ceased before 6 April 2015, enter the final date of trading DD MM YYYY

7 Date your books or accounts are made up to – read the notes

8 If you used the cash basis, money actually received and paid out, to calculate your income and expenses put 'X' in the box – read the notes

Business income – if your annual business turnover was below £81,000

9 Your turnover – the takings, fees, sales or money earned by your business
£ . 0 0

10 Any other business income not included in box 9
£ . 0 0

Allowable business expenses

If your annual turnover was below £81,000 you may just put your total expenses in box 20, rather than filling in the whole section.

11 Costs of goods bought for resale or goods used
£ . 0 0

12 Car, van and travel expenses – after private use proportion
£ . 0 0

13 Wages, salaries and other staff costs
£ . 0 0

14 Rent, rates, power and insurance costs
£ . 0 0

15 Repairs and renewals of property and equipment
£ . 0 0

16 Accountancy, legal and other professional fees
£ . 0 0

17 Interest and bank and credit card etc. financial charges
£ . 0 0

18 Phone, fax, stationery and other office costs
£ . 0 0

19 Other allowable business expenses – client entertaining costs are not an allowable expense
£ . 0 0

20 Total allowable expenses – total of boxes 11 to 19
£ . 0 0

Net profit or loss

21 **Net profit** – if your business income is more than your expenses (if box 9 + box 10 minus box 20 is positive)

£ [   ] · 0 0

22 **Or, net loss** – if your expenses exceed your business income (if box 20 minus (box 9 + box 10) is positive)

£ [   ] · 0 0

Tax allowances for vehicles and equipment (capital allowances)

There are 'capital' tax allowances available for vehicles and equipment used in your business. (Please don't include the cost of these in your business expenses)

23 **Annual Investment Allowance**

£ [   ] · 0 0

24 **Allowance for small balance of unrelieved expenditure**

£ [   ] · 0 0

25 **Other capital allowances**

£ [   ] · 0 0

26 **Total balancing charges** – where you have disposed of items for more than their value

£ [   ] · 0 0

Calculating your taxable profits

Your taxable profit may not be the same as your net profit. Please read the 'Self-employment (short) notes' to see if you need to make any adjustments and fill in the boxes which apply to arrive at your taxable profit for the year.

27 **Goods and/or services for your own use** – read the notes

£ [   ] · 0 0

28 **Net business profit for tax purposes** (if box 21 + box 26 + box 27 minus (boxes 22 to 25) is positive)

£ [   ] · 0 0

29 **Loss brought forward from earlier years set off against this year's profits** – up to the amount in box 28

£ [   ] · 0 0

30 **Any other business income not included in box 9 or box 10** – for example, non arm's length reverse premiums

£ [   ] · 0 0

Total taxable profits or net business loss

31 **Total taxable profits from this business** (if box 28 + box 30 minus box 29 is positive)

£ [   ] · 0 0

32 **Net business loss for tax purposes** (if boxes 22 to 25 minus (box 21 + box 26 + box 27) is positive)

£ [   ] · 0 0

Losses, Class 4 National Insurance contributions (NICs) and CIS deductions

If you have made a loss for tax purposes (box 32), read the 'Self-employment (short) notes' and fill in boxes 33 to 35 as appropriate.

33 **Loss from this tax year set off against other income for 2014–15**

£ [   ] · 0 0

34 **Loss to be carried back to previous year(s) and set off against income (or capital gains)**

£ [   ] · 0 0

35 **Total loss to carry forward after all other set-offs** – including unused losses brought forward

£ [   ] · 0 0

36 **If you are exempt from paying Class 4 NICs, put 'X' in the box** – read the notes

[ ]

37 **If you have been given a 2014–15 Class 4 NICs deferment certificate, put 'X' in the box** – read the notes

[ ]

38 **Deductions on payment and deduction statements from contractors** – construction industry subcontractors only

£ [   ] · 0 0

HM Revenue & Customs

Self-employment (full)
Tax year 6 April 2014 to 5 April 2015 (2014-15)

Please read the 'Self-employment (full) notes' to check if you should use this page or the 'Self-employment (short)' page.

To get notes and helpsheets that will help you fill in this form, go to www.hmrc.gov.uk/selfassessmentforms

Your name	Your Unique Taxpayer Reference (UTR)

Business details

1 Business name – unless it is in your own name

2 Description of business

3 First line of your business address – unless you work from home

4 Postcode of your business address

5 If the details in boxes 1, 2, 3 or 4 have changed in the last 12 months, put 'X' in the box and give details in the 'Any other information' box

6 If your business started after 5 April 2014, enter the start date DD MM YYYY

7 If your business ceased after 5 April 2014 but before 6 April 2015, enter the final date of trading

8 Date your books or accounts start – the beginning of your accounting period

9 Date your books or accounts are made up to or the end of your accounting period – read the notes if you have filled in box 6 or 7

10 If you used the cash basis, money actually received and paid out, to calculate your income and expenses, put 'X' in the box – read the notes

Other information

11 If your accounting date has changed permanently, put 'X' in the box

12 If your accounting date has changed more than once since 2009, put 'X' in the box

13 If special arrangements apply, put 'X' in the box – read the notes

14 If you provided the information about your 2014–15 profit on last year's tax return, put 'X' in the box – read the notes

Business income

15 Your turnover – the takings, fees, sales or money earned by your business

£ . 0 0

16 Any other business income not included in box 15

£ . 0 0

SA103F 2015   Page SEF 1   HMRC 12/14

Business expenses

Please read the 'Self-employment (full) notes' before filling in this section.

Total expenses

If your annual turnover was below £81,000, you may just put your total expenses in box 31

Disallowable expenses

Use this column if the figures in boxes 17 to 30 include disallowable amounts

17 **Cost of goods bought for resale or goods used**

£ . 0 0

32

£ . 0 0

18 **Construction industry – payments to subcontractors**

£ . 0 0

33

£ . 0 0

19 **Wages, salaries and other staff costs**

£ . 0 0

34

£ . 0 0

20 **Car, van and travel expenses**

£ . 0 0

35

£ . 0 0

21 **Rent, rates, power and insurance costs**

£ . 0 0

36

£ . 0 0

22 **Repairs and renewals of property and equipment**

£ . 0 0

37

£ . 0 0

23 **Phone, fax, stationery and other office costs**

£ . 0 0

38

£ . 0 0

24 **Advertising and business entertainment costs**

£ . 0 0

39

£ . 0 0

25 **Interest on bank and other loans**

£ . 0 0

40

£ . 0 0

26 **Bank, credit card and other financial charges**

£ . 0 0

41

£ . 0 0

27 **Irrecoverable debts written off**

£ . 0 0

42

£ . 0 0

28 **Accountancy, legal and other professional fees**

£ . 0 0

43

£ . 0 0

29 **Depreciation and loss/profit on sale of assets**

£ . 0 0

44

£ . 0 0

30 **Other business expenses**

£ . 0 0

45

£ . 0 0

31 **Total expenses (total of boxes 17 to 30)**

£ . 0 0

46 **Total disallowable expenses (total of boxes 32 to 45)**

£ . 0 0

Net profit or loss

47 **Net profit** – if your business income is more than your expenses (if box 15 + box 16 minus box 31 is positive)

£ [   ] . [0] [0]

48 **Or, net loss** – if your expenses are more than your business income (if box 31 minus (box 15 + box 16) is positive)

£ [   ] . [0] [0]

Tax allowances for vehicles and equipment (capital allowances)

There are 'capital' tax allowances for vehicles, equipment and certain buildings used in your business (don't include the cost of these in your business expenses). Please read the 'Self-employment (full) notes' and use the examples to work out your capital allowances.

49 Annual Investment Allowance

£ [   ] . [0] [0]

50 Capital allowances at 18% on equipment, including cars with lower CO_2 emissions

£ [   ] . [0] [0]

51 Capital allowances at 8% on equipment, including cars with higher CO_2 emissions

£ [   ] . [0] [0]

52 Restricted capital allowances for cars costing more than £12,000 – if bought before 6 April 2009

£ [   ] . [0] [0]

53 Agricultural or Industrial Buildings Allowance

£ [   ] . [0] [0]

54 Business Premises Renovation Allowance (Assisted Areas only) – read the notes

£ [   ] . [0] [0]

55 100% and other enhanced capital allowances – read the notes

£ [   ] . [0] [0]

56 Allowances on sale or cessation of business use (where you have disposed of assets for less than their tax value)

£ [   ] . [0] [0]

57 Total capital allowances (total of boxes 49 to 56)

£ [   ] . [0] [0]

58 Balancing charge on sale or cessation of business use (only where Business Premises Renovation Allowance has been claimed) – read the notes

£ [   ] . [0] [0]

59 Balancing charge on sales of other assets or on the cessation of business use (where you have disposed of assets for more than their tax value)

£ [   ] . [0] [0]

Calculating your taxable profit or loss

You may have to adjust your net profit or loss for disallowable expenses or capital allowances to arrive at your taxable profit or your loss for tax purposes. Please read the 'Self-employment (full) notes' and fill in the boxes below that apply.

60 Goods and services for your own use – read the notes

£ [   ] . [0] [0]

61 Total additions to net profit or deductions from net loss (box 46 + box 58 + box 59 + box 60)

£ [   ] . [0] [0]

62 Income, receipts and other profits included in business income or expenses but not taxable as business profits

£ [   ] . [0] [0]

63 Total deductions from net profit or additions to net loss (box 57 + box 62)

£ [   ] . [0] [0]

64 Net business profit for tax purposes (if box 47 + box 61 minus (box 48 + box 63) is positive)

£ [   ] . [0] [0]

65 Net business loss for tax purposes (if box 48 + box 63 minus (box 47 + box 61) is positive)

£ [   ] . [0] [0]

Calculating your taxable profit or loss (continued)

If you start or finish self-employment and your accounting period is not the same as your basis period (or there are overlaps or gaps in your basis periods) or in certain situations or trades or professions, you may need to make further tax adjustments - read the 'Self-employment (full) notes'. In all cases, please complete boxes 73 and 76, or box 77, as applicable.

66 Date your basis period began DD MM YYYY

67 Date your basis period ended

68 If your basis period is not the same as your accounting period, enter the adjustment needed to arrive at the profit or loss for the basis period – if the adjustment needs to be taken off the profit figure, put a minus sign (-) in the box

£ · 0 0

69 Overlap relief used this year – read the notes

£ · 0 0

70 Overlap profit carried forward

£ · 0 0

71 Adjustment for change of accounting practice – read the notes

£ · 0 0

72 Averaging adjustment (only for farmers, market gardeners and creators of literary or artistic works) if the adjustment needs to be taken off the profit figure, put a minus sign (-) in the box

£ · 0 0

73 Adjusted profit for 2014-15 (see the Working Sheet in the notes) – if a loss, enter it in box 77

£ · 0 0

74 Loss brought forward from earlier years set off against this year's profits

£ · 0 0

75 Any other business income not included in boxes 15, 16 or 60 – for example, non arm's length reverse premiums

£ · 0 0

76 Total taxable profits from this business (box 73 minus box 74 + box 75 – or use the Working Sheet in the notes)

£ · 0 0

Losses

If you have made a net loss for tax purposes (in box 65), or if you have losses from previous years, read the 'Self-employment (full) notes' and fill in boxes 77 to 80, as appropriate.

77 Adjusted loss for 2014-15 (see the Working Sheet in the notes)

£ · 0 0

78 Loss from this tax year set off against other income for 2014-15 – read the notes

£ · 0 0

79 Loss to be carried back to previous year(s) and set off against income (or capital gains) – read the notes

£ · 0 0

80 Total loss to carry forward after all other set-offs – including unused losses brought forward

£ · 0 0

CIS deductions and tax taken off

81 Deductions on payment and deduction statements from contractors – construction industry subcontractors only

£ · 0 0

82 Other tax taken off trading income

£ · 0 0

Balance sheet

If your business accounts include a balance sheet showing the assets, liabilities and capital of the business, fill in the relevant boxes below. If you do not have a balance sheet, go to box 100. Read the 'Self-employment (full) notes' for more information.

Assets

83 Equipment, machinery and vehicles

£ _____ . 0 0

84 Other fixed assets

£ _____ . 0 0

85 Stock and work in progress

£ _____ . 0 0

86 Trade debtors

£ _____ . 0 0

87 Bank/building society balances

£ _____ . 0 0

88 Cash in hand

£ _____ . 0 0

89 Other current assets and prepayments

£ _____ . 0 0

90 Total assets (total of boxes 83 to 89)

£ _____ . 0 0

Liabilities

91 Trade creditors

£ _____ . 0 0

92 Loans and overdrawn bank account balances

£ _____ . 0 0

93 Other liabilities and accruals

£ _____ . 0 0

Net business assets

94 Net business assets (box 90 minus (boxes 91 to 93))

£ _____ . 0 0

Capital account

95 Balance at start of period

£ _____ . 0 0

96 Net profit or loss (box 47 or box 48)

£ _____ . 0 0

97 Capital introduced

£ _____ . 0 0

98 Drawings

£ _____ . 0 0

99 Balance at end of period

£ _____ . 0 0

Class 4 National Insurance contributions (NICs)

If your self-employed profits are more than £7,956, you must pay Class 4 NICs (unless you are exempt or your contributions have been deferred) – read the 'Self-employment (full) notes'.

100 If you are exempt from paying Class 4 NICs, put 'X' in the box – read the notes

101 If you have been given a 2014–15 Class 4 NICs deferment certificate, put 'X' in the box – read the notes

102 Adjustment to profits chargeable to Class 4 NICs – read the notes

£ _____ . 0 0

Any other information

103 **Please give any other information in this space**

HM Revenue & Customs

Partnership Tax Return 2015
for the year ended 5 April 2015 (2014-15)

Tax reference

Date

Issue address

HM Revenue & Customs office address

Telephone

For
Reference

This notice requires you by law to send us a tax return giving details of income and disposals of chargeable assets, and any documents we ask for, for the year 6 April 2014 to 5 April 2015.

You can file the tax return using:

- this form and any supplementary pages you need, or
- the internet (you will need to use commercial software which you may have to buy). Most people file online. If you file online you will receive an instant online acknowledgement telling you that we have received your tax return safely. To file online, go directly to our official website by typing **www.gov.uk/file-your-self-assessment-tax-return** into your internet browser address bar. Do not use a search website to find HMRC services online.

Make sure that your tax return, and any documents asked for, reach us by:

- **31 October 2015** if you complete a **paper** tax return, or
- **31 January 2016** if you file online

Please see the Partnership Tax Return Guide for filing dates if this notice was given after 31 July 2015 or if the partnership includes a company as a partner.

Each partner who was a member of the partnership during the return period is liable to automatic penalties if the Partnership Tax Return does not reach us by the relevant filing date shown above. They will have to pay interest and may have to pay a late payment penalty on any tax they pay late.

We check all tax returns and there are penalties for supplying false or incomplete information.

Who should send the Partnership Tax Return?
If this Partnership Tax Return has been issued in the name of the partnership, then the partner nominated by the other members of the partnership during the period covered by the tax return is required by law to complete it and send it back to us. If the partners are unable to nominate someone, they should ask us to nominate one of them.

If this Partnership Tax Return has been issued in the name of a particular partner, that partner is required by law to send it back to us.

The Partnership Tax Return – your responsibilities
We have sent you pages 1 to 8 of the tax return for the most common types of partnership income. You might need other supplementary pages, which we have not sent you, for other types of income and disposals.

You are responsible for making sure that you have the right pages. Answer the questions on page 2 of this form to find out if you have the right ones.

You should make sure that the information needed by individual partners to complete their personal tax returns is given to them as quickly as possible (some partners may want to send their own returns by 31 October 2015).

If you need help:

- refer to the Partnership Tax Return Guide (included with this return, unless we know you have a tax adviser), or
- phone the number above – we can answer most questions by phone, or
- when the office is closed, phone our helpline on **0300 200 3310** for general advice, or
- go to **www.gov.uk/self-assessment-tax-returns**

PARTNERSHIP BUSINESS AND INVESTMENT INCOME for the year ended 5 April 2015

Answer Questions 1 to 6 on this page and Question 7 on page 8 to check that you have the pages you need to make a complete return of partnership income and related information for the year ended 5 April 2015. If you answer 'Yes', you must make sure that you have the right pages and then fill in the relevant boxes. If not, go to the next question.

To get the appropriate supplementary pages and notes that will help you fill in this form, go to www.hmrc.gov.uk/selfassessmentforms

Check to make sure that you have the right supplementary pages (including the Partnership Savings pages – see Question 7) and then tick the box below

Q1 Did the partnership receive any rent or other income from UK property (read the Partnership Tax Return Guide if you have furnished holiday lettings)?

YES [ ]   UK PROPERTY [ ]

Q2 Did the partnership have any foreign income?

YES [ ]   FOREIGN [ ]

Q3 Did the partnership business include a trade or profession at any time between 6 April 2014 and 5 April 2015?

YES [ ]   If yes, complete boxes 3.1 to 3.117 on pages 2 to 5 as appropriate.

Q4 Did the partnership dispose of any chargeable assets?

YES [ ]   CHARGEABLE ASSETS [ ]

Q5 During the return period has the partnership included any member who is:

• a company

YES [ ]

• not resident in the UK

YES [ ]   If yes, read the Partnership Tax Return Guide about filling in the Partnership Statement, go to hmrc.gov.uk/selfassessmentforms

• a partner in a business controlled and managed abroad and who is not domiciled in the UK or is not ordinarily resident in the UK?

YES [ ]   If yes, read the Partnership Tax Return Guide.

Q6 Are you completing this tax return on behalf of a European Economic Interest Grouping (EEIG)?

YES [ ]   If yes, read the Partnership Tax Return Guide.

TRADING AND PROFESSIONAL INCOME for the year ended 5 April 2015

You have to fill in a set of boxes for each trade carried on by the partnership and you may have to fill in a separate set if partnership accounts were made up to more than one date in the year ended 5 April 2015. Check the rules in the Partnership Tax Return Guide.
Box numbers 3.3, 3.6, 3.74 to 3.81, 3.85 to 3.92 and 3.94 to 3.96 are not used.

■ **Partnership details**

Name of business

3.1 [ ]

Description of partnership trade or profession

3.2 [ ]

Accounting period – read the Partnership Tax Return Guide, go to www.hmrc.gov.uk/selfassessmentforms

Start
3.4 [/ /]

End
3.5 [/ /]

• Date of commencement (if after 5 April 2012)
3.7 [/ /]

• Date of cessation (if before 6 April 2015)
3.8 [/ /]

• Tick box 3.9 if you used the 'cash basis', money actually received and paid out, to calculate your income and expenses – read the guide
3.9 [ ]

• Tick box 3.10 if you do not need to complete boxes 3.14 to 3.93 and boxes 3.99 to 3.115
3.10 [ ]

• Tick box 3.11 if the partnership's accounts do not cover the period from the last accounting date (explain why in the 'Additional information' box, box 3.116 on page 3)
3.11 [ ]

• Tick box 3.12 if your accounting date has changed (only if this is a permanent change and you want it to count for tax)
3.12 [ ]

• Tick box 3.13 if this is the second or further change (explain why you have not used the same date as last year in the 'Additional information' box, box 3.116 on page 3).
3.13 [ ]

TRADING AND PROFESSIONAL INCOME for the year ended 5 April 2015 – continued

■ **Capital allowances – summary**

	Capital allowances	Balancing charges
● Annual Investment Allowance (include any balancing charges in box 3.17 below)	3.13A £	
● Cars costing more than £12,000 – if bought before 6 April 2009. (You should make a separate calculation for each car.)	3.14 £	3.15 £
● Capital allowances at 18% on equipment, including cars with lower CO_2 emissions	3.14A £	3.15A £
● Capital allowances at 8% on equipment, including cars with higher CO_2 emissions	3.16 £	3.17 £
● Agricultural or Industrial Buildings Allowance. (You must make a separate calculation for each block of expenditure.)	3.18 £	3.19 £
● 100% and other enhanced capital allowances claimed (you must make separate calculations). (Claims to and balancing charges arising on Business Premises Renovation Allowance must also be included in boxes 10.4 and 10.5 respectively.)	3.20 £	3.21 £
Total capital allowances/balancing charges	total of column above 3.22 £	total of column above 3.23 £

■ **Income and expenses for this accounting period**

Read the **Partnership Tax Return Guide** before completing this section.

If your annual turnover was below £81,000 (or would have been if you had traded for the whole year) **fill in boxes 3.24 to 3.26 instead of page 4.**

If your annual turnover was between £81,000 and £15m (or would have been if you had traded for a whole year) **ignore boxes 3.24 to 3.26. Now fill in page 4.**

If the combined annualised turnover from all of your activities was **more than £15m fill in boxes 3.24 to 3.26 and send in partnership accounts and computations as well.**

In all cases, complete box 3.83 or box 3.84 on page 5, and the other boxes on page 5 if applicable.

● Turnover including other business receipts, and goods etc taken for personal use (and balancing charges from box 3.23)	3.24 £
● Expenses allowable for tax (including capital allowances from box 3.22)	3.25 £
Net profit for this accounting period (put figure in brackets if a loss)	box 3.24 minus box 3.25 3.26 £

3.116 Additional information

TRADING AND PROFESSIONAL INCOME for the year ended 5 April 2015 – continued

■ **Income and expenses for this accounting period**

You must fill in this page if your annual turnover was between £81,000 and £15m. If the combined annualised turnover from all your activities was more than £15m, fill in boxes 3.24 to 3.26 on page 3 and send in the partnership accounts and computations as well. In all cases, complete box 3.83 or box 3.84 on page 5, and the other boxes on page 5 if applicable. Read the Partnership Tax Return Guide, go to **www.hmrc.gov.uk/selfassessmentforms**

If you were registered for VAT, do the figures in boxes 3.29 to 3.64 include VAT?   **3.27** [ ]   or exclude VAT?   **3.28** [ ]

Sales/business income (turnover)   **3.29** £ [ ]

	Disallowable expenses included in boxes 3.46 to 3.63	Total expenses	
● Cost of sales	**3.30** £	**3.46** £	
● Construction industry subcontractor costs	**3.31** £	**3.47** £	
● Other direct costs	**3.32** £	**3.48** £	

box 3.29 minus (boxes 3.46 + 3.47 + 3.48)

Gross profit/(loss)   **3.49** £ [ ]

Other income/profits   **3.50** £ [ ]

● Employee costs	**3.33** £	**3.51** £	
● Premises costs	**3.34** £	**3.52** £	
● Repairs	**3.35** £	**3.53** £	
● General administrative expenses	**3.36** £	**3.54** £	
● Motor expenses	**3.37** £	**3.55** £	
● Travel and subsistence	**3.38** £	**3.56** £	
● Advertising, promotion and entertainment	**3.39** £	**3.57** £	
● Legal and professional costs	**3.40** £	**3.58** £	
● Bad debts	**3.41** £	**3.59** £	
● Interest and alternative finance payments	**3.42** £	**3.60** £	
● Other finance charges	**3.43** £	**3.61** £	
● Depreciation and loss/(profit) on sale	**3.44** £	**3.62** £	
● Other expenses including partnership charges	**3.45** £	**3.63** £	

Put the total of boxes 3.30 to 3.45 in box 3.66 below

boxes 3.51 to 3.63

Total expenses   **3.64** £ [ ]

boxes 3.49 + 3.50 minus 3.64

Net profit/(loss)   **3.65** £ [ ]

■ **Tax adjustments to net profit or loss for this accounting period**

boxes 3.30 to 3.45

● Disallowable expenses	**3.66** £	
● Goods, etc taken for personal use and other adjustments (apart from disallowable expenses) that increase profits	**3.67** £	
● Balancing charges (from box 3.23)	**3.68** £	

boxes 3.66 + 3.67 + 3.68

Total additions to net profit (deduct from net loss)   **3.69** £ [ ]

● Capital allowances (from box 3.22)	**3.70** £	
● Deductions from net profit (add to net loss)	**3.71** £	

boxes 3.70 + 3.71

3.72 £ [ ]

boxes 3.65 + 3.69 minus box 3.72

Net business profit for tax purposes for this accounting period (put figure in brackets if a loss)   **3.73** £ [ ]

SA800 2015   PARTNERSHIP TAX RETURN: PAGE 4

TRADING AND PROFESSIONAL INCOME for the year ended 5 April 2015 – continued

■ **Taxable profit or loss for this accounting period**

• Adjustment on change of basis	**3.82** £	Copy this figure to box 11A in the Partnership Statement
Net profit for this accounting period (if loss, enter '0' here) from box 3.26 or box 3.73	**3.83** £	Copy this figure to box 11 in the Partnership Statement
Allowable loss for this accounting period (if profit, enter '0' here) from box 3.26 or box 3.73	**3.84** £	Copy this figure to box 12 in the Partnership Statement
Tick box 3.93 if the figure in box 3.83 or box 3.84 is provisional	**3.93**	

■ **Subcontractors in the construction industry**

• Deductions on payment and deduction statements from contractors – construction industry subcontractors only	**3.97** £	Copy this figure to box 24 in the Partnership Statement

■ **Tax taken off trading income**

• Tax taken off trading income (excluding deductions made by contractors on account of tax)	**3.98** £	Copy this figure to box 24A in the Partnership Statement

Read the Partnership Tax Return Guide if you are a 'CT Partnership', go to **hmrc.gov.uk/selfassessmentforms**

■ **Summary of balance sheet for this accounting period**

Leave these boxes blank if you do not have a balance sheet or your annual turnover was more than £15m.

Assets		
• Plant, machinery and motor vehicles	**3.99** £	
• Other fixed assets (premises, goodwill, investments, etc)	**3.100** £	
• Stock and work in progress	**3.101** £	
• Debtors/prepayments/other current assets	**3.102** £	
• Bank/building society balances	**3.103** £	
• Cash in hand	**3.104** £	boxes 3.99 to 3.104 **3.105** £

Liabilities		
• Trade creditors/accruals	**3.106** £	
• Loans and overdrawn bank accounts	**3.107** £	
• Other liabilities	**3.108** £	boxes 3.106 to 3.108 **3.109** £

Net business assets (put the figure in brackets if you had net business liabilities) — box 3.105 minus box 3.109 **3.110** £

Represented by partners' current and capital accounts

• Balance at start of period*	**3.111** £	
• Net profit/(loss)*	**3.112** £	
• Capital introduced	**3.113** £	
• Drawings	**3.114** £	
• Balance at end of period*		boxes 3.111 to 3.113 minus box 3.114 **3.115** £

* If the capital account is overdrawn, or the business made a net loss, show the figure in brackets.

Box 3.116 'Additional information' is on page 3.

■ **Partnership trade charges**

• Net partnership charges paid in the period 6 April 2014 to 5 April 2015 (**not** the accounting period)	**3.117** £

SA800 2015   PARTNERSHIP TAX RETURN: PAGE 5

PARTNERSHIP STATEMENT (SHORT) for the year ended 5 April 2015

Please read these instructions before completing the Statement

Use these pages to allocate partnership income if the only income for the relevant return period was trading and professional income or taxed interest and alternative finance receipts from banks and building societies. Otherwise you must download or ask the SA Orderline for the 'Partnership Statement (Full)' pages to record details of the allocation of all the partnership income. Go to www.hmrc.gov.uk/selfassessmentforms

Step 1   Fill in boxes 1 to 29 and boxes A and B as appropriate. Get the figures you need from the relevant boxes in the Partnership Tax Return. Complete a separate Statement for each accounting period covered by this Partnership Tax Return and for each trade or profession carried on by the partnership.

Step 2   Then allocate the amounts in boxes 11 to 29 attributable to each partner using the allocation columns on this page and page 7, read the Partnership Tax Return Guide, go to hmrc.gov.uk/selfassessmentforms If the partnership has more than 3 partners, please photocopy page 7.

Step 3   Each partner will need a copy of their allocation of income to fill in their personal tax return.

PARTNERSHIP INFORMATION

If the partnership business includes a trade or profession, enter here the accounting period for which appropriate items in this statement are returned.

Start **1**   /   /

End **2**   /   /

Nature of trade **3**

MIXED PARTNERSHIPS

Tick here if this Statement is drawn up using Corporation Tax rules **4**

Tick here if this Statement is drawn up using tax rules for non-residents **5**

Individual partner details

6 Name of partner

Address

Postcode

Date appointed as a partner (if during 2013–14 or 2014–15) **7**   /   /

Date ceased to be a partner (if during 2013–14 or 2014–15) **9**   /   /

Partner's Unique Taxpayer Reference (UTR) **8**

Partner's National Insurance number **10**

Partnership's profits, losses, income, tax credits, etc

Tick this box if the items entered in the box had foreign tax taken off

Partner's share of profits, losses, income, tax credits, etc

Copy figures in boxes 11 to 29 to boxes in the individual's Partnership (short) pages as shown below

- **for an accounting period ended in 2014–15** ▼

from box 3.83 Profit from a trade or profession **A**	**11** £	Profit **11** £	Copy this figure to box 8
from box 3.82 Adjustment on change of basis	**11A** £	**11A** £	Copy this figure to box 10
from box 3.84 Loss from a trade or profession **B**	**12** £	Loss **12** £	Copy this figure to box 8
from box 10.4 Business Premises Renovation Allowance	**12A** £	**12A** £	Copy this figure to box 15

- **for the period 6 April 2014 to 5 April 2015***

from box 7.9A UK taxed interest and taxed alternative finance receipts	**22** £	**22** £	Copy this figure to box 28
from box 3.97 CIS deductions made by contractors on account of tax	**24** £	**24** £	Copy this figure to box 30
from box 3.98 Other tax taken off trading income	**24A** £	**24A** £	Copy this figure to box 31
from box 7.8A Income Tax taken off	**25** £	**25** £	Copy this figure to box 29
from box 3.117 Partnership charges	**29** £	**29** £	Copy this figure to box 4, 'Other tax reliefs' section on page Ai 2 in your personal tax return

* if you are a 'CT Partnership' see the Partnership Tax Return Guide

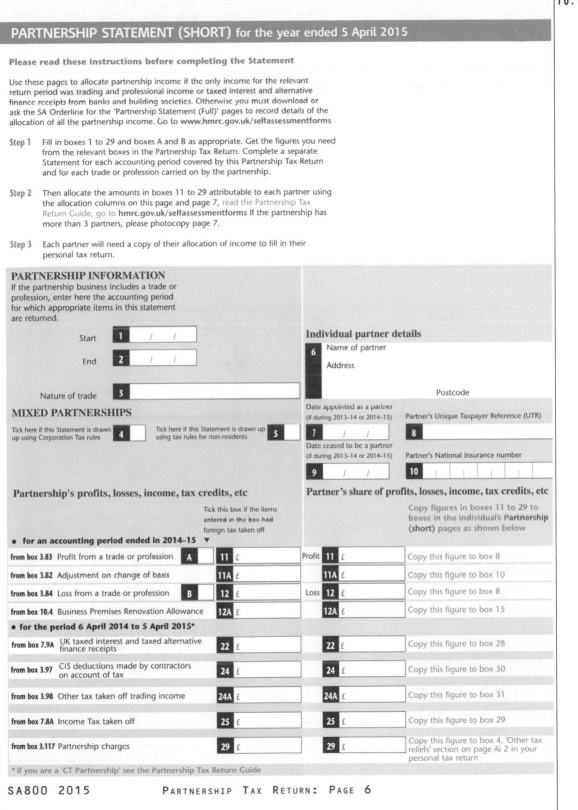

PARTNERSHIP STATEMENT (SHORT) for the year ended 5 April 2015 – continued

Individual partner details

6 Name of partner

Address

Postcode

Date appointed as a partner
(if during 2013–14 or 2014–15)

7 / /

Partner's Unique Taxpayer Reference (UTR)

8

Date ceased to be a partner
(if during 2013–14 or 2014–15)

9 / /

Partner's National Insurance number

10

Partner's share of profits, losses, income, tax credits, etc

Copy figures in boxes 11 to 29 to boxes in the individual's Partnership (short) pages as shown below

Profit **11** £ — Copy this figure to box 8

11A £ — Copy this figure to box 10

Loss **12** £ — Copy this figure to box 8

12A £ — Copy this figure to box 15

22 £ — Copy this figure to box 28

24 £ — Copy this figure to box 30

24A £ — Copy this figure to box 31

25 £ — Copy this figure to box 29

29 £ — Copy this figure to box 4, 'Other tax reliefs' section on page Ai 2 in your personal tax return

Individual partner details

6 Name of partner

Address

Postcode

Date appointed as a partner
(if during 2013–14 or 2014–15)

7 / /

Partner's Unique Taxpayer Reference (UTR)

8

Date ceased to be a partner
(if during 2013–14 or 2014–15)

9 / /

Partner's National Insurance number

10

Partner's share of profits, losses, income, tax credits, etc

Copy figures in boxes 11 to 29 to boxes in the individual's Partnership (short) pages as shown below

Profit **11** £ — Copy this figure to box 8

11A £ — Copy this figure to box 10

Loss **12** £ — Copy this figure to box 8

12A £ — Copy this figure to box 15

22 £ — Copy this figure to box 28

24 £ — Copy this figure to box 30

24A £ — Copy this figure to box 31

25 £ — Copy this figure to box 29

29 £ — Copy this figure to box 4, 'Other tax reliefs' section on page Ai 2 in your personal tax return

SA800 2015   PARTNERSHIP TAX RETURN: PAGE 7

OTHER INFORMATION for the year ended 5 April 2015

Q7 **Did the partnership receive any other income which you have not already Included elsewhere in the Partnership Tax Return?** | **YES** | If Yes, read the guidance below
Make sure that you fill in the pages for Questions 1 to 4 before answering Question 7

If you ticked the 'Yes' box and the only income was interest, or alternative finance receipts with tax taken off, from banks and building societies, fill in boxes 7.7A to 7.9A below. Otherwise download the Partnership Savings pages, go to www.hmrc.gov.uk/selfassessmentforms and leave boxes 7.7A to 7.9A blank. If you have more than one account, enter **totals** in the boxes.

Interest and alternative finance receipts from UK banks and building societies, paid **with** tax taken off for the period 6 April 2014 to 5 April 2015 (**not** the accounting period)

Amount after tax taken off	Tax taken off	Gross amount before tax
7.7A £	**7.8A** £	**7.9A** £
	Copy this figure to box 25 in the Partnership Statement	Copy this figure to box 22 in the Partnership Statement

Q8 Are the details on the front of the Partnership Tax Return wrong? | **YES** | If yes, make any corrections on the front of the form

Q9 **Please give a daytime phone number (including the area code) in boxes 9.1 and 9.2**
It is often simpler to phone if we need to ask you about your tax return.

Your phone number
9.1

or, if you prefer, your adviser's phone number
9.2

Your adviser's name and address
9.3

Postcode

Q10 **Other information**

Please tick box 10.1 if this Partnership Tax Return contains figures that are provisional because you do not yet have final figures. The Partnership Tax Return Guide explains the circumstances in which provisional figures may be used and asks you to provide some additional information in box 3.116 on page 3. | **10.1**

Disclosure of tax avoidance schemes – If the partnership is a party to one or more disclosable tax avoidance schemes, you must complete boxes 10.2 and 10.3. Give details of each scheme (up to 3) on a separate line. If the partnership is party to more than 3 schemes, details of the additional schemes must be reported on form AAG4, 'Disclosure of avoidance scheme'.

Scheme reference number or promoter reference number **10.2**

Tax year in which the expected advantage to the partners arises – year ended 5 April **10.3**

Business Premises Renovation Allowance (BPRA) – read the Partnership Tax Return Guide before you fill in these boxes. Extract from boxes 3.20 and 3.21 (and boxes 1.36 and 1.34 from the Partnership UK Property pages) the amounts that relate to any BPRA claims or charges. Enter claims to BPRA in box 10.4 and charges in box 10.5

Capital allowance	Balancing charge
10.4 £	**10.5** £
Copy this figure to box 12A in the Partnership Statement	

Q11 **Declaration** – I have filled in and am sending back to you the following:

I TO 5 OF THIS FORM		PARTNERSHIP FOREIGN	
6 & 7 PARTNERSHIP STATEMENT (SHORT)		PARTNERSHIP TRADING	
6 & 7 PARTNERSHIP STATEMENT (FULL)		PARTNERSHIP DISPOSAL OF CHARGEABLE ASSETS	
PARTNERSHIP UK PROPERTY		PARTNERSHIP SAVINGS	

I attach **11.1** additional copies of page 7. There were **11.2** partners in this partnership for that period.
Before you send the completed tax return back to your current HM Revenue & Customs office, you must sign the statement below.
If you give false information or conceal any part of the partnership's income or details of the disposal of chargeable assets, you may be liable to financial penalties and/or we may prosecute you.

11.3 **I the nominated partner,** declare that the information I have given on this Partnership Tax Return is correct and complete to the best of my knowledge and belief.

Nominated Partner Signature | Date

Print name in full here

If you have signed for someone else, please also:
- state the capacity in which you are signing (for example, as executor or receiver)
- give the name of the person you are signing for and **your** name and address in the 'Additional information' box, box 3.116, on page 3.

11.4

Index